Flipping Out?

Flipping Out?

Myth or Fact?
The Impact of the
"Year in Israel"

Shalom Z. Berger
Daniel Jacobson
Chaim I. Waxman

with an introduction by Richard M. Joel

Yashar Books, Inc.
New York, 2007

FLIPPING OUT?
Myth or Fact: The Impact of the "Year in Israel"

Shalom Z. Berger, Daniel Jacobson and Chaim I Waxman
with an introduction by Richard M. Joel

Publication of this book was made possible by a generous grant from the S. Daniel Abraham Israel Program of Yeshiva University. Learn more about this program and its benefits for students studying in Israel at http://www.yu.edu/jip/.

ISBN 978-1-933143-23-1

For information and catalog write to Yashar Books Inc., 1548 E. 33rd Street, Brooklyn, NY 11234, or visit our website: www.YasharBooks.com

Publication of this book has been sponsored by the

S. Daniel Abraham Israel Program
of Yeshiva University

Close to ninety percent of Yeshiva University students will have spent a year studying in Israel by the time they graduate college. The vast majority of these students go to Israel as part of the S. Daniel Abraham Israel Program. The SDAIP experience serves as a critical building block in their overall Torah U'Madda education as it affords our students the opportunity to root themselves in Torah, Eretz Yisrael and Am Yisrael as they begin their academic adventure and aspire to significant leadership roles within our community. As YU students, they benefit from the services and programs offered by YU Israel and effective coordination with the New York on-campus portion of their education.

Benefits in Israel

- YU Israel provides support to all program participants and serves as a resource for students and parents alike.

- Throughout the year, to supplement their Yeshiva/seminary experience, YU sponsors and runs a variety of events in Israel for program participants. Events include holiday celebrations, community service events, a battle of the bands, a choral competition, shabbaton programs, shabbat hospitality, a careers in Israel fair and *shiurim* (classes).

Financial Benefits

- Students are eligible to apply for Federal and State financial aid.

- The Israel school's tuition can be paid through YU's flexible monthly tuition plan.

Academic Benefits

- Credits from the Israel experience are YU credits and appear as such on the YU transcript.

- Students receive academic counseling and advising to ensure best use of the Israel credits toward the bachelors degree.

Learn more about the program at www.yu.edu/jip.

Contents

v

Publisher's Preface

Something unusual is happening to our children in Israel. It is now common for graduates of Orthodox high schools to spend a year learning Torah in Israel before beginning college. Some go to Israel and flip out, acquiring the surface trappings of devoted Torah scholars that seem so different from their previous ways of dressing and acting. Why does this happen? Are they brainwashed by their rabbis? Have they found an easy way to alleviate some hidden insecurity? Or are they merely inspired by a profoundly rich and spiritual lifestyle?

And how long does this newfound religious devotion last? Is it really the start of a radically different life path or is it merely a short-term religious high that becomes more moderate over time?

These are just a few of the questions that need to be asked. We all have our opinions on this subject based on anecdotes of kids we know and maybe even our own experiences. But is that really how mature and responsible community members should evaluate developments? Until now there has been very little hard data to clarify what exactly is happening in our community and that absence allowed us to judge based on the limited picture we saw with our own eyes. However, the whole story is made up of much more than a few children, and as we formulate our evaluations of this phenomenon we need to take a step back and study the facts carefully.

This book gathers together insights from three *talmidei chachamim* who are top experts on the subject, each from a different perspective. Rabbi Shalom Berger, Ed.D., and Rabbi Daniel Jacobson, Psy.D., both performed statistical studies and wrote doctoral dissertations on the phenomenon of studying in Israel for a year. Rabbi Berger, drawing on his years of experience as a leading *mechanech* (Torah instructor) in the U.S. and Israel, approaches the subject from the perspective of an educator and addresses the "what" of the changes in students—what religious changes do we see in students from the time they leave to Israel to a year after they return. Rabbi Jacobson looks at the "Year in Israel" from the perspective of his psychological training and explores the "why" of the equation—what internal and external influences on these students cause the changes that happen.

Dr. Chaim Waxman, a distinguished sociologist who hardly needs my introduction, looks at the impact of this phenomenon on the broader community from the perspective of a sociologist. How does the "Year in Israel" fit in with the historical relationship between American and Israeli Jewry, and how has it changed the American Jewish community? His decades of profound study of the Jewish community have earned him a place as one of our leading social commentators. Finally and significantly, Richard Joel adds to this impressive mix with an introduction based on his experience as the president of the Hillel college campus organization and currently the president of Yeshiva University.

It is with great pleasure that I greatly thank all of the contributors to this volume for their hard work. The development of this book was delayed by two most appropriate interruptions—the *aliyah* of Rabbi Jacobson and then later of Dr. Waxman. Mr. Joel is a very busy man whose vast talents are in constant demand. I thank him for recognizing the importance of this book and taking the time to write an introduction. Dr. Waxman is the consummate professional who maintained the highest standards of quality for all of his work. Rabbi Jacobson was kind enough to suffer through the considerable pain of revising and cutting material from his doctoral dissertation in order to make this book the best that it can be. And Rabbi Berger, my own *rebbe* from high school, was extremely gracious and diligent in converting his doctoral dissertation from a technical work into a section that is both informative and interesting to the layperson. It has been a most gratifying experience working with them throughout the process of publishing this book. Last but not least, none of this would have been possible without the immense talents of Rabbi Moshe Schapiro, whose editorial skills and keen judgment have improved this book in immeasurable ways.

I am sure that together with me, all of the authors pray that this book will help parents and students make informed choices that will improve the development of our children's religious lives and help them grow to even greater heights of Torah devotion and learning.

Gil Student
Yashar Books

How to Read this Book

This book contains discussions of an important communal issue that has multiple implications, discussions that are intended to significantly further the conversation even if they are not the final words on the subject.

Each section of the book is an independent unit and represents the perspective of its author and his specialization. Section 1 was written by Rabbi Shalom Z. Berger, an educator, and addresses the changes that take place among students. Section 2 was written by Dr. Daniel Jacobson, a psychologist, and discusses the influences on students that lead to these changes. Section 3 was written by Dr. Chaim I. Waxman, a sociologist, and tackles the "Year in Israel" in the perspective of the greater Jewish community. Each section's conclusions stand on their own. There is no need to read these sections in order.

The book has been intentionally sprinkled with Hebrew terms in order to capture a certain feel of Torah study and Israel, although only terms that are widely recognized within the Jewish community are used. There is a glossary in the back of the book for those unfamiliar with any terms. The Hebrew is transliterated into contemporary Modern Hebrew except when esthetics dictated a slight deviation.

The authors have enhanced their studies and anecdotes, both short and long. These stories and quotations have been set in a different font to stand out in the text and add personal meaning to the studies that have been conducted.

Contributors to this Book

SHALOM Z. BERGER, prior to his *aliyah* to Israel with his family in 1991, taught in New York area yeshiva high schools, inaugurating the Israel guidance center at HAFTR high school in Cedarhurst, NY. Since that time he has taught in both men's and women's one-year Israel programs and conceived and developed the on-line Israel programs website for the Orthodox Caucus. Today, when he is not busy parenting his seven children, he is on the staff of Bar-Ilan University's Lookstein Center for Jewish Education, where he is founding editor of the professional journal Jewish Educational Leadership and he directs thousands of educators around the world in a conversation about current issues in Jewish education via the Lookjed listserv, a project that he initiated. In his spare time, Shalom leads Jewish heritage tours in Poland and teaches graduate courses on Israel and Zionism.

DANIEL JACOBSON, ordained at Yeshiva University's Rabbi Isaac Elchanan Theological Seminary, is currently the Director of Student Services at Yeshivat Shvilei HaTorah in Jerusalem, and works as a clinical psychologist in private practice in Jerusalem and Gush Etzion. He received his Doctorate in Clinical Psychology from Rutgers University, writing his dissertation on "Psychological and Religious Change of Orthodox Jewish Boys During a Post-High School Year of Study in an Israeli Yeshiva." Rabbi Jacobson has a B.A. from Princeton University and studied in Israel at both Yeshivat HaKotel and Yeshivat Shaalvim. He lives with his wife Dassi and 5 children in Gush Etzion, and can be reached at dbj114@gmail.com.

CHAIM I. WAXMAN is Professor Emeritus of Sociology and Jewish Studies, Rutgers University and a Senior Fellow at the Jewish People Policy Planning Institute, in Jerusalem. He has a BA and MHL from

Yeshiva University, and an MA and PhD from the New School for Social Research. He studied in Yeshivat Kerem BeYavneh in 1958–59.

In addition to numerous articles and review-essays, his books include *The Stigma of Poverty: A Critique of Poverty Theories and Policies* (Pergamon Press, 1977; Second Edition, 1983); *America's Jews in Transition* (Temple University Press, 1983), *American Aliya* (Wayne State University Press, 1989), and *Jewish Baby Boomers: A Communal Perspective* (State University of New York Press, 2001). He also co-authored (with Rafael Medoff) the *Historical Dictionary of Zionism* (Scarecrow Press, 2000), and has edited and co-edited more than a half-dozen works in such diverse areas as political sociology, ethnicity, and social thought, among others. Most recently, he co-edited (with Uzi Rebhun) *Jews in Israel: Contemporary Social and Cultural Patterns* (University Press of New England/Brandeis University Press, 2004).

Acknowledgments

SHALOM Z. BERGER

Most of the material contained in this section of the book derives from the research that I undertook as part of my doctoral work at Yeshiva University's Azrieli Graduate School of Jewish Education and Administration in the mid-1990s. While I received support and encouragement from many, I would like to particularly thank Dr. Yitzchak Handel, who, at the time, was director of the Azrieli Graduate School, and Dr. Chaim Waxman, who was chairman of the doctoral committee.

My section of the book opens with a brief vignette describing my father, Bernard Berger, and the decisions that he faced as an American Jewish high school graduate in the 1940s. A firm believer in the power of Jewish education, he passed away a few short years ago, and I am dedicating this to his memory.

DANIEL JACOBSON

My deepest love and thanks to my best friend, advisor, supervisor, colleague . . . and wife—Dassi. Her support of all of my professional efforts is constant, and she has been patiently critiquing my work for over 12 years. My parents, Howard and Elaine, always placed our education above all else and urged us to strive for the best and always contribute to society. My in-laws, Rabbi Heshie and Rookie Billet, have been a constant source of support and encouragement. Rav Aharon Bina gave me my first exposure to the power of the "year in Israel," and my colleagues and students at Yeshivat Shvilei HaTorah have opened my eyes to new perspectives on the experience. The generosity of my dissertation subjects and mentors, Dr. Nancy McWilliams and Dr. Lew Gantwerk, provided the base for the ideas expressed here, and to them I am grateful. Finally, I thank *HaKadosh Baruch Hu* for all of the opportunities and blessings he has provided me, during my life in the United States and since my *aliyah*.

CHAIM I. WAXMAN

In memory of Rabbi Zevi Tabory z"l, the unsung hero who conceived the idea and created the Year in Israel program.

Some of the material in this part of the volume was initially presented in my paper, "Israel's Impact on American Orthodoxy," 19th Orthodox Forum of Yeshiva University, New York, March 12, 2007, and in various other articles of mine on Israel and American Orthodox Jewry.

Introduction: Reflections on Israel

As a parent of five children who have studied in Israel and another who will study there soon, God willing—and as the President of a University where eighty percent of the undergraduates have studied in Israel for at least one year—I am a great supporter of the Year in Israel program. Without doubt, the Israel experience has a profound impact on our young men and women. It is a great time for coming of age, when young people mature intellectually, socially, and religiously, and develop into outstanding citizens and proud Torah adults. Thanks in no small measure to the time they spent studying in *yeshivot* and *midrashot* in Israel, students come to our New York campuses with a deeper commitment to *yiddishkeit*, greater fervor for Torah study, and a more profound sense of *yirat shamayim*. They arrive as better students, with greater ability to apply their skills and knowledge, with a better sense of themselves and of the Transcendent.

A successful Israel experience should cement a lifelong romance with *Eretz Yisrael*, *Am Yisrael* and *Torat Yisrael*. However, too often the Israel experience can become nothing more than an elongated summer camp-like experience, where students live in a rarified atmosphere, a defined community with highly focused influences. To ensure maximal success we need careful calibration, by the schools themselves, as well as by parents and children.

The Israel experience must not stand alone, but take its place as part of an educational and experiential continuum. Students do not come to Israel straight from the womb, and they do not remain in Israel forever. There is a period before their studies in Israel, and a period of further study and personal growth after. If we as parents want to ensure success, we must take responsibility for all parts of this continuum. *Yeshivot* and seminaries must set their goals and their sights with this continuum in mind.

The best way to ensure a year of success and growth is to learn about the programs, study the options, and find the *yeshiva* or *midrashah* that fits your child the best. Parents and students should work together to define goals for the year in Israel and beyond. There is a responsibility to ask the *mechanchim* in Israel the hard questions: What are the goals in terms of Torah skills, personal maturity, *shemirat ha-mitzvot* and inspiration that can be expected from the year in Israel? What criteria will they use to measure success? Of course, as parents we must define our own expectations as well. Is the desire for our children to spend a year in Israel, where they will develop familiarity with the Israeli language, society, and culture? Or are we looking for a year where they are cloistered in a library, developing their intellectual proclivities and Torah horizons in solitude, far away from the disturbances of daily life? What can we expect of our children one year after their year in Israel? Five years after? Ten years? As my trustee Sy Syms says, an educated consumer is our best customer. So *caveat emptor*.

It is no secret that there are dangers in an undisciplined year with little supervision, without a significant adult serving *in loco parentis*. Students come to Israel with a great deal of baggage, much clean but some worn. What mechanisms are in place in Israeli *yeshivot* and *midrashot* to deal with this baggage?

In the ideal situation, young people will thrive from their independence and grow immeasurably in their year away from home. They will forge new role models who inspire them to lead lives of deeper passion and greater purpose. Sadly, a very small number of these role models can be too controlling. Rather than seeking the self-actualization of their students, they look to create students in their own image. Sometimes, when students encounter these role models they do not grow, but instead mutate. The good news is that most often young people who know themselves, who come from loving homes full of consistency and support, will grow and thrive.

But there is another caveat. You can do everything right, but you still need *mazel*. As the Gemara teaches, everything needs *mazel*, even a *Sefer Torah* that resides inside the *Beit HaMikdash*.

There is another, perhaps even more serious caveat: sometimes the Israel experience creates a feeling of entitlement in young people. Young men and women are catered to hand and foot. In many schools they do not even have to do their own laundry, or take responsibility for their meals. They begin to feel the perfect Jewish life is what they experienced in *yeshiva* or *midrashah*, that only through a life without any responsibility can one grow in Torah and *yirat shamayim*. The unfortunate paradox is that our young people spend a year in the Promised Land, only to crave the life that our ancestors lived in the *Midbar*, where bread fell from

Heaven and the Jewish people were completely unburdened with any responsibility.

The mindset we should convey is that the *Midbar* existence is not the ideal. *Yeshivot* and *midrashot* in Israel should teach that "this year is a gift to you. It is an opportunity for you to learn and grow. It is a launching pad to your future. Use it well."

Often, the only role models our children and students are exposed to in Israel come from the "Torah-only" mold. Occasionally this leads to the unfortunate mindset that everything encountered post-Israel is *b'dieved*— a disappointment, a settling, or a struggle. Consequently, far too many young men and women return to America ambivalent to, if not uncomfortable with, returning to a dual curriculum.

Parents and students have a responsibility to inquire. Israel programs need to know that we care—they want us to be involved. Visit before the year. See if it is a good fit for your son or daughter. Tell the *hanhalah* your expectations. Stay in touch with the *ramim* and teachers. Keep close contact with *madrichim*. Visit during the year and chart the progress your child is making. *Shep* a little *nachas*.

Most importantly, as parents and educators we must focus on the long-term goal: a productive and meaningful life for our children and students. We should ensure that Israel is not the pinnacle of their religious development, their personal Camp Nirvana. Let us work together to make the continuum one of ever greater opportunity and challenge, ever greater possibilities in building an integrated life based on Torah. Let us encourage a full four years of college, so that young people aren't rushed in their studies and can grow maximally in both Torah and *madda*. Let us convey the message that a Torah life is a life of ever-ascending growth, ever-increasing depth of knowledge, dedication, and fervor.

These are some of the challenges that we face collectively, as a community. This volume is intended to provoke questions, and to offer some insight into these most serious matters. I recommend that you read the essays contained in this volume and add your own voice to this important conversation. In this way we will all benefit *l'hagdil Torah u'lehaadirah*—"to beautify and expand Torah."

RICHARD M. JOEL

President, Yeshiva University

Section 1:
Engaging the Ultimate:
The Impact of Post-High School
Study in Israel

SHALOM Z. BERGER

Chapter 1

Introduction

My father was born in Williamsburg (Brooklyn, not Virginia) in 1928. After a brief spell in the local New York City public school, he transferred to Yeshiva Torah Vodaath in the third grade, where his education refocused to the traditions of his immigrant parents. After graduating from the Torah Vodaath high school in 1947, he began a course of study at City University, serving in the American Armed Forces during the Korean War, and (in his words) "hanging around" in the fledgling Lakewood *kollel* while working on my grandfather's chicken farm in Farmingdale, N.J. My grandfather had sold his sweater store on the Lower East Side of Manhattan and purchased the farm in the unsuccessful hope that his son— and daughter, who was studying nursing—would be deemed "essential farm workers" and therefore exempt from the draft.

When I asked my father why he made the choices that he did, he described the process of what passed for "College Guidance" in his *yeshiva*. One of the rabbis called each student into his office and asked about the student's plans. When a student said, for example, that he planned to go to college and study engineering, he was told that fixing cars was not a good job for a Jewish boy, and that after a few years of continued study in *yeshiva* he could get a job as a *rebbe* in an elementary school.[1] Unless *yeshiva* study offered an immediate benefit—avoiding the draft, for example—few chose to remain.

From my father's perspective, remaining in *yeshiva* meant an abdication of responsibility. Post-World War II America was a place and a time of responsibility. If it meant defending American ideals in Korea, so be it (in fact, my father was stationed in—yes—Virginia, where his most

---

1 Like most Yiddish stories, this has lost something in translation. The original, according to my sister, Shuli, was

Far vos vilstu zayn an engineer [endzineer]? Lign unter a car [kar] vern shmutsik? Ikh vel far dir shafn a teaching job [titching dzob], de vest makhn a lebn.

dangerous duty was taking the receipts from the Saturday night movie to the safe, accompanied by an armed guard).

In mid-twentieth-century America, the nation's values—and the American Jewish community—were very different from what they are today. Continued Torah study after high school was a luxury that few could afford. The Torah centers of Eastern Europe, which once drew the most committed American students, had been destroyed in the Holocaust, along with the majority of their Jewish communities. The as-yet unborn State of Israel was a foreign, distant land that did not yet have an infrastructure to support centers of Torah studies for the Diaspora.

In truth, at the moment when my father walked out of the Torah Vodaath *beit midrash* clutching his high school diploma and contemplating his future as an American Jew, the future of American traditional Jewry was at a crossroads, as well. As it stands today, the American Jewish population is, on some level, the product of its successes in the realm of developing an educational enterprise that offered something beyond the promise of a job as an elementary school teacher. The growth of the day school movement from a few dozen day schools—the vast majority of which were in the metropolitan New York area—in the late 1940s, to the hundred of such schools dotting the North American map at the turn of the twenty-first century, had a major impact on the lives and future of Jewish children in the United States.[2]

By the time the turbulent twentieth-century approached its conclusion, hundreds of parents and students were deciding that even twelve years of day school education were not enough, choosing to continue their Jewish studies in Israel before beginning college. These one-year Israel programs, now part-and-parcel of the educational experience for the majority of day school graduates, have played an important role in the educational system that has rejuvenated traditional learning and scholarship in the American Jewish community.

What goes on in these programs?

---

2 For an analysis of the growth and development of the American day school scene, see Alvin Schiff, *The Jewish Day School in America*, New York: Jewish Education Committee Press, 1966.

For more recent developments, see Jack Wertheimer, "Jewish Education in the United States: Recent Trends and Issues" in *American Jewish Year Book*, 1999, pp. 17–30 and Marvin Schick, *A Census of Jewish Day Schools in the United States*, January 2000, Avi Chai Foundation.

How do they impact on the lives of their students?

How has this educational development affected the American Jewish community?

In the coming pages we will try to examine these questions based on published research, observing the norms and mores of the institutions and, most importantly, interviewing the participants themselves.

Background: The Yeshiva

Judaism places tremendous emphasis on education, which traditionally has meant Torah study for men (Maimonides, *Hilchot Talmud Torah* 3:3). Morning prayers open with *birchot ha-Torah*, blessings over Torah study, and include a Talmudic passage that promises particular reward for Torah study (Mishnah *Pe'ah* 1:1). Such study typically takes place in a *yeshiva* —literally, the place of "sitting," where one sits and studies.

The Talmud relates the beginnings of the elementary school system with the approbation that were it not for the efforts of Yehoshua ben Gamla, the Torah would have been forgotten (*Bava Batra* 21a). On a post-secondary level, Rabban Yochanan ben Zakkai is credited with saving Jewry in the midst of the destruction of the Second Temple, by arranging for "Yavneh and its scholars," the major center of Torah learning, to be spared (*Gittin* 56a-b).

For almost two thousand years since, *yeshivot* were established as Jewish communities spread across the globe. First to Babylon, then to North Africa and Europe, Torah study traveled with the exiles' migrations. Much as a young, avid sports fan today knows North American geography by where various teams are located, the interested young Talmud scholar recognizes European cities and countries by the *rishonim* and *acharonim* (early and late Talmudic commentaries) who learned and taught there.

The processes of modernization and secularization taking place in Europe in the second half of the nineteenth century brought about a crisis in the traditional Jewish community. One reaction was the establishment of a new type of educational institution: the higher level *yeshiva*. This *yeshiva* differed from its predecessors in that it was not community-based, but instead drew students from a broad Jewish population. This new type of educational institution

comprises a community of young people, a kind of youth society, which intentionally developed the consciousness of a religious elite. The yeshiva society is characterized by a social and economic moratorium; it is isolated from everyday affairs and maintains a direct and unmitigated affinity for religious culture, as expressed . . . in the literature of *Halakha* and *Musar*.[3]

This new type of *yeshiva*, which offered a total Torah environment to its students, was reestablished in Israel and the United States after World War II, and became the dominant educational template for boys and young men within traditional Orthodox society.[4]

While accurate numbers are hard to come by, with hundreds of *yeshivot* and tens of thousands of talmidim studying in Israel today, it is generally accepted that there are more students actively engaged in Torah study now than there were at any prior point in Jewish history.

One higher level *yeshiva* stood in contrast with this response to societal change. The Rabbi Isaac Elchanan Theological Seminary, the nucleus around which Yeshiva University grew, was established in 1897 as the first advanced *yeshiva* in the United States.[5] It differed from its predecessors not only in location, but in philosophy as well.[6] The school's motto was *Torah U'Madda*: "Torah and Science." The idea that Torah scholarship could and should be joined by secular learning, almost as a religious imperative, was certainly not traditional.[7] Still, the success of Yeshiva University in teaching its graduates to participate, and even excel, in both the traditional Jewish and modern American worlds, responded to an essential need in the American Jewish community.[8] In a short time, major Jewish population centers saw a parallel growth of similarly constructed

---

3 Menachem Friedman, "The lost *kiddush* cup: Changes in Ashkenazic haredi culture —A tradition in crisis" in Jack Wertheimer, ed., *The uses of tradition: Jewish continuity in the modern era*. New York: The Jewish Theological Seminary of America, 1992, p. 182.

4 See Chaim I. Waxman, "From Institutional Decay to Primary Day: American Orthodoxy Since World War II," in *American Jewish History* 91, 3–4 (2003) pp. 405–421.

5 Gilbert Klaperman, *The story of Yeshiva University: The first Jewish university in America*. New York: The Macmillan Co., 1969.

6 Joseph Telushkin, *Jewish Literacy: The most important things to know about the Jewish religion, its people and its history*. New York: William Morrow, 1991.

7 Norman Lamm, *Torah Umadda: The encounter of religious learning and worldly knowledge in the Jewish tradition*. Northvale, New Jersey: Jason Aronson, Inc., 1990.

8 Aharon Rakeffet-Rothkoff, *Bernard Revel: Builder of American Jewish Orthodoxy*. New York: Jewish Publication Society of America, 1972.

elementary and high schools whose day was divided between secular and Judaic studies. These schools were highly Zionistic.[9] Soon the movement with which these schools were identified became known as "Modern Orthodoxy," and the schools that espoused these ideals of *Torah U'Madda* and religious Zionism became known as "Modern Orthodox day schools."

Yeshiva University differed from the traditional European *yeshiva* in other ways as well. Aside from the opportunity for the established young scholar to devote himself to the study of Torah *lishmah* (Torah "for its own sake") in the "Yeshiva Program," here could be found a choice of learning options to complement the college curriculum. Students could choose to study in the Teachers' Institute (TI, now the Isaac Breuer College, IBC), which offered a curriculum of Judaic studies that included Bible, Jewish history, Jewish philosophy and Jewish literature, a wider range than the traditional study of Talmud, and led to a Teacher's diploma aside from the Bachelor of Arts degree the student would receive in Yeshiva College. The James Striar School (JSS) was established to allow students with little or no background in Judaic studies to pursue a college degree while learning about their Jewish heritage. Such students were often highly motivated and "mainstreamed" into the Yeshiva Program or the Teachers' Institute before their graduation from college.[10] As the needs of the student community changed, more options have been added as well.

Yeshiva University's Stern College for Women was a major innovation in contemporary Jewish education when it opened its doors in 1954, making available a curriculum of *Torah U'Madda* to the female graduates of the Modern Orthodox day school system. While its Judaic studies curriculum is not identical with that of the traditional male *yeshiva*, it offers an opportunity for women to develop religiously with college-level Judaic studies courses as they advance in their secular studies. Rabbi Joseph B. Soloveitchik's involvement in teaching women Talmud, first in the Maimonides School in Boston, then in Stern College,[11] has led to a proliferation of schools in the Modern Orthodox community that teach Talmud to women.

9　Alvin I. Schiff, *The Jewish day school in America*. New York: Jewish Education Committee Press, 1966.

10　Jeffrey Gurock, *The men and women of Yeshiva*. New York: Columbia University Press, 1988.

11　Avraham Weiss, *Women at prayer*. Hoboken, NJ: Ktav, 1990.

With the developing popularity of *yeshiva* study in Israel in the early 1980s, Yeshiva University began a joint Israel program that allows students attending *yeshivot* in Israel to be officially registered as Yeshiva University students. Aside from supporting the official position of Yeshiva University as an endorser of Zionist ideals, the joint Israel program also offers a prime opportunity for Yeshiva University to recruit students. A recent survey of Yeshiva University students found that 73 percent have studied in Israel, most prior to beginning college. Almost a third of these students had not planned on attending Yeshiva University before their year of study in Israel and decided to do so in order to continue their religious studies.

Chapter 2

Who Goes to Israel to Study?

A typical North American graduate of a Modern Orthodox day school likely has attended twelve years of "double schedule" schooling, dividing his day between Judaic studies (often in the morning) and secular studies. Even with the school day extended to accommodate this load—with elementary school typically until 4:00 or 4:30 P.M. and high school until 5:00 or 6:00 P.M.—it is difficult for the average student to get the full flavor of the traditional *yeshiva* experience with its singular commitment to Judaic studies. As active participants in the "modern" world, a wide range of diversions, from sports to "the stock market game," keep the Modern Orthodox day school student from experiencing the single-minded directness of purpose encountered by his counterpart in the traditional *yeshiva*, where the primary emphasis is on Torah study.[12]

It should be noted that a variety of academic studies, as well as a rich array of anecdotal evidence, point to the success of the North American day school system as it developed over time.[13]

Doctoral studies conducted throughout the second half of the twentieth century found repeatedly that day school education has a marked impact on its students. One study examined the graduates of the Rabbi Jacob Joseph School in New York from 1925 to 1949. About 70 percent of the respondents had continued in the high school, while the others attended public school after graduation. The study found that the graduates tended to remain Orthodox, observe rituals, maintain an interest in Jewish studies, and participate actively in Jewish organizational activities. Perhaps most important, the study found that the greater the number of

---

12 William Helmreich, *The world of the Yeshiva: An intimate portrait of Orthodox Jewry*. New York: The Free Press, 1982.

13 Aside from the studies noted here, a synopsis of relevant research appears at http://www.peje.org/docs/ResearchStudiesImpact.pdf

years of formal Jewish education, the stronger the identification with Jewish values and appreciation of the benefits of day school education.[14]

A 1974 study on the impact of Jewish education on the religious involvement of adults in the Chicago area found that even attending all-day Jewish schools does not increase adult religious involvement over the level attained by those with no Jewish schooling, unless there are more than six years of such schooling. Only students who completed twelve years of supplementary Jewish education (Sunday and afternoon schools) reported that they were more religiously involved as adults. The study concludes that extensive Jewish schooling has a significant impact on adult religious behaviors, successfully accentuating religious values to which the student was predisposed, and even "converting" students from irreligious backgrounds to religious observance including keeping kosher, observing Shabbat, and prayer. Other informal Jewish education experiences, even intensive ones like a sleep-away summer camp, were found to have no lasting effect unless coupled with formal Jewish education.

Moreover, this study also found that parental religiosity is not the best predictor of any measure of religious involvement, although, it is crucial for the indirect contributions that it makes. The parents' religiosity brings the student to attend a Jewish school, participate in Jewish organizations and marry a Jewish spouse, all of which act as the best predictors of various religious involvement measures. Tellingly, the college years were found to be the most important time that long-term religious commitments were formed.[15]

The data collected in the 1990 National Jewish Population Survey led to renewed discussion of the effects and effectiveness of American Jewish education. As the survey included a relatively small number of day school graduates and had few direct questions related to Jewish education, conclusions based on the NJPS are far from clear. While some researchers found that the survey indicates a correlation between Jewish education and Jewish identification[16] and conclude that Jewish day school education is

---

14 Irving Pinsky, *The graduates of Rabbi Jacob Joseph School—A follow-up study.* Unpublished doctoral dissertation, Yeshiva University, 1961.

15 Harold Himmelfarb, *The impact of religious schooling: The effects of Jewish education upon adult religious involvement.* Unpublished doctoral dissertation, University of Chicago, 1974.

16 Sylvia Barack Fishman and Alice Goldstein, *When they are grown they will not depart: Jewish education and the Jewish behavior of American adults.* Research Report #8. Waltham, MA: Brandeis University, 1993.

the only type of schooling that slows the process of assimilation,[17] others inferred from the data that there is no significant relationship between the type of education one receives and such basic issues as intermarriage.[18]

This discussion led to a number of studies produced by researchers at the Azrieli Graduate School of Yeshiva University, which found "dramatically higher" Jewish organizational involvement among day school graduates in comparison with parallel groups of American Jews. Furthermore, their level of ritual observance and connection with Israel was found to be greater than that of their peers who did not attend day school. At the same time, these studies found that the home environment of the Jewish day school student is much more Jewishly oriented than the homes of those who do not attend day school. It is the interaction of these complementary factors that create the major differences between Jews who attend day school and Jews who do not.[19]

One final study sampled Jewish parents and their teenage children in an attempt to examine the effects of different levels of Jewish education on Jewish involvement, while attempting to control for parental and other influencing factors. While admitting that even after controlling for many factors, the children sent to the more intensive educational programs likely bring with them unmeasured—and immeasurable—Jewish resources, the clear conclusion is that Jewish education affects its students in a significant way. The more intensive the program, the greater the effect, with Orthodox day schools—where the students usually continue their studies through high school—offering the greatest impact.[20]

---

17 Mordechai Rimor and Elihu Katz, *Jewish involvement of the baby boom generation.* Jerusalem: The Louis Guttman Israel Institute of Applied Social Research, 1993.

18 Egon Mayer, "Jewish education and intermarriage among American Jews." Paper presented at the meeting of the international steering committee of the Association for Demographic Policy of the Jewish People, January 1993.

19 The Azrieli Graduate School published three separate studies by Alvin Schiff and Mareleyn Schneider. They include:

   The Jewishness quotient of Jewish day school graduates: Studying the effect of Jewish education on adult Jewish behavior.

   The far reaching effects of extensive Jewish day school attendance: The impact of Jewish education on Jewish behavior and attitudes.

   Fortifying and restoring Jewish behavior: The interaction of home and school.

   New York, Azrieli Graduate Institute, 1994.

20 Steven M. Cohen, "The impact of varieties of Jewish education upon Jewish identity." *Contemporary Jewry*, *16*, pp. 68–96, 1995.

Notwithstanding this evidence—or perhaps extrapolating from it—many educators in Modern Orthodox schools strongly recommend that their students devote a year to study in a *yeshiva* with a total Jewish environment before beginning their university studies, hoping that exposure to an all-encompassing Torah environment will instill a greater sense of long-term commitment and religious responsibility. This is especially true in an environment where many day school graduates, with the encouragement and support of their parents and schools, choose to attend college settings where their religious beliefs and practice will be challenged academically, politically and socially. As few Modern Orthodox day school graduates will attend a full-time Torah study program in the United States—indeed, for this population, such programs do not exist outside of Israel—this has meant encouraging high school graduates to travel to Israel for a year of study.

Chapter 3

Studying in Israel

Later on in this volume, Dr. Chaim Waxman presents a brief history, describing how American students traveled across the Atlantic to further their religious studies, first in pre-war Europe and later in Israel of the 1950s and '60s in the forerunners of today's Israel programs.[20a]

Still, surprising as it now sounds, full-time Torah study in a *yeshiva* in Israel was once considered an exotic experience for a Modern Orthodox high school graduate. As recently as the 1970s, Israel study simply did not appear on the map of Jewish education. When the Orthodox journal *Tradition* asked Jewish educators to comment on the Jewish day school, none discussed study in Israel post-high school.[21] In answer to questions such as "How can a Jewish day school better prepare its students for the competing lifestyles and ideologies of the campus?" or "How can a Jewish day school improve the quality of the religious life of its students and deepen their commitment to Torah?" the respondents discussed curricular change, in-service training, youth groups, and even visiting Israel during high school. A year of study in Israel was not suggested. The assumption was that few graduates, if any, would be willing to postpone college to further their Jewish education.

The situation today is very different. Interviews with administrators in some of the largest Modern Orthodox high schools in the New York metropolitan area indicate that up to 90% of their graduates choose to attend one-year post-graduation Israel programs. Well over one thousand high school graduates a year come to Israeli *yeshiva* programs prior to beginning college-level study back in the United States.

Recognizing the central place that post-high school Israel study has for its graduates, many *yeshiva* high schools now feature Israel guidance

---

20a See below, chapter 24.
21 See Walter Wurzburger, "The Jewish day school: A symposium." *Tradition, 13*, 1, pp. 95–130, 1972.

departments that rival their college guidance departments in stature, assisting seniors in choosing among available programs, in the application process, in arranging for financial assistance, and in working out transfer of academic credit to American universities. Today, in the majority of Modern Orthodox day schools, parents and students expect that, as a matter of course, the majority of graduates will spend the year after graduation in a *yeshiva* program in Israel.[22]

By the early 1990s, after one-year Israel programs had been running "full-throttle" for well over a decade, some Jewish educators began expressing reservations about the efficacy of the year and its impact on students. In published articles, administrators in both Israel and the United States questioned whether one year in Israel has any effect on students, and whether the sheer popularity of the year in Israel had diluted the experience to such an extent that it was no longer a new, powerful experience, but had become another year of Orthodox day school education in a slightly different setting.[23] More recently the concern has shifted in the other direction, the argument being that Israel study indoctrinates its participants to such an extent that it wreaks havoc with family and community relationships upon students' return to the United States.[24]

While the evidence these educators bring to support their arguments is anecdotal, the questions are important ones. *Yeshivot gevohot*—post-high school *yeshiva* programs—aim to inculcate in their students a desire for and commitment to *shemirat ha-mitzvot*, particularly dedication to continued Torah study.[25] Studies have indicated that traditional *yeshivot* have been largely successful in realizing these goals.[26]

---

22 See David Bernstein, "Perspectives from abroad: Continuing the dialogue," *Ten Da'at, 6*, 24–25, 1992.

23 Norman Amsel, "The Israel experience: A closer look from Israel," *Ten Da'at, 5*, 34–36, and Esther Krauss "The Israel experience: A closer look from America," *Ten Da'at, 5*, 32–33, 1990.

24 See Samuel Heilman "Jews and Fundamentalism," *Jewish Political Studies Review* 17:1–2 (Spring 2005), available online at http://www.jcpa.org/cjc/cjc-heilman-s05.htm

25 Aharon Lichtenstein, "*Yi'Udo shel ben HaYeshiva V'Zipiyoteha Hemenu*" [The Yeshiva student's mission and its expectations from him, Hebrew], *Alon Shevut—Kesher Bogrim, 4*, 9–34, 1987.

26 William Helmreich, *The world of the Yeshiva: An intimate portrait of Orthodox Jewry*, New York: The Free Press, 1982.

American Jewish educators are sending their students to Israel to study and experience Judaism in the hope that students will return with greater commitment to these ideals, as well as a strengthened devotion to the State of Israel.[27] Are these assumptions correct? To what extent does commitment to Judaism and the State of Israel grow during the year of study in an Israeli *yeshiva*?

Before examining the programs, it makes sense to examine the very premise of spending a year of study in Israel. Why should we assume that being "away from home" will have an impact on young people any more than an "at home" schooling experience?

---

27 Walter Ackerman, "Strangers to the tradition: Idea and constraint in American Jewish education," in H.S. Himmelfarb and S. DellaPergola (Eds.), *Jewish education world-wide: Cross-cultural perspectives.* Lanham, MD: University Press, 1989.

Chapter 4

The Impact of Studying Abroad

Up to this point we have been discussing the year in Israel from the perspective of a Jewish schooling experience. It certainly falls into that category, but for many students the major difference between high school and Israel study is the change of environment—being away from home in a foreign country. What can we expect from this travel experience?

Foreign sojourns (as they are referred to in academic studies) have become more and more popular for American college-age students. According to the Institute of International Education, the number of American college students who travel to foreign countries for study has more than doubled in the past decade, with more than 200,000 young people now taking advantage of such opportunities.[28] Although much of the attention of the research has focused on language acquisition, significant studies have also been done on the cultural and affective impact of foreign sojurns.[28b] As we will see, the studies that have been done reach radically different conclusions about the effectiveness of such programs.

Some researchers argue that foreign study causes greater increases in learning and competence than could be expected through the normal maturing process. Experiential learning, which takes place by "being there" rather than through "learning about it," stimulates motivation, memory, and eventually leads to mastery of the finer details of a foreign culture. Being exposed to new tastes, sights, sounds, and smells stimulates the mind, and, with proper support, such new experiences afford a greater sense of self-confidence.[29]

---

28 See the Institute of Global Education "Open Doors" report at http://opendoors.iienetwork.org/file_depot/0-10000000/0-1000/3390/folder/50084/Open+Doors+2006_fastFacts_FINAL.pdf. Is is unlikely that Israel yeshiva programs are included in the study, given that a total of only 812 American students are reported to have sutdied in the entire Middle East in the 2003–2004 academic year.

28b The Center for Global Education has made abstracts of current research at http://www.globaled.us/ro/index.html.

29 Betsy Hansel and Neal Grove, *Why an AFS experience accelerates learning and the growth of competence*, New York: AFS International, 1984. (ERIC ED 257 732).

Foreign study offers more to students than maturing and the development of a sense of competence. A review of dissertations and research articles that examined undergraduate college students who went to study abroad indicates that the goals of such study include "developing self-awareness, gaining understanding of another culture, becoming more objective about one's own culture, becoming more sensitive to political and social issues at home and abroad, [and] developing greater competency in a particular language or area of study."[30] American college students studying in European universities have been found to have made significant gains in self-confidence, self-esteem, appreciation of one's capabilities and worth, and understanding of the strengths and weaknesses of American culture in comparison to that of other countries.[31]

Nevertheless, a number of studies suggest alternate findings. The Council on International Educational Exchange studied college undergraduates who were randomly selected from two American universities. These students were broken into three groups: those staying on their home campuses (who acted as a control group), those studying abroad, and those studying off-campus in the United States. The study found that significant changes took place among all students in the course of their year of study, mainly with regard to tolerance of other cultures' attitudes and views. The changes could not be attributed to location, however, but to "individual receptivity, motivation, openness, personal psychology and chance experiences."[32] No clear superiority of overseas programs was shown over domestic sojourn programs in effecting attitude change. In a number of instances, more change took place among students on domestic sojourn programs than on overseas programs. For example, while overseas program participants were initially more interested in the local area of their travel than were the domestic sojourn students, upon return, the overseas students' interest in their place of study decreased until they were indistinguishable from returning domestic sojourn students.

The study found that off-campus program students felt that they would question their cultural and political values because of their experiences, but it was the students who remained in the United States in

30 Allan Pfinster, *Impact of study abroad on the American college undergraduate.* Denver: Denver University, 1972 (ERIC ED 063 882).

31 N. James, "Students abroad: Expectations versus reality," *Liberal Education, 4,* 606–607, 1976.

32 W. Frank Hull, Walter Lemke, Richard Houang, *The American undergraduate, off-campus and overseas: A study of the educational validity of such programs.* Santa Barbara, California: University of California, 1977, p. 49.

programs outside of their local communities who were more certain that their experiences forced them to do so. One suggestion is that language may be the key to some of these results, as students on overseas study programs, without significant knowledge of the host language, may have been unable to overcome the language barrier, frustrating their attempts to take full advantage of their foreign study opportunity.

One further study suggests that even if foreign study does successfully change attitudes, this attitudinal change may be short-lived. In a comparison of college juniors in upper-level French classes in the University of Connecticut—some of whom participated in the school's Junior Year in France program while the rest remained on the school's home campus—greater development was found in areas of individual independence and self-reliance, as well as in acculturation seen in the students who traveled to France. In the course of the academic year, the group in France showed an increased preference for speaking French, for eating French food, and had an increased interest in international affairs. Their counterparts in the United States did not experience these changes. Nevertheless, a follow-up questionnaire given to the students upon their return to college after the summer—fewer than three months later—indicated that these changes did not persist.[33]

From these studies it is apparent that the ability of foreign study to change the attitudes of American students is unclear. Furthermore, it is not clear whether any change that does take place is significantly different from what would have occurred as part of the normal maturing process had the student not gone to study abroad.

There is room to suggest that the experience of the Modern Orthodox day school graduate in a program of study in Israel has greater potential for success than do other foreign study programs. The student arrives in Israel with some level of Hebrew language skills and an interest in the land that is much greater than that of participants in typical American exchange programs. Twelve years of day school education have preceded the student's decision to attend this program in Israel. Nevertheless, the one-year student returns from the environment of the Israeli institution to the world of North America where he or she grew up.

What does the student find when he or she arrives in Israel? To a large extent, the experience is predetermined by the student, in the choice of a particular type of program and a specific men's *yeshiva* or women's *midrashah*.

---

33 Dennison Nash, "The personal consequences of a year of study abroad," *The Journal of Higher Education*, 47, 2, 1976, pp. 191–203.

Chapter 5

The Different Types of Programs

While American day school educators strongly recommend study in a *yeshiva* in Israel, it must be noted that the *yeshiva* programs available to the North American high school graduates in Israel are not all the same. The *yeshivot* themselves highlight many of the characteristics that are unique about them, in order to attract a student body that will be most successful in a given *yeshiva*'s environment. The differences in stress on commitment to the State of Israel, willingness to accept the validity of secular education, and attitudes toward the non-religious community are some of the major differences that might influence a student to choose to study in one *yeshiva* rather than in another. There are also differences in curriculum, with some men's programs focusing on Talmud study to the exclusion of all else, for example, and in the level of the learning program that is offered.

For the American day school graduate one distinction is fairly clear-cut. Such students, often with acceptances to the college of their choice (and deferrals) in hand, fully plan to attend university following their year in Israel. Many are even on "joint programs" in which their American universities grant college credit for their Israel study.

Clearly, few of these students will come to Israel to attend traditional European-style *yeshivot* where secular study is anathema. In fact, many of the traditional "European-type" *yeshivot*, often bearing the names of the European communities in which they originated (e.g., Mir, Ponevezh), are philosophically at odds with the education these American, Modern Orthodox day school graduates received in the United States. These *yeshivot* are often non-Zionist, objecting to a secular government in the Holy Land. Above all, the Modern Orthodox day school graduate is likely unwilling to enter an environment that rejects the values and culture of American society, which is part of his very being.

Yochanan, who came to learn in Israel having completed a BA/MA in Comparative Literature at a prestigious university, had to negotiate his study in Israel with his parents. While they valued traditional Jewish studies, and accepted his career goal in Jewish education, they insisted that he complete his graduate studies first. The deal was: finish your Masters in four years of study and then you can study in Israel for four years.

The first four years of this arrangement were difficult, but rewarding. Yochanan became active in the Jewish community on campus, participating in and leading events. At the same time, as an avid student, he excelled in his studies and became close friends with several of his professors. He felt that this first stage in his education set him well on the path of preparing him to play an important role in the lives of his students in the future.

After four years, diploma in hand, Yochanan headed to Israel— according to plan—to study in Ponevezh, a traditional *yeshiva*. His high-school *rebbe*—with whom he had continued learning throughout his undergraduate and graduate studies—had told him that it was the best *yeshiva* in the world. Having just completed a taxing academic program, Yochanan was excited to return to full-time Torah study and complete his studies, culminating in Rabbinic ordination and a career devoted to Jewish education and the Jewish community.

Culture shock does not begin to describe his arrival at the *yeshiva*. In his first interview with the *Mashgiach* who oversaw the *beit midrash*, he was told that they had made a serious exception in allowing him to attend. Few university graduates were accepted to their program. He was told that his first priority was to forget all of the *shtuss* (foolishness) that he has acquired in university.

Less than three weeks passed before Yochanan knocked on the door of one of the *yeshivot hesder*, which offered a program for American students. He needed a program that would accept him and his values. After two years of study in Israel, Yochanan felt that the appropriate place to pursue his Rabbinic Ordination was in the United States, where he went to study at Yeshiva University. Today he teaches and is the rabbi of a congregation in a large Jewish community in the United States.

There are several options for the student planning a year of study in Israel. Many day school graduates who choose an Israeli *yeshiva* program (as opposed to a program for Americans in Israel) choose a *yeshivat hesder*. A *yeshivat hesder* is one that allows Israeli students to combine their military service with traditional *yeshiva* study. These *yeshivot* are usually highly Zionistic, geared toward a mature, self-motivated student. Popular *yeshivot hesder* include Yeshivat Hakotel in Jerusalem, Yeshivat Har Etzion in Alon Shvut, Yeshivat Kerem B'Yavneh near Kibbutz Yavneh, and Yeshivat Shaalvim next to Kibbutz Shaalvim. Each of these programs has about 50–80 foreign students, who make up a quarter or more of the student body of the *yeshiva*.

Other options include programs geared specifically to American students. Such programs offer a more structured schedule, a more formal guidance program, and, in general, are more sensitive to the needs of the American high school graduate who is likely away from home for an extended period for the first time. American programs in Israel include Reishit Yerushalayim in Beit Shemesh, Yeshivat Ohr Yerushalayim in Beit Meir and Yeshivat Sha'arei Mevasseret Zion, all with between 50 and 100 students.

Although each *yeshiva* has its own distinct approach and emphasis, certain generally applicable statements can be made about the two distinct types of program that the male Modern Orthodox American high school graduate most often chooses.

Yeshivot Hesder. The *yeshivat hesder* is similar to the traditional *yeshiva* in its scholastic emphasis on Talmud study, but differs radically from its traditional counterpart in that it represents the commitment of religious Zionism to the State of Israel.

These institutions are designed primarily for Israelis. The Israeli *hesder* students commit themselves to a five-year course made up of two six-to-nine month stints in the army that interrupt their *yeshiva* studies. Ideologically, the schools and their students have come to grips with the reality and pressing need to defend the State of Israel, while they remain committed to the centrality and importance of Torah study as a way of life.[34]

When recruiting American students, these *yeshivot* emphasize that, aside from strict academics, it is expected that the atmosphere fostered by the *yeshiva* will imbue in its foreign students "an intimate connection to

---

34 See Aharon Lichtenstein, "The ideology of Hesder," *Tradition*, 19, 199–217, 1981.

Torat Yisrael, Am Yisrael, Eretz Yisrael. Developing a *talmid*'s love for learning, bond with *Eretz Yisrael*, and sense of responsibility toward Am Yisrael are the Yeshiva's primary objectives" or "a love of, and commitment to *Torah, Klal Yisrael* and *Eretz Yisrael.*"[35]

These goals are not by any means secondary. While the daily schedule of prayer and study does not, at first glance, indicate an emphasis on anything other than religion and academics, a closer examination of the schools' educational design shows how these goals are achieved. On an ordinary day in a *yeshivat hesder*, from morning services at 6:30 or 7:00 A.M. until the time that most students leave the *beit midrash* (study hall) at about 11:00 P.M., most of the day has been spent, not in lectures, but in private study groups. For all that classes are largely made up of foreign students, the American student is, on some level, removed from an atmosphere of American values and culture and thrust into an environment of Israeli life. The language he hears and is forced to speak is modern Hebrew. His roommate could be an Israeli who is his contemporary and is preparing to serve in the Israeli Defense Forces. His afternoon *chavruta* (study partner) may well be a recent immigrant from Ethiopia or the former Soviet Union.

Shabbat meals and High Holy Day services, most of which are experienced in the company of several hundred fellow *yeshiva* students, are sharply different from those he participated in during his high school years in the United States, where the score of the World Series game may have been significantly more important than the Yom Kippur service of the *Kohen Gadol* (the High Priest). Virtually every day and night in the *yeshivat hesder*, the North American Modern Orthodox day school graduate is bombarded with experiences that can have a significant impact on him over an extended period of time. Nevertheless, it should be noted that the American student will have many compatriots with whom he interacts.

The *yeshiva* is also structured to expose the student to older students who share the study hall. These *kollel* members play an important role, serving as informal role models. While most are Israeli, some of the *kollel* students are individuals who are themselves graduates of North American Modern Orthodox high schools, who attended a *yeshivat hesder*, and have returned after graduation from college to live or to study.

---

35 These phrases are all taken from recruitment literature produced by *Yeshivot Hesder*, aimed at American high school seniors.

All of this is aside from the formal educational structure of lectures in Talmud, Bible, and Jewish philosophy, as well as field trips to selected regions in Israel with Bible or *mishnayot* in hand.

American Programs in Israel. The academic objectives of the American programs in Israel are largely similar to those of the *yeshivot hesder*. The daily schedule is comparable in many ways, beginning with morning *tefillot*, followed by study sessions, lectures, and meals. There are differences, though. The language of instruction is invariably English, and all of the students come from similar backgrounds.

It appears that the emphasis in many of the American programs is on academic and religious growth of the individual, and less on commitment to Zionism and the State of Israel. In fact, these *yeshivot* advertise that their educational goal is "the acquisition of the requisite learning skills for proper independent study, particularly relevant to in-depth Talmud study. Personal guidance, *sichot*, and the study of *machshavah* texts contribute to the *middot* development of the students" or how the "Yeshiva environment of intensive study and conscientious ethical behavior leads each student to a strong personal commitment to religious study and practice."[36] One student attending a Zionist-oriented program for Americans in Israel added the following comment to the survey questionnaire: "I think that Israel was mentioned way too much in this questionnaire. One can be a perfectly *halachic* [sic] abiding Jew even if he/she despises Israel." Although this student expresses his position rather harshly, no students attending *yeshivot hesder* offered similar comments.

These *yeshivot* do, on various levels, encourage their students to involve themselves in the Israeli community through volunteer work and arranged visits to different Jewish communities, but it is an experience distinct from meeting, studying, and socializing with Israelis as a natural part of the program. While there is an attempt to bring in some *semichah* students to act as role models in the *beit midrash*, none of these institutions has a permanent *kollel* of graduate students who live in Israel.

The American programs in Israel are popular for North American day school graduates for a variety of reasons. They are "smaller, more intimate and have more levels of study for weaker students than the average

---

36 These phrases are all taken from recruitment literature produced by American programs, aimed at American high school seniors.

Yeshivat Hesder."[37] Virtually all of these programs are located in or around Jerusalem, which is a preference of many North American students who expect to be in Israel for only one year. Still, as they are directed toward a specific uni-cultural group, many of the "Israel experience" opportunities that exist in the *yeshivot hesder*—such as living and interacting with Israelis, or speaking Hebrew on an everyday basis—are more difficult to find in these programs.

Women's Programs in Israel. The differences between programs for men and programs for women in Israel reflect differences in attitude regarding Jewish education for men and women generally. While there is a difference of opinion in the Mishnah with regard to the obligation of Torah study for women, the accepted position traditionally discouraged Torah education for women (Maimonides, *Hilchot Talmud Torah* 1:13). It was understood that women should learn those laws applicable to them, such as *kashrut* and *shabbat*, but these were usually learned in practice from working at home together with their mothers.

A major change came about with the development of the *Bais Yaakov* movement, begun by Sarah Shneirer with the approval of leading Torah authorities of the last generation. Responding to the waves of secularism sweeping across Europe, she developed a program of study that would keep the Jewish girl somewhat knowledgeable and in the fold.[38]

Today, at least in the Modern Orthodox community, this innovation has been extended to offer the full range of learning opportunities for women. Still, a male high school graduate is expected by his *yeshiva* in Israel to focus his daily routine around Talmudic literature, nearly to the exclusion of all else. In women's institutions, whether Talmud is a required course or offered as an option, the emphasis is on a wide range of Judaic studies rather than on the one-dimensional study of Talmud.

This difference, as well as other traditional gender stereotypes, creates an environment for women in Israel programs that differs from that of their male peers. Oftentimes the women are expected to be more involved in activities outside the walls of the *beit midrash*, ranging from preparing

---

37 Nati Helfgot and Saul Zucker, *Guide to Israel Programs*. Paramus, New Jersey: Frisch Yeshiva High School, 1991.

38 Moshe Kahn, "Jewish education for women," *Ten Da'at*, *3*, 3, 1989, pp. 9–11.

their own meals to being involved in *chessed* projects. There are fewer opportunities to interact with "graduate students" in the *beit midrash*, as the movement to stay in *yeshiva* or to return after college for continued study is much smaller in the women's programs.

Since many traditional communal activities are male-centered, in these Orthodox programs the women are at best passive, rather than active, participants in many religious ceremonies. An obvious example are *tefillot*, where the communal prayer service itself is part of the daily curriculum in men's programs, but is largely left to personal initiative in women's programs. The *yamim noraim* experience cannot be as engaging to the student when it is not a community event and service. Even holidays that are clearly marked as offering equal obligation to women are not celebrated as such in most women's programs. Purim, about which the Gemara in *Megillah* (4a) clearly rules that women are obligated in the commandments of the day—*she'af hen hayu be-oto ha-nes*—since women played a unique role in the miracle, stands out as a day that these schools could choose to have a women's *megillah* reading; yet few choose to accept the halachic ruling permitting such a gathering.

The challenges of educating American students in Israel are handled differently by the different types of programs in Israel—indeed by every individual school. Most *yeshivot hesde*r attempt to integrate, on some level, the American students into the lifestyle of religious Israeli life. The American programs in Israel operate largely as if they were islands of American religious life in Israel. Most of the women's programs are made up of Americans, but they encourage interaction in Israeli society by offering less of the traditional isolation seen in the *yeshiva* environment.

Coming to Israel for a year of post-high school study in a *yeshiva* is a three-pronged educational experience for the Modern Orthodox high school graduate before college. On one level, it is a year of continued intensive Jewish education. At the same time, it is an experiential "foreign sojourn" of lengthy duration. Finally, it is an "Israel experience," one that challenges its participants with a culture that is so much like their own, but so different as well.

As we have seen, the literature has much to say with regard to each of these topics. Studies show that Jewish schooling has a significant impact on students—the more schooling, the greater the impact. While overseas study has an undetermined impact on the average American college-age

student, Israel visits are likely to have significant impact on their participants.[39] In this context it is reasonable to anticipate substantial change in
participants in one-year post-high school *yeshiva* study programs in Israel.

While anecdotal observations of educators in America and Israel differ regarding the impact that the Israel *yeshiva* experience has on these
students, the distinctive elements of these programs suggest that they may
have significant, long-term impact on the participants. In the words of
Rav Aharon Lichtenstein, head of Yeshivat Har Etzion:

> Many of the Orthodox youth who come to Israel to study, who
> will ultimately exercise some kind of influence in the Diaspora,
> reach this country at what I would define as a more critical stage
> of their lives. They are, as it were, young lions, younger than those
> of other sectors, and what they experience here has a more marked
> effect on their lives "back home." They come here expressly to
> study. Many of them arrive immediately after graduating from
> high school, and the religious aspect of what they learn here dove-
> tails with their studies at home when they return to the US.[40]

The only way to know for sure is by examining the participants
themselves.

---

39 For studies of the short-term Birthright program and its impact on its participants, see
Leonard Saxe, Ted Sasson, and Shahar Hecht, *Taglit-birthright Israel: Impact of
Jewish Identity, Peoplehood and Connection to Israel*, Waltham, MA: The Maurice
and Marilyn Cohen Center for Modern Jewish Studies, Brandeis University, 2006.
Available online at http://cmjs.org/files/bri2006.evaluationimpact.pdf

40 Aharon Lichtenstein, "Israeli branches of Diaspora religious movements: Indigenous
development and potential influence in the Diaspora," in *Forum on the Jewish People,
Zionism and Israel*, 60, 1987, pp. 11–13.

Chapter 6

Quantifying the Impact

What are the hopes, aspirations, and expectations from the year in Israel? The answer depends on who you ask. Professionals in Jewish education, parents, community synagogue rabbis, campus leaders, college admissions officials, *aliyah* organizations, Israeli *yeshiva* heads, siblings ... they will all have different expectations.

Even the students themselves have a variety of reasons for going to Israel, ranging from an intense desire to learn Torah, to a desire for an "Israel experience," to be able to list a prestigious Israel program on their résumé.

> In the days that I was doing "Israel advisement" in a major New York metropolitan area high school, I asked Chaya, a young woman in the senior class, to which programs she was planning to apply. She did not hesitate. Her answer was "the Gush." Aside from the gender issue ("the Gush"—Yeshivat Har Etzion—is a Yeshivat Hesder, an all men's institution), her intellectual abilities were such that a less academically demanding program seemed to be most appropriate for her.
>
> "Why 'the Gush'?" I queried.
>
> "All of my friends who went to Machon Gold came back 20 pounds heavier, but all the guys who went to the Gush came back looking great," she said.

Yes, sometimes Israel study is the means to a better figure.

But what really happens during the year of study? In an attempt to find a real answer to that matter, I asked students in Israel a series of questions examining student behaviors and attitudes on subjects that I thought were basic to the way the Orthodox community perceives itself. These questions ranged from ritual practices—like *netilat yadayim* in the morning—to their level of comfort holding their girlfriend's or boyfriend's hand and going to a "dirty" movie. Included were questions about their future plans and the place of the State of Israel in their religious worldview.

No social science study can possibly be 100% accurate. So many different experiences come into play, both before and during the year in Israel, that it is impossible to be certain what triggers a given response. In order to be as certain as possible that changes in attitude could be attributed to the Israel experience, students were approached at the very beginning of their year in Israel, and again after Pesach toward the end of that year. I also tracked down as many as I could and asked them the same questions a year later.[40a]

Overall, an analysis of the students' responses uncovered general trends that could be expected from a lengthy, powerful, all-encompassing experience. Many attitudes and behaviors reported by the students indicated greater commitment and dedication to the traditional norms and values promulgated by the schools in Israel. Specifically, when the students' survey responses were analyzed using factor analysis, three distinct areas of concern were apparent, including:

– Religious ritual behaviors and attitudes, which included:

  • Ritual practice, such as prayers, ritual hand-washing, and fasting

  • Personal modesty, including issues of modest dress and whether one would feel comfortable in mixed gender situations

  • Interaction with the secular world, for example, whether one would attend a "dirty" movie, or eat kosher food in a non-kosher restaurant

– Zionism, which included:

  • Plans to move to Israel

  • Issues of National Religious belief, e.g., that the modern state of Israel is the national homeland of the Jewish people, or that it is part of the process of redemption

– Ethical issues, which included:

40a The students' responses—before, after, and one year later—can be accessed on the Yashar Books website http://www.yasharbooks.com/Israel.html. A representative sample appears in the appendix at the end of this book.

- Questions about honesty when taking tests and in paying taxes

- Ethical behaviors, like giving charity and respect for the elderly

Factor analysis scrutinizes responses to the survey questions and produces a list of factors based on which questions were answered by the survey participants in a similar fashion. By using this method, we can see which questions the students felt were comparable, and view them as a single category, rather than as independent issues. This allows us to create scales representing percentages of respondents who scored "low" "middle" or high" before and after the year, allowing us to determine what change —if any—took place in the course of the year. Looking at these scales will give a good introduction to the changes that took place, which we will then examine in greater detail.

As noted above, the factor of "Religious ritual behaviors and attitudes" included three sets of scales: ritual practice, personal modesty, and interaction with the secular world. Less than 20% of the students scored "high" on the ritual practice scale (i.e., prayers, ritual hand-washing, and fasting) before the year in Israel; almost 70% scored "high" at the end of the year.

Just under 30% of the respondents scored "high" on the personal modesty scale (i.e., issues of modest dress and whether one would feel comfortable in mixed-gender situations) at the beginning of their year of study; 64% scored "high" by the end of the year.

At the beginning of the academic year, just under 30% of the respondents scored "high" on the scale that dealt with interaction with the secular world (i.e., whether one would attend a "dirty" movie, or eat kosher food in a non-kosher restaurant); close to 50% scored "high" at the end of the year.

Scales in the Zionism factor included plans to move to Israel and issues of National Religious belief.

Before their year in Israel, just under 30% of the students scored "high" on the plans for *aliyah* scale (i.e., living and raising a family in Israel, serving in the Israeli armed forces), while more than 50% did so at the end of the year. On the other hand, with regard to support for National Religious ideology (i.e., that the modern state of Israel is the national homeland of the Jewish people, that it is part of the process of redemption, and that all Jews are obligated to support it), just under 30% of the students scored "high" at the beginning of the year. When the year was over their attitude had not changed very much: now just over 30% scored "high."

As will be explained, it was difficult to create scales for the issues that fell under the ethics factor, since such a large number of the respondents indicated that their conduct with regard to honesty and ethical behaviors was exemplary.

The findings shed quite a bit of light on the changes that take place together with this educational experience. Let's look at each of these three areas individually.

Chapter 7

Religious Ritual Behaviors and Attitudes

Shimon ha-Tzaddik, one of the Sages of the Mishnah, teaches in *Pirkei Avot* (1:2) that the world is balanced on three things—Torah, *Avodah*, and *Gemilut Chassadim* (Torah study, religious ritual service, and acts of loving-kindness), so it should hardly surprise us that spending a year immersed in the environment of a *yeshiva* in Israel affects these particular issues.

Torah study

Virtually all of the programs—both men's and women's—focus on Torah study. A quick glance at the daily schedule makes it clear that the year's focus will be on Jewish texts.

There certainly are differences between programs. Some offer classes throughout the day, while others will offer more of a *beit midrash* environment; some offer Talmud study almost exclusively, while others offer a more diverse curriculum. The long and short of it, however, is that this year the students coming to Israel are expected to learn.

Interestingly, however, the ultimate goal for the year is not necessarily to help the students garner large amounts of knowledge, or even to master a particular area of *halachah*. The aim is to encourage the students to become life-long learners. Ideally these students will come to recognize the importance of learning to their lives as Jews, and gain the tools and desire to continue in this path in the future, whether or not they remain in a *yeshiva* setting.

In setting such a goal, the Israel programs have a solid base upon which to build. After twelve years of day school education, more than half of the students expect that it is very likely they will continue to learn with a *chavruta* (study partner) in college and beyond. More than 80% expect to have an extensive library of Jewish books in their home. Admittedly, the

35

group that comes to Israel is self-selecting, and the less motivated high school graduate has deliberately chosen to forego Israel study. Nevertheless, the schools these students attended seem to have done something right.

As important as this foundation is, however, the experience in Israel brings commitment to lifelong Torah study to an entirely new level. Following one year of full-time study, more than 75% of the students expect to continue their learning into adulthood, and fully 90% of them anticipate that their library of Jewish texts will be a central part of their home.

How does this added commitment come about?

Yehuda came to *yeshiva* with a major concern—what was he going to do all day? Gemara in high school was one thing. Although it was a double period, he liked his *rebbe*, did well on the tests and could always look forward to gym, which was the next period on most days. Yehuda enjoyed an academic challenge as well as the next guy, but he also enjoyed taking in an occasional movie and spending time just unwinding with his friends. He came to Israel because that's what "everybody" did, and chose a *Yeshivat Hesder* because that's where the Israel advisor told him "the real learning" went on—and Yehuda wasn't someone who went second-best on anything.

"When I first walked into the *beit midrash*, I was overwhelmed. There was a room with about 300 people in animated discussion, with *Gemarot* open in front of them and other books strewn about. These people didn't just learn Torah, they cared about Torah. In all honesty, I wasn't sure that I cared as much as they did."

The first few weeks were difficult. What first got Yehuda involved wasn't the intellectual challenge of text study, but the experience of the *yamim noraim* davening.

"Back home I always went to the *minyan* that was going to finish fastest. I just wanted to get home to read the paper or take a nap. Here I was, davening all day, and I didn't even realize that it was the mid-afternoon. I can't tell you what it was; it may have been a combination of things. I was surrounded by hundreds of people who wanted to be there. The tunes that they sang as a group were so powerful that I just got drawn in. The closest I had ever been to that before was *lehavdil* at a rock concert at the Garden. Any thought that I had about switching to a 'less serious' program ended right there."

After the Sukkot vacation, Yehuda returned to *yeshiva* determined to make a success of himself there.

"I was used to being at the very top of my class. Here I was starting at the bottom rung. After a week or two I realized that the other students weren't smarter than me, but they knew an awful lot more, and I needed to catch up."

Yehuda began to study Mishnah—the six volumes edited by Rabbi Yehuda HaNasi that are the basis for all discussions in the Gemara —with Kehati's commentary, written in modern Hebrew.

"Studying Mishnah straight wasn't the most challenging—or interesting—thing to do in the *beit midrash*, but I was driven to know as much as everyone else in the *beit midrash*, and I stuck to it."

His efforts bore fruit and soon he was moved into the *Rosh Yeshiva's* top-level *shiur*, an unusual feat for an American student from a co-ed high school."

The *yeshiva* experience is all-encompassing in a way that no day school in North America can ever be. The environment is such that students are surrounded by an impressive community of learners, not only in the *beit midrash*, but in day-to-day activities as well.

Even getting into a taxi in Israel can be an experience. A traditional—but not necessarily *kippah*-wearing—driver may engage his passengers in conversations about the weekly Torah reading or *mishnayot* that he was reviewing. One of my recollections from my own days as a student in Israel is going to my Israeli friend's home for Shabbat. His father was a businessman who had moved to Palestine with his family as a teenager just before the establishment of the State of Israel. He regaled the guests with stories about living in Petach Tikva in 1948, and the difficulties in finding a non-Jew to whom they could sell the community's *chametz* before Passover, since they were in a virtual state of war with their Arab neighbors (someone solved the problem by remembering the Seventh Day Adventist who lived as a hermit in a cave outside of town). What was most impressive, however, was when he turned to his son, asking "so, what are you learning in *yeshiva* these days?" and the conversation that ensued on the topic. When I asked him how he was conversant in the material, he answered that he had been learning *daf yomi* on a regular basis for the past ten years. Every day he prepared the page, attended the class, and went home to review it. The man had been through the entire Talmud several times!

While Talmud Torah is valued in the Modern Orthodox community in North America, in most homes it does not permeate the atmosphere as it does in many communities in Israel. The experience in Israel—both inside and outside of the *yeshiva*—encourages students to see Torah study as part-and-parcel of their identity as a practicing Jew. At a particular juncture in life when the student is beginning to break loose from home and parent and choose his or her own path, the influence of the *yeshiva* environment, its faculty and surroundings, can have a major influence on the young people studying there.

At the same time, these young people do not appear to be swept up by a cult-like phenomenon. Even as they accept the Mishnaic dictum *V'Talmud Torah k'negged kulam*—popularly translated as "the study of Torah is equivalent to all *mitzvot*," they recognize that there is still a "real" world to which they will be returning. Although more of them think that it is "very likely" that they will learn in full-time *kollel* for at least a year (4% in the pre-test vs. 10% in the post-test), but they do not all see themselves as rabbis or teachers (6% saying that such a goal is "very likely" and less than 15% saying "somewhat likely"), where the numbers planning those careers remains unchanged from the beginning to the end of the year.

Avodah

For a typical Orthodox Jew, ritual law and practice is the basis for what defines his or her Jewishness. Rashi, the masterful medieval commentator on the *Chumash*, early in his work questions why we need all of the stories that appear throughout *Sefer Bereshit*: why not start with the first *halachah*, the first law given to the Jewish People in Chapter 12 of *Sefer Shemot*? Traditionally, the Code of Jewish Law—the *Shulchan Aruch*—is the basic book against which behavior is measured.

Children growing up in Orthodox homes and day schools interact with ritual from their first memories. Their lives are full of religious responsibilities and instructions, ranging from saying *berachot* on food to Shabbat restrictions. Some of these rituals are home-based, while others take place in the public sphere, where certain behaviors are expected. Yet others are private, in the sense that aside from God, no one will ever know whether a particular act had been performed. All of these rules and regulations are taught to children throughout their childhood and adolescence, yet according to the responses there is a wide discrepancy between the levels of performance of different kinds of practice.

Reciting *Birkat Hamazon*—grace after meals—is one of the few (perhaps the only) *berachot* that is a Biblical obligation, and we find that a comfortable majority of students (62%) coming to Israel indicate that they either "always" or "usually" recite it. It is likely, however, that the relatively large number of people who perform this mitzvah do so not so much because of its source in the Bible, as because throughout their childhood it was sung—first at family meals, then in schools, summer camps, and so on. Much smaller numbers (less than half) report performing certain other daily rituals either "always" or "usually"; these include morning hand-washing, *Netilat Yadayim*, or reciting the blessing of *Asher Yatzar*, which praises God for allowing the performance of basic natural functions, a *berachah* recited after using the bathroom.

The experience of a year in *yeshiva* is one of transformation for these students. By year's end, three quarters or more of the students report that these behaviors have become part of their daily routine on a regular basis.

I am not sure that research can prove what brings about this change of behavior, but this is what Dan told me, when I met him for lunch at one of the eateries near Yeshiva University.

It is hard to say what exactly made me "turn the corner," although a lot of it had to do with what I saw around me. At home my father—who always went to *shul* on Shabbat—seemed more concerned with the social aspect of things. He ran the kiddush club at the end of *Keriat ha-Torah*, and never seemed concerned with the small things. He chose which of the three *minyanim* to go to on Yom Kippur based on which one had the longest break. When I got to *yeshiva*, I met people who wanted to be in *shul*. The words, the ceremonies, all seemed to have so much meaning for them.

I remember that on my first Rosh Hashana, seeing the *Rosh Yeshiva* with his father, who was hard-of-hearing. They made sure to stand right next to the man who blew shofar so that he would be able to fulfill the mitzvah. I thought about how hearing the shofar back home never meant so much to me, and here I stood with people who leaned forward to make sure to hear every sound— and if there was a mistake they went over from the beginning. It made me want to understand why this was all so important, and for the first time I actually paid attention to what was in the *Machzor*. Instead of talking to my friends about the World Series on Rosh Hashana I ended up discussing whether it was a day to do *teshuvah*—and if not what was it. It was that experience, I guess, that made me realize that all that stuff that I had been told to do since I was a kid meant something. It wasn't just something to do to make me different.

An interesting note is the question of fasting on minor fast days. Although in its origins fasting was likely connected with repentance and introspection—and days connected with the destruction of the Temple are certainly appropriate opportunities for that behavior—today the fast days on the calendar are perceived more as a religious obligation, to refrain from eating, than an opportunity for spontaneous spirituality. The fast days have one tremendous advantage over the other rituals that we have examined: they come only once a year. Young people (boys, in particular) saw lasting a whole day without a morsel of food as a challenge; in this way, fulfillment of this ritual may have little to do with religious devotion.

We find, in fact, that two thirds of the students in the pre-test say that they fast "always" or "usually," and the response level reaches 90% after a year of study in Israel.

To explain this shift in behavior, it is important to note that these students have been learning *halachah* for twelve years prior to arriving in Israel, and undoubtedly have known many of the *halachot* that—based on their own testimony—they did not perform prior to arriving in Israel. The *yeshivot* do not generally lecture their students on the importance of reciting *Asher Yatzar* or *Birkat Hamazon*; the *yeshivot* assume that these basic ritual behaviors are common practice. These behaviors appear to change during the year due to the students living in an environment where these are the norms of conduct. The values of the *yeshiva* environment differ significantly from those of the students' community at home.[41] It is not the learning *per se* that brings about the change; rather, it is the total environment (of which, obviously, learning is an important factor).

It is important to note again that this different lifestyle is not merely the lifestyle of the *yeshiva*, but is the lifestyle of the larger Israeli commu-

---

41 See, for example, Shalom Carmy, "Rejoinder: Synthesis and the unification of human existence," *Tradition*, 21, 4, 1985, pp. 37–51.

nity in which the student lives. Certainly in the *yeshivot* which are contained within their own communities or on enclosed campuses, the lifestyle all around is one that supports adherence to ritual practice. Still, even when leaving the precincts of the *yeshiva*, the student comes into contact with a society that is more observant than the American Jewish community. In the words of one Jewish sociologist, "Israeli society simply lends more social support, significance, and legitimacy to Jewish ritual practice than American society does."[42]

This all-encompassing atmosphere of religious, ritually practiced Judaism, foregrounded as a norm of behavior, is a powerful force that has an impact on the American day school student every day during the year of study in Israel.

Personal modesty

When I was an American student in a *Yeshivat Hesder*, my seat location in the *beit midrash* made me the prime choice to be tour-guide for an hour. When a group of tourists would come to visit the *yeshiva*, one of the administrators would walk into the study hall looking for an English speaker to spend half-an-hour with them. For me this was an opportunity to take a break from my day, and I enjoyed meeting people and talking to them.

After a while I came up with my standard spiel. I would show them the Second Temple period wine-press at the entrance and talk about our centuries-old connection to the Land of Israel. Then I would take them inside and talk to them about the concept of a *Yeshivat Hesder*. Finally, I would take them to the balcony that served as the women's section on Shabbat where they could see the *beit midrash* in action, and I would take their questions.

Once a group came, walked with me through the standard tour, and looked down at the *beit midrash*. One woman, who looked to be in her sixties, stared in fascination at the activity below. She inquired as to the different classes, and asked me to point out who the teachers were. After gazing at the scene below for a few minutes, she looked at me and said ". . . and you are telling me that all of those young men are celibate?!"

---

42 Samuel Heilman and Steven M. Cohen, *Cosmopolitans and Parochials: Modern Orthodox Jews in America*. Chicago: University of Chicago Press, 1989, p. 140.

I was taken aback by the question, and needed to think about it for a moment. While I did not see myself as celibate, as a single eighteen-year-old I was not sexually active. After a moment I explained that Judaism does not believe in celibacy; that there were, in fact married students in the *beit midrash* below, and that those of us who were not yet married, certainly intended on getting there one day in the future.

Of all the issues that a healthy 17- or 18-year-old young adult has to face, questions of developing a sexual identity are probably the most crucial, yet the least discussed. An Orthodox Jewish youngster who grows up exposed to the values and mores of modern American society cannot help but be challenged by the incongruity of the standards taught in *yeshiva* and what he or she sees on television and the movies. No longer a "Leave it to Beaver" community, the messages on the big—and small—screen shout that anyone who is not engaged in at least thinking about sex (if not actively pursuing it) has something wrong with them.

Of course, Judaism does not forbid sexual relations, and perceives them as not only permissible but as a mitzvah, when pursued in the proper setting—that is, within the context of marriage. Students are well aware of this, and the topic of marriage is on their minds, certainly in women's programs.

> Chaim and Michal were getting married. They hadn't told anyone yet, but they had decided back in eleventh grade that they were going to live their lives together. Like Mottel the Tailor and Tzeitel in Fiddler on the Roof, they had "made each other a pledge."
>
> It wasn't as though this was totally unexpected. They had grown up in the same neighborhood, davened in the same *shul*, and had gone to the same school. There were months of not talking to each other followed by spending every waking moment together. "We were normal, Modern Orthodox kids," tells Michal. "We had our whole lives planned, from the colleges we were going to, the wedding date—approximately anyway—kids, jobs. We knew what we were going to do. But first, we were going to learn in Israel. It was part of the schooling that all of our friends went through. And we were going to spend time together there, too."
>
> Both Chaim and Michal got into their first choice for college, received deferrals, and chose the Israel programs that they would attend. For Michal it was pretty easy: "there weren't many women's programs where I could continue learning Gemara like I did in high

school. I was good at Gemara. I liked the give-and-take of the discussions as well as the analysis that followed. Chaim and I had been *chavrutot* in high school and there was never an issue there."

Chaim had a harder time deciding where to study. The idea of being full-time with Israelis was daunting, and he was concerned that his Hebrew was not good enough to follow a high-level *shiur* in that language. "When push came to shove, I just couldn't sign up for a *Hesder Yeshiva*. Lots of my friends from high school who came back during Pesach vacation said that some of the American programs were on the same level as the *Hesder Yeshivot*. I wanted to be near Jerusalem—that's where Michal was going to be—so I decided to go to one of the American programs just outside the city."

The year began much as they had planned it. They talked on the phone, got together on Fridays and once or twice during the week. After some initial adjustment time, they each became acclimated in their programs and began to enjoy their studies, their teachers, their new friends and the atmosphere of being in Israel. Chaim's parents came for Sukkot and Michal joined them for Yom Tov meals and davening. Everything seemed as it should be.

"I guess it started around Chanukah, Michal recalls. My program had three days off and I called Chaim to schedule stuff to do together. Chaim said that his *yeshiva* had no vacation during Chanukah—'they say that Chanukah is when you are supposed to learn extra'—was the way he put it. I realized that more and more 'they' were telling him what to do. And they weren't only telling him what to do with his time. They were telling him what NOT to do with his time. And talking to me was one of those things."

Chaim remembers it a bit differently, although he agrees with the bottom line. "When you sit and learn all day, and you realize how important—how central—learning is to being a full, practicing Jew, you understand that you can't let everyday things distract you. Sure Michal was important to me, but she had to understand that everything has its time and place. I wasn't getting married at 18. Hanging around with her was fun, but it wasn't essential for me just then, the way learning was. She just had to let go."

Michal suspects that there were a number of factors in the collapse of their relationship. She believes that the men's programs discourage any interaction with women, but especially with women who are, themselves, studying Gemara, an area that is perceived as being off-limits to women in traditional Jewish society. True to her training, she points to a passage in the Talmud in *Kiddushin* 29b that discusses whether a man should first study Torah or get married. "The Gemara quotes two opinions. Rav Yehuda quotes Shmuel as saying that you should first get married. Rabbi Yochanan responds, saying, 'someone with the responsibilities of marriage will be able to study?' Everyone in the story recognizes that marriage is important. I understand that Chaim's rabbis didn't want guys to waste their time spending time with girls when they should be in the *beit midrash*, but our situation was different. We were getting married!"

For all their exposure to contemporary culture, it is clear that the sexual mores of the Orthodox community are significantly more conservative than that of the general population. The statistics most often quoted for the general population in the United States indicate that more than half of high school teenagers are sexually active. While there are no hard numbers in the Orthodox community, the phenomenon cannot possibly be close to that. Teenage pregnancy has never been a serious problem in the community, and it isn't only because Jewish teens know more about contraception. According to their responses, day school graduates may be at least somewhat comfortable holding hands with their girlfriends or boyfriends, but only a quarter would be very comfortable "being intimate" with their fiancée after they are engaged.

The year in Israel is a watershed as far as these behaviors are concerned. For many students who attended co-ed Modern Orthodox schools back home, in Israel they are placed in single-sex settings where casual interaction with the opposite sex is actively discouraged. By year end, the number of students reporting that they would feel "very comfortable" or "somewhat comfortable" holding hands with their girlfriend or boyfriend is half of what it was at the beginning of the year (less than two thirds of the students), and even fewer than that would be comfortable being alone with them. Similarly, those students who say that they would be "very comfortable" being intimate with their fiancée has dropped to under 10%.

A former student of mine approached me to ask for advice. Beyond being a talented teacher, she is the granddaughter of a prominent American rabbi whose positions and philosophy had played an important role in molding the contemporary Jewish community in North America. She wanted my help in finding a job.

I didn't beat around any bushes. "If you want to work in one of the one-year programs you have to start covering your hair. No one will hire you otherwise." I asked her if she wanted to consider working in the Conservative Yeshiva. She did not, as she identified completely with the Orthodox community and did not want to be perceived otherwise. Her argument was simple. "My mother didn't cover her hair. My grandmother didn't cover her hair. The wives of the community rabbis where I grew up did not cover their hair. Why should I ignore generations of tradition in order to fit the model of what has recently become the definition of Orthodoxy?" While her logic was impeccable, she still wasn't going to get hired.

A further indication that these students are thinking about marriage is the change that takes place in their attitudes toward hair covering. There are clear *halachot* obligating married women to cover their hair after marriage, although the practice was almost unheard-of even in the most religious circles in America in the 1950s. (It should also be mentioned that the issues discussed above, such as holding hands, were also kept in the breach in that generation, where young men and women met at social dances sponsored by organizations like the Religious Zionists of America.) In answer to the question "does your mother cover her hair in public?" 50% of the respondents replied with an emphatic "never," and only 17% responded "often." Yet even before their year in Israel study began, more than half of the women surveyed in this study indicated that it was at least "somewhat likely" that they would do so, and after a year in Israel, more than three quarters felt that way.

The men were less concerned with this issue, although at the close of the year nearly 70% felt that it was "very important" or "somewhat important" to them that their wives cover their hair.

Of course, there are issues of sexuality not connected with marriage at all, which are, on some level, probably unique to religious communities. Recreational activities that general society perceives as being basically neutral carry significance according to traditional norms of behavior in the Orthodox Jewish community. Two examples that appeared on the survey asked about "mixed swimming" and attending movies that contained sexual themes.

If we look at the responses to both of these questions, it appears that prior to their Israel study, the majority of students viewed these activities as normative. About 60% say that they are at least fairly comfortable participating in them; less than 17% say that they would be "very uncomfortable" in those settings. The numbers switch by the end of the year, where we find only 12% of the students saying that they would be "very comfortable" going mixed swimming or attending racy films, while about 60% would be, on some level, uncomfortable with these activities.

Perhaps more than any other single finding, this change points to the difference between the experience that Israel offers to adolescents on the cusp of adulthood in contrast to what the alternative—the American college campus—proffers. This alternative to the *yeshiva* is not simply a set of generic values espoused by American society at large, but an environment where the basic values and belief system of the Modern Orthodox day school graduate is challenged daily. As one of my email correspondents wrote to me, "call it naïve, but I like to believe that the campus culture with its unabashed emphasis on hedonistic indulgence in sex, drugs, and alcohol, and its intellectual milieu wherein 'faith' is treated as a dirty word, need not necessarily 'reflect the world around us'." The Israeli *yeshivot*, on the other hand, preach *tzeniut* (modesty) by way of practice, as well as the importance of valuing a person for themselves, rather than making them into sex objects.

Chapter 8

Moral/Ethical Development

Gemilut Chassadim

For many years after I came on *aliyah* I worked full-time at a program for women in Jerusalem. The students were, by-and-large, highly motivated academically and community-wise. Invariably we got a fairly large number who had been the valedictorians of their graduating class in high school, presidents of their student councils, or head counselors in summer camps.

The school was always looking for ways to engage the students as members of the Jewish community, both scholastically and socially. Some years students successfully published an academic journal that included articles penned by the faculty and by the students themselves. Recently the school has developed a program that mainstreams special-needs women, who have their own academic track for part of the day, but who participate in much of the programming—both academic and extra-curricular—that goes on throughout the year.

Tova, the director of the program, is rightfully proud of these activities, which she sees as part of the educational message of the institution. Teaching about Judaism and about being a passionate, active Jewish woman is not only about studying texts, it is also about being a caring, supportive member of the Jewish community.

Some time ago a phone call came to the office asking for some help. A family of recent *olim* were in an emergency situation, with the father hospitalized, the mother overwhelmed with children, and no natural family support network available to them. Tova recruited students who quickly made a sign-up sheet to arrange for shifts in childcare and household help for this family. She also called a number of other one-year Israel programs to solicit their assistance in helping out this family in a difficult situation. When the director of

47

another program responded to her request by saying, "we don't do *chessed* on Wednesdays," she threw up her hand in exasperation. "I didn't know that *chessed* was limited to certain days of the week!" she exclaimed.

As the Mishnah in *Pirkei Avot* indicates, Judaism is not focused solely on religious ritual and study. Aside from intellectual and ritual demands, the expectation is that the truly religious person will grow from those activities and transfer his or her religious devotion into an impeccable moral and ethical life.

All too often, we get caught up in the minutiae of the ritual or the four cubits of the *beit midrash*, and lose sight of a third—perhaps primary—goal. In the words of one observer of the Jewish community:

> While we have created many observant Jews, we have not created many religious Jews. When it is possible for a Jew to don *tefillin*, be rigorous in his *kashrut*, live a life marked by many *chumrot*, and yet be lax in his *bein adam l'chaveiro*, something is not right. Students of Torah are considered to have "succeeded" when they know this or that Gemara and are expert in certain areas of *halakha*. But the noblest internal possibilities of the Jew—*bitahon*, awe, humility, courage, loyalty, *hesed, 'ahava*— are by and large not an integral part of the learning program—as if *middot* and general spiritual development will somehow take care of themselves.[43]

At first glance the data collected in this study would appear to support this anecdotal observation in the case of one-year Israel programs. There did not seem to be the same degree of change in this category as there was regarding ritual behaviors and attitudes, or, as we will see, toward Israel and Zionism. Surprisingly—or, perhaps, not so surprisingly—the area of ethical behavior, which included such questions as charity, honesty, and concern for others, seemed to show little, if any, such change.

When discussing this initial finding with colleagues, it aroused some debate, and a call from some to rethink the traditional curriculum, to place a greater emphasis on these concerns. It was my belief that the text study was not the critical issue here; rather it was the environment that should

---

43 Emanuel Feldman, "Observant Jews and religious Jews," in *Tradition*, 26, 2, 1992, pp. 1–3.

be changed. If students found themselves in a setting where these were clearly the values of the institution and community, they would internalize the message, making it their own.

Upon a reexamination of numbers, however, it appears that based on the students' responses, these concerns are largely misplaced. While it is true that there is little change with regard to these issues over the course of the year in Israel, this can be explained in a simple, straightforward manner. According to their answers, the values of *chessed* and *emet*—of charity and truth—have been so well inculcated in day school graduates that there is not much room for positive change.

Even before the year of study in Israel began, when students were asked, for example, whether they would be totally honest when filling out their tax return, more than 80% indicated that it was "very likely" or "somewhat likely." A mere 3% said that it was "very unlikely." Only 3% thought that it was "very likely" that they would cheat in order to pass a college exam; 70% said that it was "very unlikely." 85% of day school graduates think that it is likely that they will be giving 10% of their earnings to charity and more than three quarters report that they "always" or "usually" offer their seat to an aged person. These results, stemming from the influences of home, school, and community in North America are hard to improve upon.

One area that falls into this category, which does not garner the same responses, is the question about speaking *lashon hara* ("evil words" or "gossip"). Here, only 1% thought that they successfully refrained from speaking ill of others "always," and only about a quarter of the students felt that they are usually successful in this area. There is some improvement in this pattern at year's end, but not nearly the kind of change is witnessed as we have seen regarding religious ritual behavior, commitment to Torah study, or heightened sensitivity to issues of personal modesty.

With regard to *lashon hara*, we are witnesses to the honesty of the respondents, who recognize their own shortcomings with regard to interpersonal relationships. This is one mitzvah widely discussed and universally recognized as difficult to keep. The statement by one-third of the students that, at the end of a year of study, they "always" or "usually" refrain from speaking *lashon hara*, is an indication of heightened awareness and sensitivity to that commandment, stemming from a year of emphasis on the care and concern that a religious person should have with regard to everyday behaviors.

One question that should be asked is why graduates of Modern Orthodox day schools do not embrace traditional Jewish values of Torah and *Avodah* to the same extent that they report accepting those areas that we have dubbed *Gemilut Chassadim*.[44]

Here, it is essential that we think about the role that general society plays in the development of children today. We have already observed that many of the messages that are broadcast by the media run counter to traditional Jewish values. Generally speaking, secular society places tremendous value on personal choice and freedoms. The idea that people should be confined in their movements, limited in what they can choose to eat or wear, restricted in what they can study or challenge, is anathema in today's world. In particular, attitudes toward personal modesty and sexuality presented as societal norms in movies, television, and the internet, run counter to what the *yeshiva* perceives as the religious ideal.

Traditional values do restrict freedom of behavior. Within the framework of *halachah*—a framework that is subject to different definitions—day schools work to acculturate students to the norms of Judaism that present an "alternative lifestyle" to what appears to be accepted in the larger community. At the same time, the power of the values and mores of American society at large is very strong; moreover, children's homes do not necessarily support rejection of those societal values.

When dealing with issues of morals and ethics, these tensions do not exist. On some level, the message given by the world at large is harmonious with that of the home and the Jewish day school. "Good deeds" are praiseworthy, as are honesty and integrity. A dishonest politician is recognized as corrupt and, if he is reelected, it is despite his misdeeds, not because they are seen as praiseworthy. With a confluence of parallel messages, it is fairly easy for the day school student to accept that those values are appropriate ones, which should be held close and valued as Jews.

---

44 Here I am in somewhat of a quandary with regard to accepting the results of the survey responses at face value. Do students really expect that they will not cheat on tests and will always offer their seats to the aged? If I choose to reject their self-evaluation, however, then how can I accept any of their answers? For the more cynical among us, the question to be asked here is why these students are more comfortable admitting that they do not perform the religious precepts taught in day school than they are admitting that they fall short in matters of ethics. I believe that the answer to this question is the same as the answer to the question presented in the body of the article.

Chapter 9

Attitudes Toward Israel

Aside from the basic aims and goals of the one-year Israel programs—
Torah, *Avodah* and *Gemilut Chassadim*—all of which are the traditional
objectives of traditional *yeshivot*—this year of study clearly has an impact
on another crucial area of Jewish concern, the Land of Israel. For all that
ease of travel and communication has made Israel so much more accessible and so much less exotic than it once was, there are still major differences between attitude and practice in Israel and the contemporary
Diaspora communities. The North American Jewish community has
become comfortable enough for some to argue that they no longer have a
sense of being in *galut*, as did their great-grandparents in Poland and
Russia. Furthermore, under the influence of the philosophy of
Rav Avraham Isaac Kook, religious Zionists have transformed *Eretz
Yisrael* into a pillar of Judaism, a position unfamiliar to many committed
Diaspora Jews for whom Zionism means support for the Jewish state,
rather than feeling obligated to live there.

For someone who reads the Bible, the Land of Israel is the Promised
Land. The seeds of the Jewish nation were planted there, and—as the nar-
rative of *Sefer Bereshit* informs us—with strife and difficulty, these seeds
grow there. Jews may be driven out of their land, but they are destined to
return, even from the depths of Egyptian slavery or Babylonian exile. The
prayer of return to the land—in the exclamation "Next Year in
Jerusalem!"—is not only sung at the end of the service on Yom Kippur
and at the close of the family *seder* on Pesach: it is repeated daily in the
prayers and blessings recited by a practicing Jew.

Over the centuries, tens of generations of religious Jews in the
Diaspora may have prayed fervently for a return to the land, having looked
forward to a divine response to their supplications. Nevertheless, it was
only with the establishment of the State of Israel in 1948, the successful
defense of the country in 1967, and the country's evolution into a modern,

51

Western economy in the late twentieth century, that living in Israel became a viable possibility for most Jews. Ironically, now that it is relatively easy to fulfill the dreams of generations of Diaspora Jews, the reasons to become an *oleh*—to "move up" to Israel—have dissipated for many. From the perspective of most North American Jews, the threat of anti-Semitism is no more frightening than concerns about terrorism that exist in Israel. Discrimination against Jews in the American Diaspora is for all practical purposes non-existent today. While the economy in Israel has improved, it is still easier to make a living elsewhere.

The students who come to Israel for the next year are aware of the place's uniqueness—on a philosophical and spiritual plane. Upon their arrival in Israel, more than half of them agree that they could live a fuller Jewish life in Israel, and 63% indicate that they see the modern State of Israel as part of "the process of redemption" of the Jewish People. This perception of modern Israel as the ideal place for them as Jews and as central to the destiny of the Jewish People does not translate into a desire to be part of it. Less than one-half think that it is "very likely" or "likely" that they will move to Israel (only 13% think that it is "very likely"), while only about one-third perceive it as an issue that will be important for them when they date. Even fewer think that they will likely serve in the Israeli army. From a religious perspective, less than one-third "strongly agree" or "agree" that there is a religious imperative to live in Israel.

The year in Israel affects many of these perceptions. After their year in Israel, more than half agree that *halachah* requires them to live in Israel. Close to 70% now report that it is "very likely" or "likely" that they will move to Israel. More significantly, the commitment that they personally feel toward such a move is now mirrored in what they expect from their potential spouse. Not surprisingly, the spiritual and philosophical elements also show change, with more than 70% now agreeing that they see Israel as part of the process of redemption and believe that they can live a fuller Jewish life in Israel.

After a year in Israel, students react more favorably with regard to their plans to live there, reflecting their new-found ability to function in a society that was foreign, which is now familiar. They meet people whom they perceive as role models, who have come on *aliyah*, and appreciate this act as a positive value. After a year of study in Israel, the American youngster expresses the belief that it is possible—even desirable—to commit oneself to living in the State of Israel. Having developed relationships, Israel becomes a "second home," and with the ease and relative low cost of travel today, many come back to visit, to study, to intern. Some even make the decision to return for good.

> Sara's parents were both immigrants, and to make it worse they were a "mixed marriage." Her father was born in a DP camp in Germany after World War II and her mother was originally from Libya, having come to the United States via Italy following Kaddafi's rise to power. Childhood, as she remembers it, was a kaleidoscope of emotion and confusion—she related that the film "My Big, Fat Greek Wedding" described her life pretty accurately—and going to Israel for a year was an opportunity to move beyond her somewhat stifling home situation.

> Although it was directed at students from North America, the program that Sara chose to attend worked hard at giving the students a taste of Israel. The *Madrichot* had lists of people who lived throughout the country—both native Israelis and *olim* from America—who were willing to have students for Shabbatot. "On *Parashat Chayei Sarah* I just needed to be in Hebron for Shabbat. The school didn't have anyone who lived there, so I found out what the telephone prefix was and dialed numbers at random. After a couple of misses—the Arabs of Hebron share the same prefix—I got one of the rabbis in town who was happy to host my friend and me," Sara recalls. The school also set her up with a family in the Old City of Jerusalem who "adopted" her. She developed a relationship with the kids in the family and felt comfortable dropping in.

> After her year was over, Sara went to Stern College, where she was active in the Israel club, and in developing programs for college students who wanted to participate in Sherut Le'umi-type programs during their college vacations. These programs were housed in Israeli development towns, and spending two months there allowed for a greater understanding of Israel, its needs and its people.

> Her mother was never excited about Sara's participation in these programs, or her growing interest in Israel. The experience of the Jewish community in Libya, where she had seen her father killed in his store by an Arab robber and had watched as the anti-Zionist sentiment came to affect the local Jewish population, made it clear to Sara's mother that the Middle East was no place for a good Jewish girl. "I didn't run away from there for you to go back there," Sara quotes her mother as saying. "It's funny, though. When my

mother was in Bnei Akiva, her group got into boats planning to row to Israel and were brought home to their distraught parents by the Libyan Navy. But she says that that was the idealism of her youth and that today she knows better. You don't need to take a rowboat today to come to Israel, and for all that I am not unaware of the existential threat, day-to-day life in Israel is not all that threatening. She doesn't seem to get that."

With her parents' somewhat reluctant agreement, Sara continued visiting Israel regularly and participating in internship programs there. She stayed in touch with her adoptive family and joined them at their *semachot*. When she dated, one of the most basic issues for her was whether the guy saw himself as an Israeli when it came to family and career. "Coming back from my year in Israel, I had two goals in life: to move to Israel and to have a big family."

When her parents want to visit their grandchildren today, they come to Israel where, Sara says, her father is thrilled to see the development of the State since his first visit in the 1950's. Her mother is "coming around," as well.

It is important to note that not all of the programs in Israel are the same. Not only do the different programs offer their students varying experiences during the year, but the students self-select the programs based on their own preparedness and desires. One example of this is in the area of *aliyah*. As might be anticipated, students who attend *Yeshivot Hesder* express greater interest in *aliyah* than their peers who come to study in American programs. 37% of the students in *Yeshivot Hesder* score "high" regarding their plans for *aliyah*, nominally higher than their peers in women's programs in Israel, 34% of whom score "high" and significantly higher than the students attending American programs, where only 11% do so.

By year's end it is the women who show the greatest commitment to *aliyah*, with 61% scoring "high," compared to 59% of *Yeshivot Hesder* students and 42% of the students who attended American programs.

Still, there are a number of areas that show little change. Even as they have become committed to living in Israel, these students still cannot conceive of themselves wearing an Israeli army uniform. They also did not see serving in the Israeli army as an imperative for all Israeli *yeshiva* students either before—when 14% strongly agreed—or after, when 16% strongly agreed. The long-standing tradition of at best reluctant participation in the military on the part of Diaspora Jews cannot be undone in just one year.

Perhaps of even greater interest is the reluctance of the one-year students to accept some of the popular National Religious dogmas that are part-and-parcel of the *dati le'umi* school system in Israel. While there is a general perception that the values of the American Modern Orthodox community are identical to that of the National Religious community in Israel, in truth there are many differences between them, ranging from the centrality of the State of Israel, to contemporary Jewish life, to the openness that should be shown to ideas and philosophies whose roots are found in cultures other than Judaism. Influenced by the thought of the Rav Avraham Kook as interpreted by his son Rav Zvi Yehuda, a generation of activists grew who influenced not only the educational system, but the entire country's social and political discourse.[45] While recent political realities are seen to have largely broken the messianic belief in *Eretz Yisrael Ha-Shelemah* of the religious right, the students surveyed in this study were prescient in their reluctance to take on those beliefs as their own, even as they accepted other values prevalent in the Israeli *yeshiva* setting.[46]

---

45 See for example, Richard Hoch, "Sovereignty, sanctity, and salvation: the theology of Rabbi Tzvi Yehudah ha-Kohen Kook and the actions of Gush Emunim" in *Shofar* 13,1, 1994, pp. 90–118 and Ella Belfer, "*BeTzipiyat haYeshuah haShelemah*: the messianic politics of Rav Avraham Yitzchak Kook and Rav Zvi Yehudah Kook" in Moshe Sokol, ed. *Tolerance, Dissent, and Democracy: Philosophical, Historical and Halakhic Perspectives*. Northvale, NJ: Jason Aronson, 2002, pp. 311–361.

46 Admittedly, American students may not accept the National Religious belief system, because many of the heads of Israeli programs catering to these students do not subscribe to these beliefs themselves. A prime example is Yeshivat Har Etzion, a *Yeshivat Hesder* whose reputation is politically moderate. Rabbi Aharon Lichtenstein, one of heads of the *yeshiva*, has questioned the widely accepted view in Israel that the contemporary State of Israel is the beginning of the redemption. See, for example, his interview with an organization called "Realistic Religious Zionism" that appears at http://tzionut.org/articles_details.asp?id=61

Here is a translated excerpt from the interview:

This concept [of *at'halta de'geulah*] is a clouded one. I do not feel that we will soon be in messianic times. I would like to believe that the . . . entire process of returning to *Eretz Yisrael* is meaningful not only politically, but also in that there is a return to the historical arena and to another type of living—this is an important turning point in history of *Knesset Yisrael*. . . . However, I do not see every small step as part of the redemptive process. Here, there is certainly a debate: to what extent do you think in material terms and to what extent do you think in spiritual/ethical terms. And here, I disagree with [those who follow Rav Tzvi Yehuda Kook]: the parameters which they describe [to show that the

Only 11% of the surveyed students strongly agreed with the statement "the modern State of Israel is the fulfillment of the *nevu'ot* of our prophets" before they began their year of study; after the year was over 13% of these students strongly agreed.[47] A fairly robust 50% of the students strongly agreed that the modern State of Israel is the national homeland of the Jewish people, but that figure does not change even after a year of study, when 53% strongly agree.

The year in Israel does not open an entirely new page in the lives of American Orthodox students who come for a year of *yeshiva* study. Having completed years of study in traditional Jewish schools back home, they come with a foundation of Jewish tradition and knowledge, of practice and feeling. Exposed to a raw, intense experience that supports this foundation, many students begin to erect an edifice composed of study, behaviors, and values that take the education they have received to the next logical level.

This idea is supported by the fact that as students undergo change in their attitudes over the year they appear to become more committed in their thinking in ways that show development in the context of previously held ideas, rather than an acceptance of radical new ones. As an example, let us examine the students' *aliyah* plans. It is an accepted maxim—

---

geulah has arrived] are in my opinion not spiritual enough. The geopolitical [improvements] and the fact that agriculture is thriving, I do not belittle them; but when I open the Tanakh, first and foremost [I see] discussed a flowering of a spiritual kind . . . . Of course *yeshu'at Hashem k'haref ayin* . . . , but if we are looking at historical developments, we are far from the social improvements [which are expected]. There is a famous Chinese proverb: a march of thousand kilometers begins with one step. In that context, there is *at'halta*, . . . but where are we on this march, on the first kilometer or the 999th? I would guess, neither. So: *at'halah*—yes, but this is not a central ingredient in my day-to-day awareness, that I expect that tomorrow, I will awaken and . . . [these dots are in the original].

47 It is worthwhile noting that a recent Pew report (August 2006) found that, among white evangelical Christians, there is widespread support for the statement that the contemporary State of Israel is the fulfillment of biblical prophecies. "Among religious groups, white evangelical Protestants stand out for their widespread belief that Israel was given by God to the Jews (69%), and that Israel is the fulfillment of biblical prophecy (59%). Majorities of black Protestants also share these points of view. White mainline Protestants and Catholics, by contrast, are much less likely to see a religious dimension to the establishment of the state of Israel." See the full report at http://people-press.org/reports/display.php3?PageID=1084.

although one that I do not believe has been examined in a serious way—that "out-of town" communities are more encouraging of *aliyah* than New York metropolitan area communities. This idea is supported by our study, which found that prior to their year of Israel study, nearly half (46%) of the students who come from outside the New York area scored "high" regarding their plans for *aliyah*. Fewer than 30% of students attending New York area schools scored "high" on that question. As we have seen, the impact of Israel study made all of the students more committed to living in Israel. Now two thirds of the "out of town students" scored "high" regarding their *aliyah* plans, while about half of the New Yorkers did so. Although changes do take place, they are proportionate with originally held positions.

Another example is the question of commitment to Torah study. It is generally believed (again, I am not familiar with rigorous studies of this question) that students in co-educational schools are "less religious" than those in single sex schools, a belief that would lead to the conclusion that such students should show less commitment to studying Torah than their peers who attend more "more religious" programs. Again our study supports this notion. Among New York area schools, students in co-ed schools lag behind their peers who attend either all-boys or all-girls schools with regard to commitment to Torah study, where 23% score "high" vs. 43% for students in all-boys schools.

Following their year in Israel, changes took place among all the different groups, but again, the movement parallels the originally held positions. Now 42% of students who attended co-ed high schools score "high" with regard to their commitment to Torah study as compared to 73% of the students who went to boys' high schools.

Does change occur? The evidence indicates that it does. What the numbers show, however, is that the students are building on their previous beliefs and knowledge to reach another place. They are not rejecting the old, rather they are using it as a foundation to move to the next level.

Chapter 10

Does the Change Last?

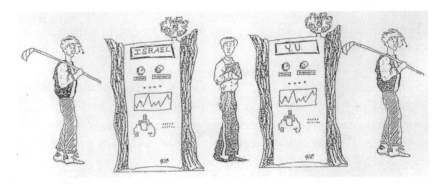

A *Hamevaser* Purim perspective on Yeshiva University students pre- and post-Israel study. From *Hamevaser*, Purim 5750. Copyright 1990 by *Hamevaser*. Reprinted with permission.

In comparing the students' responses before and after their year-long experience in Israel, profound changes are observed that have taken place in the course of their sojourn. The people they meet, the friends they make, the hours of study, the places that they visit, all add up to a significant moment at a critical juncture in life, one that may affect them over the long term. But what happens when the year is over? Some studies of students who travel on extended programs seem to find that, while the short-term effects seem momentous, they fade away relatively soon after returning.

One study we have referred to told of French language majors in their junior year in a state university. This study found that the students who spent an academic year in France reported returning to the United States in June well acculturated. The students now spoke French, enjoyed French cuisine, preferred to date French men and women, and showed a greater interest in international affairs. Nevertheless, a follow-up survey at the beginning of their senior year showed that one summer back home undid all of these changes.[48]

These findings do not surprise students of social psychology. Brief trips away from home usually cause little emotional discomfort beyond the inconvenience of jet lag. Longer sojourns, however—particularly those that carry with them the promise of an intense experience—have been researched and found to offer fairly predictable outcomes. Perhaps the simplest approach presents the experience as a "U-curve," with the sojourner beginning on an emotional "high" brimming with excitement and anticipation (the top left point of the "U"). As time passes and the initial enthusiasm is replaced with the challenging reality of an unfamiliar language, a foreign culture, among other factors, the traveler becomes disenchanted with the experience (the bottom of the "U"). Generally speaking, however, as the foreign becomes familiar, and the values of the new culture are assimilated and become more approachable, understandable, and acceptable, the excitement and enthusiasm returns—together with the newly attained values—as the experience draws to a close (the top right point of the "U").[49]

Further studies suggest that the "U-curve" should be expanded to explain the experiences of the sojourner upon return to his or her home society. The suggestion is to extend the "U" to a "W," indicating that something similar happens when the student comes back to familiar stomping grounds. The student returns, excited about his or her newly found values (the top middle of the "W"), oftentimes not recognizing the cultural dissonance that they will create among people who have not shared such a foreign experience. The rejection brings about a sense of despair (the second trough of the "W"), regaining equilibrium (the right-hand point of the "W") only after a "cooling off" period that allows for a tempering of the new and a return to some core foundational values.[50]

What happens to the day school graduates whose "foreign sojourn" was to an Israeli *yeshiva* program? Before attempting to answer this question, it is important to note that these students do not return to the

---

48 Dennison Nash, "The personal consequences of a year of study abroad."

49 Arthur Church, "Sojourner adjustment," *Psychological Bulletin, 91(3)*, 1982, pp. 540–577.

50 John Gullahorn and Jeanne Gullahorn, "An extension of the U-curve hypothesis," *Journal of Social Issues* 3, 1962, pp. 33–47.

same environment that they left. They will not be returning to their pre-Israel schools; rather, they will be choosing colleges and universities where they expect to pursue higher education in environments that may be very different from what they had at home or in *yeshiva*. Their choice of what to do after the year in Israel may be affected by their experience during that time. Will they return to the college of their choice according to their original plan, or will they choose a campus that will offer them a more intensely Jewish experience while pursuing their undergraduate studies? Or, perhaps, they will choose to postpone their university level study and elect to remain in Israel and continue their "foreign sojourn."

An examination of some of the same questions considered above shows that the changes taking place during the year of study in Israel remained basically intact one year later. With respect to the three questions about commitment to Torah study focused on earlier, we found that before the year in Israel, about half of the students anticipated learning with a *chavruta* when they finished college (those answering "very likely" or "likely"); after the year was over, that number rose to more than three quarters of the students. That number stays virtually the same one year later. If anything, the commitment seems to have grown during the post-Israel year, as more of those students say that it is "very likely" that they will do so now (45%) than did at the end of the year (39%). At the end of the year in Israel, 90% of the students said that they expected to have a large collection of *sefarim*; one year later, 99% of the respondents thought that they would. Finally, although the same percentage of students think that it is "very likely" that they will learn in a *kollel* setting at some point later on in their lives (10%), more of them think that it is "somewhat likely" that they will (22%) than did immediately after the year was over (15%).

Similar findings are evident in both ritual behaviors and concern for personal modesty. Activities like ritual hand-washing in the morning (immediately after the year, 75% report washing "always" or "usually," vs. 79% one year later), grace after meals (88% vs. 92%), and saying *Asher Yatzar* after visiting the bathroom (81% vs. 89%) are as strong one year later, and the responses even show signs of greater commitment.

Concern with *yichud*—being secluded with one's girlfriend or boyfriend—where more than half (56%) of the students reported feeling "very comfortable" or "somewhat comfortable" before the year began, and less than one-third (30%) felt that way at the end of the year, one year later 32% reported those comfort levels. The students report similar consistency in their responses to the question about intimacy with their fiancée, where the percentage of students who felt "very comfortable" or somewhat comfortable dropped from 39% to 17% during the year of Israel study, and remained at 19% one year later.

Aside from areas of study and ritual, commitment to Israel—on both a theoretical and practical level—also remains virtually unchanged. Before their study in Israel, a little over half of the students (53%) "strongly agreed" or "agreed" that they could live a fuller Jewish life in Israel. Three quarters felt this way after the year (74%), a number virtually unchanged one year later (76%). Before the year, less than a third (30%) expressed agreement with the statement that *halachah* requires that one live in Israel, while more than half (55%) agreed with it at the end of the year, and 53% one year later. Finally, 43% saw moving to Israel as "likely" or "somewhat likely" before the year began, 68% thought so when the year was over, the same percentage as one year later.

These results indicate the power of the Israel *yeshiva* experience. Supportive, as it is, of prior, deep-seated religious beliefs, the changes that take place have the potential to be much stronger than those of other overseas programs. Even the environment to which the student returns is, today, conducive to sustaining the changes that took place during the year of study in Israel. Certainly the student returning to Yeshiva University lives in such an environment. On-campus Jewish communities have developed in a number of secular colleges that also support a continuity of belief and action in these areas. The ease of communication and travel now allows alumni to remain in close contact with their teachers, peers, and schools. Today all of the Israel programs have websites that include *divrei Torah* and alumni news. A prime example is Yeshivat Har Etzion's "Virtual *beit midrash*," which allows its alumni—and anyone else with email access—to participate in lectures from the *yeshiva* in Israel in a variety of formats. These connections all help explain the strong long-term connection that the alumni retain with their Israel programs.

Shanah Bet

> Josh was the ideal high school student. His success in his general studies subjects—math, in particular—was matched by his devotion to, and accomplishments in, *Limudei Kodesh*. No one was surprised when he was accepted to Harvard and chose to attend the premier *Yeshivat Hesder* in Israel.

He continued to shine in *yeshiva*, and found both personal and academic satisfaction with his studies, so much so that as the end of the year approached he decided that he wanted to remain in the Jewish environment to which he had become so well acclimated. Ideally, in his mind, this meant spending a second year in *yeshiva*. If circumstances did not allow that, he was willing to settle on attending Yeshiva University.

"I can't say that it was an easy decision. For years my goal was to go to Harvard, so it wasn't something that I just forgot about. After lengthy conversations with my *Rosh Yeshiva* I was convinced that spending *shanah bet* in *yeshiva* and attending YU was not going to limit my intellectual or professional opportunities in a significant way. As the *Rosh Yeshiva* pointed out, today what is really important is where you go to graduate school—and YU has as good an acceptance rate to the best graduate schools as you can find anywhere. The argument made so much sense to me, that I could not imagine my parents, or anyone else objecting to it."

Actually, when word got back to Josh's high school, it was the Jewish studies principal who raised the first objection. Future students' ability to defer admissions to Ivy League schools would be jeopardized if today's students did not uphold their commitments to return to those universities after their year of study in Israel. Moreover, as this administrator told me, "the *yeshivot* in Israel are so committed to Torah study, but what about Torah values? How can these students be encouraged to renege on a signed commitment to the university that saved their spot for them? Is dishonesty permissible in order to learn Torah?"

In Josh's case, his parents felt that he was not only backing out of a written agreement with Harvard, but out of a verbal understanding with them as well. Their feelings on this matter were so strong that they actually signed his name to the letter of agreement that the university sent to his home, indicating on his behalf that Josh would, in fact, attend school there in the fall.

"I was faced with a terrible dilemma. I had come to believe that this was the wrong choice for me, but I loved and respected my parents and understood that they felt betrayed by my change of plans. Signing the acceptance letter against my will was so out of character for them that it sort of shocked me into understanding that I had gone too far." Josh returned to the U.S. for college and attended Harvard, where he excelled. He even arranged to spend his junior year as a visiting student at YU.

A new phenomenon derived from the year of study is *shanah bet*, a decision to stay a second year. While only 6% of students report that they come to Israel planning to spend more than a single year there, by year's end almost one third of the students decide to stay. While many of these are students who had originally planned to study at Yeshiva University, the number clearly includes others who had no such plans. It is worth noting that Yeshiva University offers a full year of academic credit for Israel study, which makes the choice to continue Israel study less of a postponement of life for YU students than it is for others.

Thus, at least some of the responses that we have seen are colored by the participation of those students who never really left Israel. We can hardly be surprised that those *shanah bet* students who remained under the same influences in their Israeli *yeshivot* retained the changes and became, if anything, even more committed to the values espoused by those programs.

It is important to note that the decision to stay in Israel for a second year does not necessarily indicate a major change in future plans. A small number have decided to stay in Israel for college study. The percentage of students planning to attend Yeshiva University remains virtually the same. There is a small shift away from the Ivy League schools and a small shift toward local schools, where presumably the student will live at home. The overall changes, however, are not so great.

Where will you be next year?

	Pre-test	Post-test
YU	49	37
Local College	18	16
Ivy League	27	17
Israel	6	31

Where will you go to college?

	Pre-test	Post-test
YU	56	57
Local College	18	20
Ivy League	27	21
Israel	–	2

Given the various choices open to students who finish their year of study in Israel, it makes sense to separate out the answers of the students based on where they ended the year after their *shanah alef* year—in Yeshiva University, in secular colleges, or on a *shanah bet* in Israel. By doing this, we can examine the change that occurs within each group regarding their attitudes toward Torah study, ritual practice, and Israel, information we have followed throughout this study. Here we make use of factor analysis, a statistical method that allows us to combine similar questions and create scales, which then can be studied. In effect, it allows us to look at a whole range of attitudes and behaviors that make up one category, and follow the changes at the three peaks of the "W" curve— when the students first come to Israel, at the end of their first year, and at the end of the year that follows.

Let's look at the numbers. Take, for example, the scale of "Commitment to Torah Study," which was made up of the questions about having a *chavruta*, attending *shiurim*, owning *sefarim*, and so on. This table shows how those students who ended up in different programs the year after their *shanah alef* reported their attitude and commitment to Torah study before they came to Israel (pre-test), at the end of that year (post-test), and one year later (follow-up study).

Commitment to Torah study

	LOW	MIDDLE	HIGH
Pre-test			
Yeshiva University	22.2	38.9	38.9
Secular College	39.6	34.0	26.4
Shanah Bet	17.0	34.0	49.1
Post-test			
Yeshiva University	5.7	41.4	52.9
Secular College	11.8	37.3	51.0
Shanah Bet	0.0	18.0	82.0

	LOW	MIDDLE	HIGH
Follow-up study			
Yeshiva University	13.5	38.7	47.7
Secular College	22.2	30.9	46.9
Shanah Bet	0.0	12.3	87.7

We are not really surprised to find that those students who ended up remaining in Israel reported the highest commitment even before the year started, nor that those students who eventually went to secular colleges reported the weakest commitment (recall that we saw earlier how relatively few students planned on *shanah bet* study before the year began). The shifts, however, are worth considering in more depth. After the year in Israel, the number of students who attend secular colleges scoring "high" in their commitment to Torah study almost doubles, and is comparable to those students who will attend Yeshiva University. There is some tailing off of the high scores in both YU and secular colleges one year later, while the *shanah bet* students—not surprisingly—become even more committed than they were beforehand.

What happens to the students whose interest and commitment to Torah study wanes? The drop-off is greater in secular colleges than in YU, which can be explained by the more supportive environment to be found on the Yeshiva University campus. Nevertheless, an impressive number of students continue to report that they remain committed to the values that they gained during their year in Israel.

Other scales show similar results. An examination of the ritual practice scale, made up of questions about participation in prayer, reciting *berachot*, engaging in ritual handwashing, fasting on communal fast days—among other aspects of observance—again shows that the students who would choose to stay in Israel for a second year already came to Israel with the highest level of commitment, while those who were to attend secular colleges came with the lowest level of commitment. Unlike Torah study, however, the increased sense of responsibility to ritual has greater staying power among all groups. The numbers reported by the students who attend YU remain virtually the same, while the minor drop-off that is seen among the students scoring "high" among the students in secular colleges indicates a move to the "middle" level, with no fall-off beyond that.

Ritual practice

	LOW	MIDDLE	HIGH
Pre-test			
Yeshiva University	19.7	36.6	43.7
Secular College	34.6	48.1	17.3
Shanah Bet	7.3	36.4	56.4
Post-test			
Yeshiva University	4.4	27.9	67.6
Secular College	15.4	28.8	55.8
Shanah Bet	0.0	13.3	86.7
Follow-up study			
Yeshiva University	4.5	27.0	68.5
Secular College	15.7	32.5	51.8
Shanah Bet	0.0	8.8	91.2

Given the perception of the American college campus as a place of sexual freedom, the scale of personal modesty should be of particular interest. In this context, "personal modesty" is comprised of questions about traditional halachic restrictions on sensual or sexual interactions between genders, such as *yichud*—being in closed quarters with a member of the opposite sex—and *negiah*—physical contact between men and women—and intimacy. As before, the students who were to end up studying in secular colleges were the lowest scoring on the scale of personal modesty. With regard to this scale, however, the norms and values of the *yeshiva* did not bring them to the same level as their peers, as was the case with the Torah study scale. The changes that took place in Israel brought a much higher percentage to score "high" on this scale than they reported before the year began; nevertheless, it remains much lower than their peers attending YU or staying in Israel. It is interesting to note, however, that those students who indicate a greater commitment to the demands of *halachah* in this area retain that level of commitment even after a year on a secular college campus, even as those whose commitment was middling found the atmosphere of the college campus not conducive to these values, and we find a drop to "low" from the middle group.

Personal modesty

	LOW	MIDDLE	HIGH
Pre-test			
Yeshiva University	15.3	49.2	35.6
Secular College	39.6	35.8	24.5
Shanah Bet	23.1	34.6	42.3
Post-test			
Yeshiva University	7.0	18.6	74.4
Secular College	11.5	42.3	46.2
Shanah Bet	0.0	6.0	94.0
Follow-up study			
Yeshiva University	5.4	21.6	73.0
Secular College	21.4	33.3	45.2
Shanah Bet	2.3	4.6	93.1

So do we find that there are differences between the students? Of course we do. From the numbers it becomes clear, however, that many of these differences existed prior to the students' arrival in Israel at the beginning of the year. Furthermore, the statistics show that the impact of the year in Israel is significant and changes the attitudes and behaviors of kids who come to Israel, no matter where they came from and whatever choices they make about where to go after Israel. Finally, unlike the French students whose accents and actions fade away within two or three months after they leave France, day school graduates largely retain the values that they gained in Israel, even if they do not return to an environment that specifically supports those values.

Chapter 11

Conclusion

What does this mean to the American Jewish community?

For one thing, it means that for a good number of Jewish children today, exposure to Jewish thought and study does not end after twelve years of day school education. More and more, children from homes that are committed enough to send them to day school take it for granted that there will be another year—or even two—of heavy-duty Jewish learning. As we have seen, coming at a critical moment in life, this experience has the potential to make a real difference in lifelong decisions made by these young people regarding their continued education, whom they will marry, what their role in the Jewish community will be, and where they will live.

Moreover, the experience has simply become part of the sociological scene in the Jewish community. Popular novels refer to the Israel study as one of those things that young Jewish people do. Tova Mirvis' novel *The Outside World*[51] is clearly aimed at the community whose values it is meant to spotlight, but the coming-of-age story that revolves around the changes that young people undergo as a result of their Israel study and the strains that it puts on their relationships with their parents and family is for general consumption. When, in Faye Kellerman's *Jupiter's Bones*,[52] Decker argues with Rina and her son Sammy about the dangers of studying in "the Gush" because of its location "over the Green Line," advocating instead study in Kerem B'Yavneh or Shaalvim, the expectation is that the reader—even the non-Jewish reader—will have a sense of what is being discussed.

The acceptance of these programs as part-and-parcel of the educational experience for Orthodox Jewish high school graduates has probably played a role in broadening the scope of Israel study, as well. The success

---

51 Tova Mirvis, *The Outside World*, New York, Knopf, 2004.

52 Faye Kellerman, *Jupiter's Bones*, New York, William Morrow and Company, 1999.

of American Orthodox day schools in retaining its graduates "within the fold" led first to the development of similar types of day schools in the other denominational streams, and more recently to a movement of non-affiliated "community Jewish day schools." The current trend in Israel is the opening of new, year-long programs, which offer a wider range of options to students—both non-traditional study options within traditional *yeshivot* and non-*yeshiva* options. The development and success of the birthright Israel program, as well as the encouragement offered by the Israeli government to long-term programs in Israel through their support via MASA grants, can certainly be seen as building on the successes of the one-year *yeshiva* programs.

But the real impact of these programs is on the students themselves. Upon their return to American colleges and universities, there is certainly some level of culture shock as the students who have spent one or two years cocooned in an environment very different from that of the campus see their values challenged and compromised.

Some Jewish educators, discussing whether the secular college campus is an appropriate place for a good Jewish girl or boy who has returned from Israel say things like:

"Be aware that you're going into enemy territory and if you want to come out alive then you need to be on a mission and stay focused. If you succeed then you can come out with lots of medals, hopefully not purple hearts . . ."

"If your goal is staying religious then you're playing with failure. Your goal needs to be to introduce all Jews to Judaism and make a *Kiddush Hashem* in every thing that you do."

"Here are three reasons that people stop being religious –
    a. physical/social needs—everyone else is doing it . . .
    b. emotional—issues, low self-esteem, depression
    c. intellectual—heretical ideas and courses."[53]

---

53 Several such discussions have taken place on Lookjed, an online discussion group for Jewish educators, which is a project of the Lookstein Center for Jewish education at Bar-Ilan University.

Even as there are perceived threats to religious commitment of the alumni of *yeshiva* programs in Israel, there are also those who are working to make the college campus more accommodating to the needs of the Israel returnee. Aside from the traditional mainstays of Orthodox Hillel rabbis and Habad houses, the Jewish Learning Initiative (JLI) sends young couples who are Religious Zionists and have, themselves, experienced life on American college campuses, to act as mentors to day school graduates in universities across the United States.[54] Anecdotal evidence points to such grassroots efforts as offering a lifeline to Israel alumni in these settings.

Yeshiva University is not immune to the tensions that are bound to exist between the values of the *beit midrash* and those of a traditional liberal arts education. Recent defection of Israel program alumni from Yeshiva University to other settings perceived by them as more sensitive to a Torah focused lifestyle[55] are certainly one of the catalysts to discussions between the dean of Yeshiva College and the rabbinic faculty about the appropriateness of certain college courses from a religious standpoint.[56] While these frictions have always existed—and such leadership figures as Rabbi Joseph B. Soloveitchik seemed at peace with them—it appears that the groundswell of concern shown by the Israel alumni have played a role in bringing these issues to the fore.

But the effects of Israel study are apparent well beyond the walls of the academy. While the almost universal popularity of the year-long Israel experience is relatively recent, more than a generation of students have already gone through this process, and the effects on the Jewish community

---

See, for example, the conversation entitled "Yeshiva in Israel after high school" at http://www.lookstein.org/lookjed/read.php?f=1&i=5159&t=5159 and the more heated discussion entitled "Preparation for life on the college campus" at http://www.lookstein.org/lookjed/read.php?f=1&i=2660&t=2660. All of the quotes are from that discussion.

54 For information on this initiative, see http://www.jli.co.il

55 Zev Eleff, "Ten Sha'alvim alumni depart Yeshiva after a year for less academic alternatives," in *The Commentator*, August 22, 2006, available online at http://www.yucommentator.com/news/2006/08/22/Features/Ten-Shaalvim.Alumni.Depart.Yeshiva.After.A.Year.For.Less.Academic.Alternatives-2204991.shtml

56 See Zev Eleff and Eitan Kastner, "Reconciling Institutional Divides: Rosh Kollel and YC Dean Begin Dialogue," in *The Commentator*, September 11, 2006, available online at http://www.yucommentator.com/news/2006/09/11/Features/Reconciling.Institutional.Divides-2259824.shtml

are clear. In many places in America today the demands and expectations of the Jewish community from their day schools have risen —together with a willingness to pay for excellence in Judaic studies alongside general studies. Branches of *Kollel Torah MiTzion*, a movement of in-school *kollelim* that bring faculty and fellows from Israel to learn and teach both in the school and the local synagogues, now exist in communities across the United States and around the world.[57] Every *Bet Knesset* worth its salt arranges for scholars-in-residence throughout the year— oftentimes *Roshei Yeshiva* and *Rabbanim* at the Israeli *yeshivot*—to offer high-level lectures and *shiurim* to their congregants.

Having made these observations, the proverbial question must be asked: is it good for the Jews or bad for the Jews? There is a perceived "slide to the right" that is being discussed more and more in the context of the future direction of American Orthodoxy. The changes that have been observed and commented on range from the superficial garb of young people who are abandoning the knitted *kippah* for a black fedora to punctiliousness in religious ritual and attendance at *daf yomi shiurim*.[58] What role have one-year Israel programs played in this sociological shift? Is such a change a reason for concern?

Probably the first group to express apprehension about the success of Israel programs in bringing students to greater levels of commitment to Jewish learning and ritual were parents, some of whom perceived the changes in their sons and daughters as "flipping out," i.e., as a rejection of their value system.[59] "Flipping out" manifests itself in a change of outward appearances (including a change of dress and hairstyle), college and professional choices, and a changed attitude toward secular society and culture.

There is no doubt that some superficial changes are evident in outward appearances, and, as we have seen, there are certainly indications of greater concern for some areas of *halachah* that are bound to create tension in the home. Children who return after a year of Israel study who will

---

57　For information on the *Kollel MiTzion* project, see http://www.torahmitzion.org/eng/

58　See Samuel Heilman, *Sliding to the Right: The Contest for the Future of American Jewish Orthodoxy*, University of California Press, 2006.

59　This terminology was popularized by Blue Fringe, a band made up of students in one-year Israel programs. The lyrics poke fun at the changes that take place among the men and women who attend these programs.

no longer participate in outings to the beach with their families, boys who are reluctant to kiss their aunt who comes to visit, or girls who will not be seen outside the house wearing pants, will certainly raise eyebrows—if not tempers—in many a Modern Orthodox home.

It is interesting to note, however, that with regard to some of the more central issues having to do with life decisions, students' responses in our study do not seem to indicate a major shift in their thinking. As noted above, there is an increase among those students who think it likely that they will spend a year studying in *kollel* (4% saying that it was "very likely" in the pre-test vs. 10% in the post-test); nevertheless, there is virtually no change in the number of students planning a career in the rabbinate or in Jewish education.

Similarly, there does not seem to be much change in college choice. When asked "in what college do you intend to study?" the number of students responding with plans to attend YU, a local college, or an Ivy League University remained largely unchanged after a year of study (with YU getting just over half of the students, the local schools about 20% , and the Ivies about a quarter of them), although almost a third indicated that they were now planning to remain in Israel a second year, subsequently returning home for university level study.

Moreover, it is unreasonable to expect that our children will be mirror images of ourselves. In general American society today, it is not unusual for children to move out of their parents' homes post-high school and to expose themselves to experiences that will help mold themselves as individuals—experiences that can take place on the college campus, in foreign sojourns, in volunteer work, at the workplace, or in the military. These encounters often challenge the values and attitudes of the participant who experiences them at a particularly delicate moment in his or her personal development. It is the age of rebellion—obviously not for all young people, but for many of them—providing an opportunity for searching out ways of identifying themselves as individuals, unique and separate from their parents.[60]

But these observations are not limited to parents. One prominent observer of the American Jewish scene describes the Israel programs much as we have in our analysis, writing:

---

60 James Fowler, *Stages of Faith: the Psychology of Human Development and the Quest for Meaning.* New York: HarperCollins, 1981.

The *yeshiva/midrashah* experience in Israel is extraordinary. Here, where there are no pressures of getting grades—since most students have already been accepted to college—one finds young people who are ready for a change. They are in the period of identity quest and role moratorium. For many of them, this is their first extended period away from their parents. It is spent in what is essentially a total institution, cut off from their parents and everything that is familiar to them. Being in a *yeshiva* is being where the key element of life is sitting side by side with a peer, in a protective environment where the rabbis and religious teachers are the only adult models, where all one has to do is study Torah and absorb the holiness of the place (both the school and the Land of Israel) and where one is told that by doing so one fulfills God's plan.

He argues that following this intensive Israel study, many students choose to remain in Israel where they become *haredim* or right-wing settlers. Furthermore, he claims, "[t]hose who came back home came back ready to transform the Orthodox world into a far more fundamentalist one."

In concluding he draws a parallel between the *beit midrash* and the *Masjid*, between rabbis and imams, warning, "[i]f one considers what has happened to the rich culture of Islam as it has devolved into Islamist fundamentalism as a model, the Jews who espouse this option would do well to rethink their strategy."[61]

While the questions posed in our survey dealt with a broad range of issues and did not focus on those of fundamentalism, the collected data presented in this study does not support this thesis. Without question the year in Israel is a powerful experience, an educational event whose intensity is unparalleled in the framework of traditional day school education. Students, away from their parents for an extended period for the first time, assume the values of the *yeshiva*. Do they become more knowledgeable about their Jewish heritage? Do they become more committed to Jewish law and Jewish learning? Do they affirm their commitment to building a Jewish family, and begin to consider the possibility that its place will be in Israel? Do they come to see themselves as critical to the future of the

---

61 Samuel Heilman, "Jews and Fundamentalism," *Jewish Political Studies Review* 17:1–2, Spring 2005. Available online at http://www.jcpa.org/cjc/cjc-heilman-s05.htm

Jewish people? The answer to all of these questions is an emphatic "yes!" At the same time, few—if any—of these students drop their plans for the future and move to settle the hilltops of the West Bank. In fact, the overwhelming majority continue to express their plans to complete their college educations in America and indicate a continued willingness to come to terms with the world around them.

Concern for the well-being of "non-fundamentalist Modern Orthodoxy" may likely be based primarily on a specific definition of "Modern Orthodoxy." This is not the place to split hairs about how to define Modern vs. Centrist Orthodoxy.[62] However, we may briefly examine how leading Modern Orthodox thinkers have defined the term, and how today's Israel alumni are playing a role in fulfilling their vision of this movement.

The question of the appropriate level of acceptance of, and interaction with, the general community is not new. It appears to have become an issue beginning with the Babylonian Diaspora following the destruction of the First Temple.[63] The issue famously came to a head during Second Temple period times, with the war between the assimilating Hellenists and the Hasmonean traditionalists. Our focus, however, is on the contemporary American scene.

In 1976, Rabbi Shlomo Riskin—then a community rabbi at the Lincoln Square synagogue in Manhattan and today rabbi of the community of Efrat and head of Ohr Torah Institute in Israel—set down his vision for Modern Orthodoxy as a vibrant, crucial part of the American Jewish community.[64] He opened by noting a "shift to the right" taking place in

---

62 I recall hearing Rav Yerucham Gorelick, upon whom one of the protagonists in Chaim Potok's *The Chosen* and *The Promise* is based, assuring one of his students that he could discuss the young man's dating. Speaking Hebrew in his heavy Yiddish accent, Rav Gorelik said, *"Efshar le-saper li. Ani ish moderni!* " ("You can tell me. I am a modern person!")

63 See the Gemara in TB *Sanhedrin* 39b: "In one verse it is said, After the ordinances of the nations that are round about you, have ye done (Ezekiel 11:12); while in another it is said, After the ordinances of the nations that are round about you, ye have not done (Ezekiel 5:7)—How is this contradiction to be reconciled? As follows: Their good ordinances ye have not copied; their evil ones ye have followed."

64 Shlomo Riskin, "Where modern Orthodox life is at—and where it is going," *Jewish Life*, Spring 1976 pp. 27–31. In a sidebar to the article, a comment is included indicating that the article was adapted from a sermon delivered by Rabbi Riskin in Lincoln Square Synagogue, a center and symbol of Modern Orthodoxy in the 1970s.

American Orthodoxy, pointing to an article that appeared in the 1965 issue of the *American Jewish Yearbook* that made this point, and asked what the Modern Orthodox community could do to offer a real contribution to Jewish life in America.[65]

Riskin attributed the move to the right to a number of factors, including a shift in the value system of general society—particularly with regard to sexual mores—that encouraged committed Jews to seek sanctuary in a more "closed-off" community and a lack of passion endemic in the Modern Orthodox community. He concluded by calling on the Modern Orthodox community to respond by "provid[ing] an environment for the commitment to Torah study and Torah living as an absolute," arguing that "only when we strive to pursue *Kedushah* and *Emunah* in our daily lives, will we produce in American Orthodoxy the fiery commitment which will enable us to endure, and ultimately to prevail."

More than 20 years later, Rabbi Avi Weiss—Rabbi of the Hebrew Institute of Riverdale and founder and Dean of Yeshivat Chovevei Torah—published his view on Modern Orthodoxy. In it he lists a number of central issues that distinguish between Modern Orthodoxy—which Weiss prefers to call "Open Orthodoxy"—and its right-wing co-religionists. He sums up the unique vision of this movement by arguing that "Open Orthodoxy is open to secular studies and views other than those of their rabbis; open to non-Jews and less observant Jews; open to the state of Israel as having religious meaning; open to increased women's participation; open to contact with the Conservative, Reform and Reconstructionist movements; and open to public protest as a means of helping our people." Now comes the challenge. Weiss argues that "[t]he key to strengthening Open Orthodoxy is the reconciling of more rigid halachic practices, which I believe are positive, with our own ideological agenda." Weiss readily admits that "it is a tension that is difficult to live with" and that the inability to do so plays a role in the shift to the right. He explains this movement as stemming from the sincere search "for genuine religious expression in prayer, Torah study and halachic observance. Too often, what they see, however, is an Open Orthodoxy that is open ideologically, but compromising in its halachic standards. . . . Hence, the challenge today is for Open

---

65 The article in question, entitled "Orthodoxy in American Jewish Life," was authored by the sociologist Charles Leibman, who was prescient in noting this trend well before it became widely understood.

Orthodox parents and institutions to be ideologically open, while intensely committed to *halakha*."[66]

Rabbis Riskin and Weiss recognize that the future of "modern" or "open" Orthodoxy depends on creating a cadre of learned, thoughtful, passionate young people, who will be committed in a primary way to the traditional values of Torah and *mitzvot* even as they take up the challenge of interacting with the contemporary world in a serious way. While neither of these activist rabbis have been satisfied with a call to action—both have opened educational institutions, Riskin in Israel and Weiss in the United States—in a sense, their calls for nurturing such a group of young people have been answered by the emergence of the one-year Israel programs. As we have seen, these programs have made a significant impact on individual students, on Jewish institutions of higher learning, and ultimately on the American Jewish community at large.[67]

I recently had the opportunity to spend a long weekend with a group of fairly typical Modern Orthodox couples on a trip in Eastern Europe. As many of them had children who were in their high school and college years, the conversation turned to one-year Israel programs. One father told me that he would not let his son consider going to Israel. "I have a good kid. I don't need him to go to some *yeshiva* where they will tell him that what his 'old man' does isn't good enough. He'll end up coming back a religious fanatic and will marry a girl who only wears skirts and covers her hair." Another couple talked quietly—and proudly—about their son's choice to continue his studies in a "right-wing" *yeshiva* in America after learning in Israel for the year. The most interesting story came from a woman who told me the following:

> My son, Moshe, was always a tough kid. I simply do not remember a day growing up that we didn't have a fight. He argued about everything—what he was going to wear, whether he was going to go out with his friends, what was being served for dinner. If there was nothing to argue about he would pick on his kid sister.

66 Avraham Weiss, "Open Orthodoxy! A modern Orthodox Rabbi's creed," *Judaism*, Fall 1997, 46, 4, pp. 409–421.

67 See also Walter Wurtzberger's presentation on the Rav's understanding of "modern Orthodoxy" in "Rav Joseph B. Soloveitchik as *posek* of Post-modern Orthodoxy," *Tradition*, Vol. 29, 1994. Haym Soloveitchick's seminal "Rupture and Reconstruction" in *Tradition*, Vol. 28, No. 4 Summer 1994 also touches on a definition of Orthodoxy—both "modern" and *haredi*—and its development over time.

He went to Israel with one goal in mind—to take a year off and play a lot of tennis. In fact, he chose a *yeshiva* based on its proximity to the tennis courts. In December, around Chanukah time, I had a business trip to Israel, and I called him and suggested that we go out. All of my friends who visit Israel take a whole group of kids out to eat, and I figured that I had to do my share of supporting the local Israeli eateries. When I called to confirm the time and place, Moshe told me that he wasn't bringing any of his friends. That he wanted to talk. I have to tell you—I was frightened. I hadn't had a civil conversation with him . . . ever. What would the two of us do by ourselves?

When we met at the restaurant, it wasn't just that he was wearing a white shirt—his whole demeanor was different. After 15 minutes I said, "What's with you Moshe? What happened?" And he just said, "Ma, I'm in a different place." He changed his college plans and is in the Touro College joint program where he learns in a serious *yeshiva* half-day and goes to college. He has his head screwed on straight. I don't care that he wears a hat now—he's a mensch!"

Ultimately the post-high school choice is a very personal one. The educational institutions to which we send our children will have an impact on them—and ultimately on their children and their communities, on Israel and on the Jewish People. The world is now a fast-moving place and the challenges and choices faced by today's youth are significantly different from those of the last generation. The opportunities are different, as well. As parents and teachers, our task is to help our children successfully face those challenges and create a better reality of future generations of Jews in Israel and in the Diaspora.

Section 2:
In Search of Self:
Psychological Perspectives
on Change During the
"Year in Israel"

DANIEL JACOBSON

Chapter 12

Introduction

The year in Israel has become a rite of passage for many *yeshiva* high school graduates prior to embarking on their college experience. Dr. Shalom Berger describes in depth the content of the religious and spiritual impact of this year. Unfortunately, many people see the change *only* through this religious lens. In reality, however, there is a whole other, psychological aspect of this process. The failure to understand the deeper picture regarding change can have a negative impact on all parties involved, while incorporating this perspective can change the experience from all angles. Students may be better able to handle the psychological challenges of the year and the twists and turns of readjustment upon their return home, if they better understand the impact such programs can have. Parents may more smoothly negotiate conflicts that arise with their children when viewing them through more nuanced lenses. Finally, Israeli *yeshivot* may more sufficiently appreciate the difficulties of adjustment to Israel, the impact of different *yeshiva* interventions, as well as the need to prepare students for return to family and community.

One caveat is in order: this section is based on my doctoral dissertation, my rabbinical tenure in the United States, my experience in an Israeli *yeshiva* program, and my work as a clinical psychologist working with *yeshiva* students. Inasmuch as the bulk of this work has been with boys, this chapter focuses more on the male Israel experience. In many areas, there are similarities with girls, but there are certainly many differences as well.

Goals of Study in Israel

Ariel, a student in our *yeshiva* high school, is deliberating whether to go to Israel for the year. Although I usually encourage our students to go, his reasons for going seem so shallow—to get away from home and have fun. Maybe he'll just waste the year?!

Students have a variety of reasons for studying in Israel, but there is significant overlap in their goals. Most perceive learning and spiritual growth as important goals for themselves before going to Israel, and many more acquire these goals during study in Israel. Before going to Israel, however, students also harbor less serious reasons, such as having fun and following the crowd. Many students explain that their desire to learn was somewhat subconscious prior to going to Israel.

It's very weird, because I had two separate goals [before going to Israel] and they completely contradicted each other. So how that was supposed to work out I don't know. One of them was, not really a goal, just all my friends are going to Israel, and I want to be a year away with my friends in a different country away from parents and have a great time. You know everyone comes back and loves it. At the same time, I was realistic and I knew that everyone who comes back has gotten more religious and I wasn't afraid of it. I knew that something was going to happen and I welcomed it a little bit.

These students explain that there are manifestations of their subconscious interest in intense learning and spiritual growth in their choice of *yeshiva*.

I went to have fun. I go places to have fun. That was the main goal. Well I certainly did not go to Israel to learn, but I did know that I was going to *yeshiva*. And a *yeshiva* has certain regulations. I chose a *yeshiva* that has regulations on purpose. At some point I was supposed to go to _____ (a *yeshiva* without strict rules), but the whole year can go by [there] without anything happening. So I decided on _____ specifically because it has regulations. You know when I say it's all for fun, there was something in the back of my mind, "you know I can't just have fun because that can't happen."

Certain students explain that seeing older students who had changed in Israel gave them some direction as to what their religious growth might entail.

The guys who came back from *yeshiva*, I wanted to strive to be more like that. There was a certain demeanor or way they carry themselves and are serious about learning . . . . When you see a product that looks impressive, it's meaningful.

This phenomenon of "seeds of change" resonates with Kenneth Pargament's suggestion that "the theory of spontaneous generation of religion fails as much in the religious case as it does in the biological. Even when religion seemingly comes out of nowhere a closer analysis often reveals evidence of religious availability."[68]

Even those who were more consciously interested in learning or spiritual growth explained that they "had no idea what that meant" prior to their study in Israel. The focusing of goals during study in Israel manifests itself in several ways. For many, it entails setting their spiritual sights higher.

By the end, my goal was to not have a limit of "this is what I'm gonna be religiously," but just to keep going and keep as many *halachot* as I can and be as good a Jew as I can, in action and in learning, and to be a better person also.

Other students explain that their appreciation of the magnitude of the goal grew over the course of the year.

I think all my goals from before remained, but I realized they were not going to happen as quickly as I hoped. I realized that it was more of a lifetime pursuit and would encompass all of my existence, as opposed to being another nice little characteristic.

Inasmuch as goals are a manifestation of one's *weltanschauung*, these examples demonstrate a considerable, though not necessarily radical, change during study in Israel. This is different from the religious change literature, which generally focuses on religious conversion. Pargament[69]

---

68 Pargament, K.I. (1997). *The psychology of religion and coping.* New York: The Guilford Press.

69 Ibid.

defines religious conversion as "an effort to re-create life; the individual experiences a dramatic change of the self, a change in which the self becomes identified with the sacred." While change among *yeshiva* students is often significant, it is not necessarily comparable to a conversion in its scope. Many of these students, growing up in Orthodox homes, describe having had a degree of prior affiliation with the sacred. Thus, while the experience certainly entails a change in the self, with an increased identification with their Orthodox Judaism, students' goals manifest a degree of this even before study in Israel.

Chapter 13

Types of Change

I went straight from high school to college. My best friend Jacob went to Israel for the year. When I saw him over Pesach, he was wearing *tzitzit* and kept wanting to "go learn." He wore tanktops and hated Gemara before he went to Israel. What's going on?

Among students who undergo meaningful religious change in Israel, there is a wide range of religious observance during high school. During high school, most students see themselves as observing Halachah within the norms of the Modern Orthodox community, and are comfortable with their level of observance.

For students who are less observant than their families, this behavior is not necessarily a function of rebellion, but rather a feeling of apathy regarding observance.

As you go through high school, 10th 11th 12th, you become less afraid of the teachers, so by 12th grade you just come in at 9 A.M. after davening for class.

An unusual, but not uncommon, phenomenon is something that one student termed his "delay button." Many students feel that their observance during high school is not ideal, but do not yet feel the need to change.

I viewed that as being the best I could have been [at that time]. I admitted it as being hypocritical; I didn't think of it as the right way to live Jewishly, but I felt it was the right way to live for myself in the context that I was living in. I think I always had in mind that I would become more *frum* when I got back [from study in Israel]; that was always in mind. There was just a delay button.

85

The phenomenon of change in Israel is baffling to many parents. Where does the spark for change originate? The answer for this subgroup is that the seeds were already planted pre-Israel, and the Israel experience simply provided the climatic conditions necessary for germination.

Ritual Observance

> My older son learned seriously during his year in Israel two years ago, and remains very dedicated to his Judaism during college. My younger son Noam has just returned, however, and talks about going to the Mir or Ner Yisrael ("to a real *yeshiva*"). Did they go through the same experience?

Any interested observer of the "Year in Israel" phenomenon has noted the trend of students to become "more religious" than their previous selves and than their parents. In analyzing the process of change with regard to religious observance, it is critical to understand students' self-perception of their increased religiousness. Increased precision in observance is nearly universal as a meaningful part of the change. The specific changes vary, but these often include more stringent observance of *kashrut* and Shabbat and more restricted contact with the opposite sex for non-marriage related purposes. For boys they also include practices, such as increased care in praying three times daily with a *minyan*, and wearing a *kippah* and *tzitzit*. Girls often become more stringent or conservative in their style of dress. While students often struggle separately through each specific change in observance, they perceive the overall array of new behaviors as a single unit: "That's the only way I can describe it. Every *halachah* I know I try to keep."

The focus on behavioral change is consonant with Judaism's intimate involvement with the mundane, addressing the entire spectrum of human experience, including areas such as agriculture, civil law, marital law, and the holiday cycle. For many students, however, this new level of observance is inextricably intertwined with a new phenomenology, experiencing one's life as revolving around the service of God.

Although the behavioral changes are more overtly detectable, one student explained that the basis for change is the shifting of perspective.

> I think it's more in terms of ideology than acts. The importance of being observant. Rabbi _____ spoke to us . . . . He said

that if you don't believe that this world is a corridor to the next world, this world is the most depressing thing; it's just a time clock to dying. He also made a comment about a t-shirt he saw in New York: "the person who dies with the most toys wins." That molded my ideology.

This change in *weltanschauung*, in turn, creates pervasive behavioral change:

> I realized that religion was defined by what you eat and keeping *Shabbat*. I realized it takes up more of your daily activities. You know, making *berachot* on food, wearing *tzitzit*, making a *berachah* after the bathroom, learning at night. These were all things that I hadn't really considered before, that I didn't really know existed. Well I knew they existed, but they weren't considered an option.

Rav Joseph B. Soloveitchik[70] has demonstrated extensively that Jewish Law focuses on "outward action," but he also seeks the creation of a particular religious "inward experience." For example, the Rambam and *Shulchan Aruch* list numerous behavioral requirements surrounding the proper place, cleanliness of body, and verbal recitations in order for prayer to be deemed halachically approved. However, R. Soloveitchik demonstrates that these behavioral requirements are merely the necessary means toward the end goal of an inner experience, an encounter, with the divine.[71] Similarly, the rabbis enacted numerous restrictions and obligations on the mourner during the *shiva* period. Here too, careful analysis of the sources reveals that such rules and ritual practices constitute the vehicle allowing the mourner to properly experience and express his or her grief.[72]

In comparison to the internal experience Christians face as their religious observance changes, Jewish students are more behaviorally focused. Nonetheless, their experience of a core inner change is consistent with the phenomenon that, for deeply religious individuals of all faiths, religion

---

70 Soloveitchik, R.J.B. (2000). *Family redeemed*. U.S.A.: Toras HoRav Foundation.

71 Soloveitchik, R.J.B. (2003). *Worship of the Heart*. Jersey City, NJ: Ktav.

72 Soloveitchik, R.J.B. (2003). *Out of the Whirlwind*. Jersey City, NJ: Ktav.

pervades their being such that their psychology can only be understood by understanding their religiousness. Indeed, their religious outlook becomes deeply woven into the fabric of their perception and interpretation of life events.[73]

The nature of a student's experience cannot be understood merely from viewing the externals. While the manifestations of change in observance tend to be similar, the students' experiences of the changes differ. Some of the young men and women feel the change to be an outgrowth of their previous observance.

> I think . . . my relationship to God got deepened. I still read a lot [of philosophy] and that speaks to me a lot. I think basically everything I had in high school has just been, let's say, it's deeper and more intense than it was. There was no radical change. I was dedicated to *halachah* before, but now I'm more careful about certain areas. I have trouble with some of the same things that I did in high school: sexual things, how I treat other people. The same areas that I was *nichshal* (failing to observe) before are there. I personally think I'm doing much better, but there hasn't been an eradication of any challenges. But there's the pressure and guilt factor that I should be less *shayach* (associated) to those things now.

Other students, however, feel their new observance entails a radical shift from their previous mode: "I just keep everything stricter. It was a pretty drastic change . . . I'd say my character has changed. I try to act in a manner consistent with Jewish beliefs."

These distinctions will be more fully clarified in later discussion of the students' identity formation. It is critical, however, not to underestimate the implications. The two above students, for instance, might have looked quite similar upon return from Israel in external appearance and halachic observance. However, their experiences of reintegrating into their families and communities in America were radically different.

---

73 McIntosh, D.N. (1997). "Religion as schema, with implications for the relation between religion and coping." In Spilka, B. & McIntosh, D.N. *The Psychology of Religion: Theoretical Approaches.* 171–183. Boulder, CO: Westview Press.

This spectrum of change among students stands in contrast to the traditional literature on religious change, which has focused on radical religious shifts. The notion of change as a more nuanced growth process has been written about primarily in the secular humanist framework of personal growth.[74]

More recent psychological literature on religion, however, has noted the presence of differing types of change. Kenneth Pargament differentiates between "conservational" religious change and "transformational" religious change. In the former, the goal is to change in order to maintain and solidify the individual's present identity, while in the latter the goal is a replacement of the former self with a new sense of being. "The convert attempts to give up not just old 'love objects' (e.g. alcohol, sex, unfulfilling relationships, anger, guilt, or helplessness), but the life built around them. In their place, the convert looks for another organizing force, a new 'center of loyalty'."[75] Indeed, among Year in Israel students, there are profound inner distinctions between those who have found a new center of loyalty versus those who have reorganized themselves around the same center as before.

Involvement in Torah Study

> Our son Daniel sounds like he's studying 15 hours a day—is everything alright over there?

Prior to study in Israel, most Modern Orthodox students only study *Limudei Kodesh* as academic subjects in school. For boys undergoing meaningful change, the study of Torah beyond academic requirements becomes universal. However, many describe Torah as becoming more than simply one of their extracurricular activities. Rather, it becomes an encompassing experience that is the focus of their life pursuit.

The causes behind the drive to study, as well as the boys' experience of it, are far from uniform. Among those describing Torah study as an encompassing aspect of their life, many derive great pleasure from the activity.

---

74 Pargament, K.I. (1997). *The psychology of religion and coping.* New York: The Guilford Press.

75 Ibid.

Before going to Israel, I understood that you have to learn in
order to know history and *halachah*, but to learn it all the time?!
It's boring. Why would you do that? After studying in Israel, my
attitude changed. I loved it. It's an intellectual experience where
sometimes, after doing it for a few hours, you're on a different
planet.

The presence of pleasure as a driving force in these students' process
of change can be understood from both a religious and psychological perspective. Religiously, many strains of Jewish tradition have taught that
enjoyment of religious living is acceptable and even mandated. Hence,
many Jewish commentators translate the Biblical verse "[You will be pun-
ished] because you have not worshipped the *Lord*, your God with joy and
goodness of heart."(Deuteronomy 28:47).[76] Similarly there is a Talmudic
debate regarding the cause for the nazirite's requirement to bring a sin-
offering (Tractate *Nedarim* 10a). One opinion states that the nazirite is
culpable for depriving himself of the pleasures of the world. Some Jewish
thinkers have also averred that one should take pleasure in one's learning:
"The essence of the *mitzvah* of Torah study is to be happy, rejoice and take
pleasure in one's studies. Then the words of the Torah become absorbed
into his blood."[77] Essentially, in this perspective, religious growth does not
entail perpetual struggle in all mitzvah performance, but rather a process
of developing a taste for the finer (spiritual) aspects of life.
Psychodynamically, the process of change can be understood simply as a
manifestation of Freud's pleasure principle, with the transfer of focus
from childhood pleasures to more intellectual ones.[78]

Others, however, do not enjoy Torah study, but feel it to be an encompassing, meaningful obligation, "something I had to do." These students
describe an array of different reasons and manners in which they feel
Torah study to be meaningful for them. Some feel that it connects them
with a larger mission, "a responsibility because I'm Jewish, just to preserve our heritage." Others feel learning to be their primary vehicle for
connecting with the divine.

---

76 Greenberg, J. (1995). *Iturei Torah*. Tel Aviv: Yavneh.

77 Bornstein, A. (1931). *Introduction to Eglei Tal*. New York: Abraham Isaac Friedman.

78 McWilliams, N. (1994). *Psychoanalytic Diagnosis*. New York: The Guilford Press.

I sort of see it as discipline. Not an intellectual discipline, but a way to continue your connection, your relationship with God. It's weird because it shouldn't necessarily have to bring you towards God. For instance, you're learning *Bava Metzia* (laws of ownership and contracts), but when you finish it seems to have this weird affect on you, like you feel like a better person in a way. Like you're really using your mind the way it should be used.

For others, it is not the process of learning, but the content of learning that is meaningful.

First of all, I feel like you have to know everything in order to do it. But you can't just learn straight *halachah*, you have to know the whole Gemara . . . . Also, through learning, your observance level becomes better. People also say they learn because it connects them with Hashem. That's not me. I learn because I want to know the whole Torah . . . . It's the desire to be a *talmid chacham*, to give *shiur*, to know, but not the actual learning . . . . In Israel, I created this sense of wanting to know everything . . . . I want to learn it, *chazar* (review) it, know it, and move on to the next thing. Everything adds up and I'll have a broad base of knowledge.

Paradoxically, not all who become engrossed in learning describe themselves as intellectually curious people before going to Israel.

I generally hate reading, I just can't sit and read . . . . That idea never came to me; it still doesn't come to me. My idea of having free time is playing basketball. I never hated learning more than anything else; I just hated reading. Now learning is everything.

Another student explains the importance of learning outside of an academic structure.

I think [in high school] my classes began and ended by semester. After I got my grade I forgot about the course. [After study in Israel] I was very aware that my learning had more long-term implications and that it was much more [related to] eternal things, and that what I was doing was part of a grander scheme . . . my learning was something that transcended that by a lot.

Back in the United States, the study of Torah also serves as a conduit back to inspired times.

> When I go to Y.U. (Yeshiva University) and learn with my *chavruta*, I think the learning provides me with different things now then it used to. Right now it's like a breath of fresh air; it takes me back to *yeshiva*. I guess that's also the environment. It warms my heart; opens up/wakes up my *neshamah*.

The experience of these students who do not usually enjoy Torah study, but still feel encompassed by the study of Torah and are driven to study it, can also be explained both religiously and psychologically. The second opinion in the aforementioned Talmudic passage regarding the nazirite takes a more monastic approach; the nazirite requires atonement at the conclusion of his naziritic period for abandoning the holiness of his restrictive living and returning to the pleasures of the world.

The phenomenon of change and dedication in the absence of pleasure can also be understood psychologically. In the latter half of the twentieth century, psychological thinkers raised challenges to the Freudian pleasure principle, and suggested that there are other inner motivational forces that are as powerful as pleasure. Erik Erikson suggested that individuals are driven primarily by the need to meet the challenges of their particular life stage, in this case identity formation.[79] Similarly, Carl Rogers (1961) proposed that individuals' need to grow and find fulfillment is their strongest motivation.[80] Thus, *yeshiva* students are driven to dedicate themselves to Torah study by the need to find identity and fulfillment, even though it does not give them hedonic pleasure.

In his seminal work, *Man's Search For Meaning*, Victor Frankl suggested that the human drive to meaning is exceedingly powerful. Based on his experience in concentration camps, Frankl observed that many people were able to survive the torturous conditions because there was some point of meaning in their life.

The students' perspectives in many cases echo writings on the phenomenology of Torah study in the Jewish tradition. Rabbi Aharon Lichtenstein explains that the study of Torah serves both as a means to learning *halachah* as well as an experience of connection with the divine

---

79 Erikson, E.H. (1950). *Childhood and Society*. New York: Norton
80 Rogers, C.R. (1961). *On becoming a person*. Boston: Houghton Mifflin.

and with Jewish tradition.[81] Despite its deeply intellectual nature, for some students Torah study is more religiously than intellectually focused. Along these lines, Kenneth Pargament lists Bible study as one of many religious acts that connect the religious devotee with God.[82]

Ethics

The area of ethical growth is rarely addressed in popular discussion of the process of change during study in Israel. Indeed, few students conceive of this as the focus of their change. Shalom Berger has found that students' change is much more focused on *bein adam la-makom* than on *bein adam l'chaveiro*.[83] Nonetheless, many individuals do perceive themselves as having become more ethical or interpersonally sensitive over the course of the year. Some students describe this growth as a behavioral change resulting from direct rabbinical discussion of the topic. For most, however, this is seen as an outgrowth of a general change in persona.

> I think it was a matter of attitude change. I can't say I've eliminated my bad traits because I still get frustrated with people . . . . On a Sunday I was driving my brother to *shul*, and I was driving a minivan down a street with cars parked on both sides. As I was driving, a minivan came the other way, and I had to move to the right. As I did that I brushed up against a parked car, and I didn't think anything happened. But I turned around and saw that the rearview mirror was cracked and hanging by a thread. So I pulled over to the right, and my first thought was "drive away." But I stopped and wrote a note, which I don't know if I would have before Israel. I'm just trying in my attitude to be more positive toward people. It turned out afterward the rearview mirror had been broken all along.

Alternatively, many students see ethical progress not as a qualitative change, but rather an improvement of previously good interpersonal traits.

---

81 Lichtenstein, A. (2003). *Leaves of Faith*. Jersey City: Ktav.

82 Pargament, K.I. (1997). *The psychology of religion and coping*. New York: The Guilford Press.

83 See above, chapter 8.

I remember just walking down the path back to my room. It was a nice cool night. For some reason, I saw a stray dog, and I thought "I bet it's hungry." So I went to my room and got some milk or water, maybe some food, and I brought it outside to bring to the dog. One of my roommates asked me what I was doing, and I just thought about how I probably got that from my mom.

This phenomenon contrasts with the typical path of Christian religious changers. For some Christian changers, ethical and interpersonal change is at the heart of their change.[84] Thus, in eight types of religious individuals, one group is termed "socially oriented servants." The *yeshiva* students do not fit this prototype, as evidenced by their failure to mention this as a focal religious change. Nonetheless, there is anecdotal evidence that even converts whose change does not focus on social justice feel a natural inclination to help others. In his interviews with converts, Edwin Starbuck (1899) found such a phenomenon. One subject explained that after conversion, "I had more tender feeling toward my family and friends," while another "felt in harmony with everybody, and all creation and its Creator." This appears to be reflected among some *yeshiva* students as well in their assertion that ethical improvement was an outgrowth of their general religious change.

Connection with Israel

Shalom Berger has also noted a dearth of growth in the Zionism of students during a year in Israel.[85] Nonetheless, many students do intensify their connection to Israel, in some manner, during the year of study. However, students identify with Israel on different planes. For some, it is a spiritual or mystical connection with the land.

My feelings about Israel were previously not very intense . . . . Being there allowed me more time to appreciate things more . . . . I wouldn't say you love Israel more because you become more religious, but for me they came together.

---

84 Pargament, K.I. (1997). *The psychology of religion and coping.* New York: The Guilford Press

85 See above, chapter 9.

Others describe their connection in terms of feelings for the religious community in Israel.

> I loved Israel. It became like my home. As soon as I came back I said "after college I'm going back for another year." Or hopefully one day I'll move there. And hopefully we will in a couple of years. It's just unbelievable. I love Israel, especially coming back to America; I realized you just can't be on the level you can be in Israel. At least for me I felt that way with all the distractions and other stuff here.

For some, the connection is via the wider Israeli nation.

> It was really living there. Two of my roommates were Israeli . . . it really felt like being part of something, a nation. I felt guilty, my roommates were soldiers putting their butts on the line, and I wasn't. And the Intifada, everyone felt so bonded by that experience. I remember it was *motzei* Rosh Hashana, the alarms were sounding in the *yishuv*. We weren't allowed to leave, and people were scared. That experience really connected us. The entire year, the experience of our parents [being] nervous at home and all of us trying to maintain sanity and calm really bonded us . . . . Even if you're not doing anything there, you suffer with the people who suffer, you laugh with people, with the history. [In America], it's a moment of pain and then it passes. There, you feel like you're part of some process.

The Process of Religious Change and Identity Formation

"My older sister came back from Israel very different; what happened to her over there?"

For the family member or friend of many a returnee from "*shanah ba'aretz*" there are many questions regarding the process of change, that is, "how did this happen?"

The phenomenon of change in Israel entails both religious and psychological components. This interplay of psychology and religion has critical implications for all of the involved parties in *shanah ba'aretz*. While the phenomenon of change in Israel is generally viewed as an issue of "religion," it is a psychological process on many levels. First, the process of late adolescent change is a universal aspect of psychological development, as will be discussed below. Second, the psychological makeup of the individual helps shape the change process, and for good or bad, the change process has psychological implications on the student. It is critical for students, teachers, and parents to understand these psychological aspects of the change process.

Spiritual Moments

> "My high school did a lot of *kumsitz* singing on school shabbatons, but I was never particularly into it. For some reason, the spiritual stuff seems to be sinking in more?!"

Although students change in many different ways, spiritual moments are almost universally directly or indirectly important in the process. Some types of spiritual experiences are common both before and during study in Israel, while others are unique to the Israel experience.

Many students who have undergone religious change in Israel tend to forget the spiritual experiences that they had during high school, although they recall them upon being asked. This phenomenon is indicative of two things. First, contrary to popular belief, religious change almost always has its roots in prior experiences. Second, students tend to focus on the change process as a new experience, and forget that it had its base in previous family and school-based experiences.

The importance of earlier experiences as a foundation for change is also consistent with the literature on religious conversion. A case study of a born-again Christian portrayed an apparent first-time religious inspiration that was actually grounded in subtle, earlier internalizations of spirituality. While tripping on drugs, Tim entered a bathroom:

> I'm thinking this is pretty cool, bathroom, you know, commode, tub . . . somebody talking to me that has a lot of influence, a lot of pack, a lot of punch behind him, cause I responded like, "OK God, what do you want?" I was looking in the mirror and it says "all your life you have believed in me" . . . . This Scripture started to filter through my head, and I couldn't remember what it

was. I couldn't identify it as I can now. It was John 3:16, and it's just that I remember parts of it from when I was a kid.[86]

Elsewhere, Pargament explained the implications of this case study:

Religion seemingly emerged out of nowhere to help him get his life back together. Through the interview, however, it became clear that Tim did not come to this critical moment empty-handed, and his conversion did not grow out of a void. He brought with him a set of religious resources, burdens, and predispositions, and these factors played an important role in his experience.[87]

While the nature of these *ruach* experiences is similar before and during study in Israel, there are also multiple differences between them. First, the frequency of these experiences differs in *yeshiva* where they are "all over the place." Students explain that the impact of these experiences is also different. During high school, these spiritual highs tended to be more fleeting in nature.

At Camp . . . we would sit in a circle and sing slow songs. I was always a fan . . . . When I say it was a spiritual moment, I mean, I was sitting and schmoozing with my friends, but . . . . sometimes, on the last Shabbat of camp, that's when someone gets up and tells one of those meaningful stories. I remember one *tish* after my junior year, in camp. One of my old counselors gave a great speech. I guess I felt into it, excited. I don't know what it meant. It didn't translate into learning or going to davening the next day. There was no higher for me. I never knew what was higher than that. What does that mean?

Pargament reported that the presence of varied reactions to the same religious experience is a universal phenomenon.[88] Thus, only some people

86 Pargament, K.I., Royster, B.J.T., Albert, M., Crowe, P., Cullman, E.P., Holley, R., Schaefer, D., Sytniak, M., & Wood, M. (1990). *A qualitative approach to the study of religion and coping: Four tentative conclusions*. Paper presented at the meeting of the American Psychological Association, Boston, MA.

87 Pargament, K.I. (1997). *The psychology of religion and coping*. New York: The Guilford Press.

88 Ibid.

respond to religious inspiration with the "a-ha" experience, predictive of religious change. The differences in experience may be due to the environment, maturation, or other factors. One student explained that his pre-Israel spiritual moments only had a temporary effect because "I don't think I was looking for an impact."

Alternatively, sociologist Roger Straus suggests that it is not the experience but the follow-up that is determinative: "It is not so much the initial action that enables the convert to experience a transformed life but the day to day actions of living it."[89] The encompassing spiritual atmosphere of the *yeshiva* is more likely to facilitate the internalizing of the experience.

Yeshivot in Israel tend to receive the credit (or blame) for religious changes in students. In reality, however, religious growth processes generally have meaningful roots in high school experiences. While pre-Israel spiritual experiences generally have less impact, they should not be dismissed. One student suggested that, while there was no overt impact of his pre-Israel *ruach* experience, he believed that it did leave an impact under the surface.

> A lot of times during the summer, guys are pretty wild. And it feels like everything is just about having fun and enjoying yourself, so when I felt I had a chance to do something religious I was happy about it. And I felt good about myself. At the time I was heading one way in my mind and that shifted me. Even though I didn't act any more religious, in my mind I think I was.

Most students report a conversation as the turning point of their year. These conversations are usually with a charismatic figure and entail emotional heightening. One student described such a moment during study in Israel.

> This is toward the end, but I had a cousin in Israel that I was close with. He's a *rosh kollel*. He has a small *kollel* in Meah Shearim. He's a very special person. I used to learn with him when I was in the _____ Yeshiva . . . . Every time I spoke with

---

89 Straus, R.A. (1979). "Religious conversion as a personal and collective accomplishment." *Sociological Analysis*, 40, 158–165.

him was a religious moment. One incident I remember [was on] Sukkot in his house. I remember the lights had gone off and the room was dark. The meal was over, and we were in the sleeping *sukkah*. I was setting up my bed with my friend. And we just got to talking. I remember we just sat there with the moonlight shining on his face. He's someone I still respect very much, and he's a *Chasidish Litvak* (spiritual scholar). He has a lot of feeling, a lot of emotion. He speaks very passionately about his relationship with *Hakadosh Baruch Hu*.

Although spiritual conversations are experienced in a similar manner before and during study in Israel, conversation in Israel tends to leave a more lasting impact. One student captured the poignancy and permanence of these conversations in describing them as "Kodak moments, defining moments."

Among these students, some describe the nature of the conversation as a positively focused one, helping the students to better see the alternatives to the status quo.

I had a little schmooze with my *rebbe*, and he basically outlined the idea of Judaism being a part of you. You're not just going to learn, but it's the change in attitude that's more important, because then everything snowballs. It took me about a month to get used to it because everybody says you go to learn.

Other students explain that a negative focus forced them to reconsider their previous conception of themselves, the world, or Judaism.

It was a Sunday night *erev* Yom Kippur, speaking with a *madrich* and *shanah bet* (second year) guy. So the *madrich* said to me, "you don't believe in God at all," and the conversation took off from there. You find . . . people do whatever they want. You serve yourself, not God. That's believing in yourself, not in God.

Regardless of the positive or negative nature of the impacting conversation, this trend stands in contrast with the most common Christian change experiences. In his classic study of converts, William James presented the following individual's experience as typical:

> The Holy Spirit descended upon me in a manner that seemed
> to go through me, body and soul, I could feel the impression, like
> a wave of electricity, going through and through me. Indeed, it
> seemed to come in waves and waves of liquid love; for I could not
> express it in any other way. I can recollect distinctly that it seemed
> to fan me, like immense wings.[90]

The Christian convert's spiritual, almost "prophetic," turning point
stands in stark contrast to the *yeshiva* student's experience of change
through conversation. In all likelihood, this is attributable to differences
between Christianity and Judaism. The Jewish system of *halachah* may
engender a more grounded, intellectual approach than many strains of
Christianity. This, in turn, manifests itself in the nature of the change
process.

A small number of students have traumatic experiences that serve as
a spiritual catalyst. For instance, one American student who was wavering
in his commitment to Orthodox Judaism became firmly entrenched after
experiencing the shock of witnessing a terror attack in Jerusalem. The frequency of spiritually meaningful traumatic experiences for *yeshiva* students appears small relative to the general literature on conversion, where
it is noted that some form of emotional distress was involved in the change
process of most converts.[91] This is certainly not the case for religious
change during study in Israel.

There is a small minority of students who experience significant
change without any discrete moments of inspiration that they can pinpoint.

> I wish I could tell you I went to the *Kotel* and had a spiritual
> moment, but I didn't. I didn't have one of those crazy moments.
> It wasn't like a "boom." It wasn't "wow now I see God." People
> assume you get brainwashed. They see you go to Israel and come
> back completely different and assume something happened, [that]
> it was a click. It was gradually, slowly over time, it just happened
> through one rabbi. It happened through me trying to poke holes in

---

90 James, W. (1997). *The Varieties of Religious Experience*. New York: Simon &
Schuster.

91 Kox, W., Meeus, W., & Har, H. (1991). "Religious conversion of adolescents: Testing
the Lofland and Stark model of religious conversion." *Sociological Analysis*, 52,
227–240.

everything he said. I wanted to be that one person who finds the hole in the Torah and disproves Judaism. Every conversation, every philosophical debate we got into, he would just rock me. Not that he was smarter; not that he was a better debater. Bottom line was he was debating for God and I was debating for crazy American society views. It wasn't one time; it was months of his disproving every view that I had over time that got me.

While *ruach* and conversation are not uncommon spiritual experiences before as well as during study in Israel, inspiration through prayer and learning is more uniquely experienced during the *shanah ba'aretz*. Although prayer and learning are not new experiences in Israel, they are apparently experienced differently.

One student described how prayer inspired him in Israel.

So my *kollel* guy said to me "whether you believe it or not, just daven fifteen minutes a day, do it in English, do it in Russian. I don't care. Just ask God to show you the truth, and I promise God will take you there" . . . . I can't say there was that one day "boom," when it started, but gradually I just started getting this feeling that just felt so right.

Another student described the way in which learning had spiritual meaning to him.

Oh there were so many spiritual moments in *yeshiva*. I think just learning Gemara was a spiritual experience. It was a feeling, after you work at it for an hour and get the idea, you feel like you're part of it, part of the *mesorah*. The [rabbis in the Talmud] were arguing; now you understand why and what the whole deal is. Now you know what they knew. The whole year was basically one great spiritual experience.

At times the change catches a student by surprise.

Gradually, just one day I'd do something extra. One day I was bored and I'd pick up a *sefer*. Like, instead of reading *Sports Illustrated*, I'd do something more Jewish-oriented. And it pretty much built from there.

Interestingly, even among students with multiple "*ruach*" moments during their study in Israel, it is uncommon for this to serve as the primary catalyst of change. Thus, even for the spiritually oriented individual, an intellectual component is necessary to effect identity change.

Chapter 14

Turning Points

"Parents from New York have been requesting that we schedule vacation in late January to coordinate with their visits to Israel. Although we want to be accommodating, this time is the heart of *Choref Zeman*. Won't breaking up the students' *yeshiva* experience have a serious impact on their growth?"

Although friends and family are generally introduced to the "changed" individual at a discrete time, change is not typically sudden. The academic year in Israeli *yeshivot* consists of five periods. The first period, *Elul Zeman* (the period of the Hebrew month Elul), consists of five weeks from the opening of the year until Yom Kippur; the second period is the two-week Sukkot holiday break following Yom Kippur; the third period is the five-month *Choref Zeman* (Winter Period) following Sukkot until two weeks before Passover; the fourth period is the month-long *Pesach* (Passover) break; the fifth period is the two-month *Kayitz Zeman* (Summer Period).

There is wide variability regarding the timing and discreteness of change. While for a significant minority the process is gradual with no defining moments, the majority of students can point to a time in the year of their most significant change. Most point to *Choref Zeman* as the critical juncture, although others specify one of the other time frames.

At a certain level, logistics warrant *Choref Zeman*'s place as the primary turning point, as it is the longest of the periods, spanning five to six months of the ten-month year. One student explained that the season also contributes.

Some time around Chanukah is when I started getting serious, and I'm trying to remember why .... When it gets cold in _____ Yeshiva, there's very little reason to leave. I'd just go from my room to the *Beit Midrash*.

However, some students explain that the uninterrupted nature of the extended time period is also critical. Marc Galanter has similarly documented the importance of separation from larger society in the change process for those who join a charismatic religious group.[92]

Several of the other periods are more surprising times for a turning point. Inasmuch as the learning and *yeshiva* atmosphere are generally the impetus for change, it seems surprising that some students experience a turning point early in the year during the Sukkot break.

> I ended up going with my friends to Netanya (coastal resort town) over Sukkot. I decided that what they were doing is not for me any more, but it could be a nice vacation. I don't necessarily have to do what they do. You know, in high school I had friends who were eating non-kosher [while I didn't], so I could do the same here. But it didn't happen that way. I ended up going back to what I used to do. And then I had no place to go for the first days of *yom tov* and my friend had an apartment, and said we could sleep there on the floor. And then afterward, we'd find a hotel or something to sleep at.
>
> We ended up staying [in Netanya] for the entire Sukkot, and there were just guys coming in off of the street, you knew 'em, you didn't know 'em. There were girls coming in off of the street. People passing out on the floor drunk. A lot of smoking . . . . There were crazy things going on. I was sleeping all day and staying up all night. Right at the beginning I realized "this is not for me," but I had no other situation at the time. So it just became "this is what I'm doing." So once I got back to *yeshiva* after Sukkot, I was like "o.k. I'm gonna learn now. I'm gonna start trying to change."

For these students, it seems that hitting a spiritual "rock bottom" was the impetus for change. This concept of a crisis point as the impetus for change is omnipresent in the literature on the psychological change in the process of recovery from addictions. It is particularly prevalent in the 12-step (e.g., Alcoholics Anonymous) approach.

---

92 Galanter, M. (1989). *Cults: Faith healing and coercion*. New York: Oxford University Press.

There are less common instances in which an event at the very end of the year may effect change in a student who has not previously undergone a significant shift.

> This happened one Shabbat in Meah Shearim after [the holiday of] Shavuot. We stayed at one kid's uncle's house, who's a *rebbe* in _____ Yeshiva. So in the afternoon, I went to take a nap and so did one friend. The other friend said "I'm going to learn." He said, "should I wake you up?" So my friend said, "yeah wake me up in an hour." So I said "wake me up in an hour too." So three, four hours later I get up and go to the *beit midrash*, and realize these guys had been learning straight through. So I thought "these guys are great. Look at me I'm such a bum." It hit me. So we went to the *rebbe*'s for *shalosh seudot*. After *havdalah*, he starts asking us questions on the Gemara, and I had no idea what he was talking about. And the other guys were asking him *kashyas* back and forth. And I'm sitting there like an idiot. And while we're sitting there, I realized that I wasted an entire year. I got back to *yeshiva* that Saturday night and started really learning. That was one moment that changed me in learning and in every way. I started learning *mussar*, I started davening better, getting to *seder* on time. Everything started to have meaning.

Drives to Change

"Some of the students in our Israel program change more quickly and others more slowly. Why is that? Is the quicker change necessarily less psychologically healthy?"

In addition to the content and timing of the change, it is also important to understand the phenomenological experience of the internal drives behind the process of change. Besides experiencing change as a step toward a truer or more meaningful mode of living, astute students are also able to pinpoint the psychological and emotional aspects of the change process.

Although each student's change process is unique, two prototypes seem to emerge. In analyzing their psychological motivations, some students describe themselves as dissatisfied with their previous mode of living, while others had been satisfied, but became inspired to change nonetheless. This distinction between "dissatisfied changers" and "inspired changers" is important in understanding a number of aspects of the change process.

The dissatisfied changers, motivated by psychological difficulties or at least a feeling of being internally unsettled, are a typical example of religious change. In the literature addressing religious conversion, there is an almost universal perspective of religious change as a reaction to psychological distress. Psychoanalytic thinkers have explained conversion as an attempt to maintain mental health in the face of potential mental disintegration. Researcher Pehr Granqvist points out that there are correlations between religious change and prior psychopathology.[93] In fact, Ken Pargament has gone so far as to suggest that trauma or conflict is a prerequisite for a conversion experience.

> Radical change does not come easy. Some type of stressor, tension, conflict, or uneasiness seems to be a prerequisite. The trigger may be an important transition or major negative events, such as the death of a loved one, a health threat, a divorce, or a critical loss.[94]

The Jerusalem based psychiatrist team of Witztum, Greenberg, and Dasberg have also noted that *ba'alei teshuvah* (returnees to Orthodox Judaism) in a certain Jerusalem neighborhood were more likely to suffer from mental illness than native Orthodox Jews. Thirteen percent of the patients referred to their clinic were returnees, while returnees were estimated to be well under 5 percent of the local population.[95] It is unclear, though, whether their psychological stress helped generate religious change or vice versa.

Psychologists have described dissatisfaction as a source of religious change from several angles. Sigmund Freud described conversions as an attempt to resolve Oedipal aggression toward the father by submitting to

---

93 Granqvist, P. (1998). "Religiousness and perceived childhood attachment: On the question of compensation or correspondence." *Journal for the Scientific Study of Religion 37* (2), 350–367.

94 Pargament, K.I. (1997). *The psychology of religion and coping.* New York: The Guilford Press.

95 Witztum, E., D. Greenberg, & H. Dasberg. "Mental illness and religious change." *British Journal of Medical Psychology,* 1990, 63, 33–41.

the father figure of God. Others have suggested that conversion results from an inability to live with ambiguity. Victor Frankl demonstrated that a search for meaning can resolve angst within the psyche. Cognitive psychologists have suggested conversion as an attempt to achieve intellectual order and escape cognitive confusion.

It appears that those who are "dissatisfied changers" are more likely to have a discrete point of change, while those who are "inspired changers" are more likely to change gradually. Additionally, there are "dissatisfied changers" who experience their turning point during the Sukkot break, absent any *yeshiva* influence. The contrast between the *yeshiva* environment and the more hedonistic alternatives, and their dissatisfaction with the latter, apparently spurs change. The process of change for "dissatisfied changers" may be similar to the experience described in Christian conversion experiences. As discussed earlier, the conversion literature has long described change as being driven by negative factors and entailing a discrete turning point.

For dissatisfied changers, there are a few different strains of dissatisfaction that drive them to change. For some, this feeling of dissatisfaction is focused on their previous lifestyle.

> I guess before I went to *Eretz Yisrael* I was just not happy with what I was doing . . . . Yeah, there was for sure one point for a few days in the summer before Israel—July, August, when I felt like that. All my friends were doing drugs and stuff, and everyone was just out for themselves. It was stupid. I remember coming home from work at 5:30 one day and saying "this is so stupid." It didn't stop me except for that one day, but . . . .

For others, however, the feeling of dissatisfaction focuses on accomplishment in learning.

> Looking around and thinking "these guys learned so much and I haven't really learned." That clued me in. I said "I don't know what's gonna happen in the fall, but I have a job to do, and I became very determined and very focused." It was a feeling that I'd wasted a lot of my time. I was just sitting in the B.M. (*Bet Midrash*) and looking at my Gemara or sitting in my room and reading a book. Seeing how much other people had accomplished made me realize.

The change process for "dissatisfied changers" and its psychological ramifications is a source of intense debate. Is the *yishuv ha-daat* (inner peace) a sign of deep healing and growth or a pathological façade of health that will crumble? This popular debate has its roots in both psychological and rabbinic literature. Traditional psychoanalytic thought treated such religious change as a psychologically defensive maneuver that would merely paper over psychological difficulties. Victor Frankl, however, argued the opposite based on his experience in concentration camps. He observed that finding a source of meaning and purpose provided a source of psychological stability for prisoners even in the most degrading circumstances. Similarly, he argued that psychological problems often have an "existential vacuum" at their core. Addressing this vacuum not only provides life direction, but also heals the psychological symptoms: "There is much wisdom in the words of Nietzsche: 'He who has a why to live for can bear almost any how.' I can see in these words a motto which holds true for any psychotherapy."[96]

In more recent years, researchers have described religious change from a perspective more related to the experience of "inspired changers." Kenneth Pargament agrees that there is generally dissatisfaction behind change. At the same time, he describes the inspiration that often stands behind change as well. He defined religious conversion as "an effort to re-create life, [in which] the individual experiences a dramatic change of the self, a change in which the self becomes identified with the sacred."[97]

One student described his own process of inspiration and "identification with the sacred":

> Nothing in particular drove me . . . . It was just over a period of time, living in Israel and there are no academic classes, just everything is learning, Gemara, *mussar*. It just overwhelmed me, took me over and that's how it happened.

The inspired changers are an aberration in comparison to other religious changers in Western society. In fact, the very existence of wide-scale religious change among happy people is a unique phenomenon. This discrepancy probably reflects two issues. First, psychological problems may be generally necessary to shake adults from inertia in order to undertake

---

96 Frankl, V. (1963). *Man's Search for Meaning*. New York: Washington Square Press-Simon & Schuster.

97 Ibid.

religious changes. On the other hand, during adolescence, identity change lies at the core of the normal developmental trajectory, and therefore can take place without the prod of psychological upheaval. Second, as noted earlier, many of the students in this study underwent meaningful—but not radical—change. Trauma may be a prerequisite for radical changes, but not for more subtle ones. The inconsistency of the students' overall experiences with the more negative perspective of researchers may, once again, be a function of degree of change. Perhaps "radical change" is generally driven by negative emotions or cognitions, while more subtle change need not be.

There also seem to be psychological differences between these two groups undertaking study in Israel. "Dissatisfied changers" seem more likely to change earlier in the year, during *Elul Zeman* or early *Choref Zeman*, while "inspired changers" are more likely to change in *Choref Zeman* or in a slow process over the course of the year. After undergoing change, dissatisfied changers become more psychologically comfortable, similar to the typical experience of converts.

> Some of my friends say or think that after they went to Israel, or after they decided that this is the way they want to live their life, and they wanted to stay in the *yeshiva* world and continue with it, that they found *yishuv ha-daat* and they are much happier. In a way I'm very attracted to that. It's true. If you feel like what you're doing is right all the time.

Another individual explained that "*yeshiva* was like a safe haven. When I think about *yeshiva*, I never imagine a time not smiling."

It seems clear to me that there is no sweeping generalization as to whether the change of these dissatisfied changers is psychologically stable. The critical question, rather, is how one determines the stability and healthiness of change in each case. Frankl suggests that the degree of genuineness of the new values is the critical factor in distinguishing stable and unstable change.

This distinction has an important application for one-year *yeshiva* students. In assessing a "dissatisfied changer," we might ask ourselves a number of questions. Does his intensity in learning feel sincere or serve as a source of competition with others in "*hatmadah*"? Does his newfound dedication to a mitzvah appear primarily to be in the service of God or serve as a bludgeon in discussions with parents? How comfortable does the student feel with his new identity?

For "inspired changers," on the other hand, the year in Israel can be a time of increased emotional stress, even for those who describe the year as successful. Students suggest a number of different causes for emotional difficulties, including academic frustration and growing pains.

In Israel I would be like "this is great I'm having a good time," but at a particular time I could be in the *Bet Midrash* for four, five, six days on end learning, trying to learn as much as possible, and I wasn't enjoying it. Maybe I'd learn for twenty minutes and I'd have an epiphany and that would be great. But the rest of the time I'd sit there for five, six hours and I wasn't enjoying it. I'd be sitting and sitting hoping to come to a time when I would enjoy it, and it did come. We had a *sugya* (Talmudic passage) where everything fell into place over three weeks, right before Pesach. I was on a high. I was like the happiest person in *yeshiva*. But most of the time it was not like that.

Sometimes this frustration entails feelings of guilt: "when I was going through certain changes . . . it's a depressing feeling. I thought if I'd been learning in high school, I could have been [so much more]." One student explained how the serious nature of the *yeshiva* environment changed the focus of his prior emotional difficulties.

In high school, I would get depressed about my mom's health, and what would I do if she died. But that was out of my hands. In Israel I got depressed because I was failing, and it's much more depressing when you blame yourself . . . . I would go 45 hours without sleeping, and I was taking sleeping pills.

For others, the process of going through religious change and identity formation is a grueling experience.

It was also a feeling of "I don't know what I want to do with my life. O.K. I haven't been doing anything till now, but what do I want to do now? Do I want to be part of this weird Judaism thing and learn and every day have to worry about davening three times a day?" It's a big transition.

Yet others found the loose structure allows mental health problems to creep in: "a lot of things are not worth thinking about, but you just can't

help it. So in Israel when there's so much time to sit and think, it's hard."
Many students experience subclinical symptoms, which make life uncomfortable but not debilitating.

> When I was in Israel there were times that I was sadder and
> more down than I had ever been any time in my life. The begin-
> ning was the hardest. I was very very frustrated at the beginning.
> My parents came to visit, and I spent five days with them in the
> hotel, and I remember forcing myself to put on a happy face. I had
> to show them how much I'm enjoying it. You know this is great,
> but inside I was like "I hate this place I want to go home."

But for others, there are diagnosable symptoms.

> Towards the end of Sukkot, I started thinking about things a
> lot religiously. Sometimes I couldn't necessarily think about
> learning because I was thinking about these things . . . . I was hav-
> ing problems with thoughts in my head that I couldn't get rid of
> and stuff like that. It was problems with obsessions, not regular
> O.C.D. I don't know if it would have happened without going to
> Israel, but, of course, it's a chemical imbalance. But I didn't know
> how to label it then . . . . It was really bothering me. It was very
> hard; I didn't know what was going on. If it was a *yetzer hara*
> kind of thing or a punishment.

The psychological stress these students experience may be due to the
process of religious change, general adolescent development, and the
experience of study abroad. A 1991 study noted that religious change is
generally stressful, and that most converts have some form of emotional
distress during the process.[98] A different study noted that adolescents
undergoing all kinds of transitions also tend to experience decreased sense
of well-being.[99] Similarly, Jolene Koester found the beginning of study
abroad to be an emotionally difficult time for American college students.[100]

---

98 Kox, W., Meeus, W., & Har, H. (1991). "Religious conversion of adolescents: Testing
    the Lofland and Stark model of religious conversion." *Sociological Analysis*, 52,
    227–240.

99 Berk, L. (1994). *Child Development*. Needham Heights, MA: Simon & Schuster.

100 Koester, J. (1984). "Communication and the intercultural reentry: a course proposal."
    Communication Education, 33, 251.

This conception of *yeshiva* "blues" as a transient phenomenon related to transition is supported by the students' psychological state upon their return to the United States. Later in the year and after return to the United States, both "inspired" and "dissatisfied" students are generally happy. This fits in with the finding among converts that, while those with psychological problems are more likely to change, religious change generally does not cause psychopathology.

Chapter 15

Impediments to Change

"As a senior in high school, I saw the guys coming back after a year in Israel. The way they described it, the process of becoming more serious sounded so simple. My own experience feels more like two steps forward and one, two, or three steps back."

The process of change is not a simple forward march, as it may seem to the outsider. In the midst of students' religious shifts there are a number of factors that impede the process of change. Many students perceive these impediments as obstacles to growth. However, others portray them as constructive forces that help maintain a balanced change process.

The nature of these hindrances varies widely. The most prevalent impediment relates to prior relationships that might be compromised by change. For many, this is the primary force that stands in the way of their change. These social ties take two primary forms. First, many students have friends either in Israel or in the U.S. who are not undergoing change. Occasionally these friends exert direct pressure against change. More often, however, the student is simply concerned about losing the friendship by changing from the person he has been.

Second, the religious changes that students undergo often include changes in their perspectives on coed relationships, usually restricting heterosexual socializing unless it is for the purpose of finding a spouse. Many students thus realize that, by progressing with their change process, they will eventually feel compelled to terminate relationships with friends of the opposite sex.

The phenomenon of religious change being restrained by social factors runs contrary to the usual notions of the interplay of religion and social interaction. Both philosophers and psychological researchers have noted the deep connection between the two, with the search for greater social intimacy often serving as the prod to religious change. As one convert explained to Kenneth Pargament, "ours is a friendly place, but I joined [my church] for something more than friendliness. It was familiness I missed and wanted."[101] The search for social connection as a drive to change is not absent in conversion to Judaism. Like other major religions, community is a focal aspect of Jewish life.[102] Rather, the pull of friends away from change seems to be more intense among "year in Israel" students due to the unique place of friendship during the adolescent period.[103] Additionally, there are simultaneous social factors pushing students toward change, such as the change of peers and the possibility of entry into a new community.

The fact that students change despite the social impediments disproves the notion of religious change as a simple solution to emotional problems and discontent. For these students, the decision to change entails giving up pleasurable activities. Rather, this phenomenon is in line with the approaches of Erik Erikson and Carl Rogers that the need to find identity and meaning can override the pleasure principle.

Some students report that their family ties are a significant impediment to change. In some cases, this entails a fear of creating a deep chasm between themselves and their families.

> My mom always says, "You're going to grow distant . . . ." I always say "no that's not true," but it is. That held me back a lot; it still does. Even though rationally people tell me it's in my hands to be as close or as far as I want, in reality that's not true.

Others worry about dealing with the more direct emotional reaction of their family to their changes.

> It was also hard that in Israel everyone was praising me for getting into things because nobody was expecting that to happen so fast. But when I came home in December, I went from a hero to zero. My family and friends were like "what are you doing?" All I got was praise praise praise from one side, and then I got

---

101 Pargament, K.I. (1997). *The psychology of religion and coping*. New York: The Guilford Press.

102 Jacquet, C.H., Jr., & Jones, A.M. (Eds.). (1991). *Yearbook of American and Canadian Churches, 1991*. Nashville, TN: Abingdon Press.

103 Berk, L.E. (2001) *Development through the lifespan*. Boston: Allyn &Bacon.

home and I was like the enemy. I had an aunt say to me "you were our favorite nephew what did you do to yourself." There I was thinking "I'm doing the most important thing in my life, getting closer to God. Living for the first time." And everyone who loved me was telling me how much they were disappointed in me . . . . It kind of knocked me off of my pedestal.

Some students feel more secure in their family relationships, but nevertheless feel more subtly tempered by their familial connection.

Even in high school I was very close with my parents, and I still am. When I come home from school, I'll sit with them for an hour or two just talking with them. So I guess, I don't like to see that as a something holding back, because I'm happy about that, and I feel lucky that I have it. But I guess it did hold me back to some degree because I could have become "crazier" (more religiously extreme) if I divorced myself from my family.

These students' family-based hesitations are developmentally normal. During the stage of separation-individuation, it is typical to encounter struggles of connection and abandonment in the relationship between parents and children.

Israeli psychologist Dodi Tobin also notes that the influence of parents in the change process may be stronger in the era of cell phones. Many parents recall the days of reserving a time slot for an international call from a Jerusalem post office. Only ten years ago, students usually spoke with parents no more than once per week due to the difficulty of procuring a pay phone, while today contact is much more frequent. Nonetheless, this effect may be more meaningful for girls than for boys. In Tobin's study of current *yeshiva* students, 43% of girls, but only 20% of boys, spoke with their parents at least three times per week.[104]

Significant numbers of students describe internal emotional processes, including laziness, fear, and doubt as impediments to change. Some experience laziness or inertia as the primary factor.

---

104 Tobin, D.F. (2000). "Parent-child relationships in the context of a year of study in a post-high school yeshiva program in Israel." *Atid Journal*.

I immensely enjoyed, you know I was living a life chilling with friends and just basically enjoying life. So that was really great. I wouldn't be enjoying myself as much. You know I could be playing football instead of learning or doing *chessed*. It was tough to let go of some of the things that I don't do so much any more.

For other students, fear of change is the primary factor.

There's always some sort of fear of the unknown. What am I going to be like? If I take this step, if I do this one extra thing, people are going to look at me differently. And if I do this, then I'm also going to have to do this. People are going to expect me to do this. I was a little scared of this.

For yet other students, doubt is the prime factor holding them back. This doubt usually entails philosophical questioning or discomfort with accepting a more stringent and conservative notion of Judaism.

I guess I was also frustrated with the way a lot of the guys went to Israel, had their first religious experience. I don't know, it's very arrogant and elitist, but I'm gonna say it anyway. Not about myself necessarily. You take something very exciting and powerful and give it a big group. And not everyone's ready for it and thinking about it. And it's frustrating to be part of that group. That sort of makes me feel that this religion is not working.

Many of the students see the array of impediments to change as obstacles to growth. However, others portray them as constructive forces that help temper change to allow them to change without becoming extreme.

I think a lot of me doesn't want to become extreme . . . . The deepest person is very intense, or has progressed a lot, but at the same time is not extreme. And maybe because of *ga'avah*, I never wanted to become extreme. Maybe because of *ga'avah*, but I always wanted to become great, and so I felt that in order to do that I couldn't be extreme. Even though I was caught up at a certain point in the Yeshivish thing. But any time someone started saying "this is *assur* that's *assur*," that set me on edge. So I don't know if that held me back a little bit.

Why is it that emotional impediments to change are more common among these students than among converts? First, the change here is generally part of an ongoing process rather than a discrete event. Thus, there is more opportunity for the student to be aware of emotional hesitations. Moreover, the emotional struggles may be an element of the age-appropriate separation-individuation process.

Chapter 16

Influential Individuals

"As a *yeshiva* high school, we sometimes rely on Israeli *yeshivot* to 'finish off the process for us.' At a recent staff meeting, we discussed how to incorporate some of the 'Israel experience' into our students' high school experience. How exactly do Israeli educators have such a deep impact on their students?"

For students undergoing change there are almost invariably one or more individuals who are instrumental in the process of change. Rebbes often take on a more intense role for students than they had in high school. Among other reasons for this, the context allows more opportunities for extended conversation.

I don't know if everybody felt this way, but I felt like I had a special relationship with him. We had a very good intellectual relationship. Some people went with him to Tzfat, but we went out to dinner to talk. It was just very nice. We talked for 2–3 hours. Mostly intellectually discussing issues that Jews struggle with. Sometimes personally directed. I still speak with him, not just for advice . . . sometimes just to share the experience. I think he has a strong personality and I gained a lot just from speaking with him about regular things.

The setting of Israeli *yeshivot* also engenders more informal contact, which allows for more rabbinic influence

Rav _____ was my *rebbe*. I always remained very close with him. I went to his house for meals on Shabbat. I loved him. I wanted to be like him. I wanted to act like him.

Students also gain admiration for the community of which the *rebbe* is a part.

You're exposed to these people who [live in] an entire community of *talmidei chachamim*. A community where you really think, at least on the outside, it's pleasantville-perfect, utopic. Everyone's *frum* (pious), really *frum*, good people. Not just on the outside but on the inside. And they know so much, and they're so inspiring. And living it, you don't want to leave that. Even if you weren't learning at all, you feel like it's having a really big effect. Just being in that environment.

While some students describe constructive criticism from a *rebbe* as helpful, most students note the importance of their *rebbe* taking an encouraging rather than critical role in the process of change.

I had a conversation with Rav _____ about leaving *yeshiva* early to go to Europe for two weeks, and he was vehemently against it, and was railing into me. He was sinking his teeth into me trying to convince me not to. And I remember thinking that was a real turnoff . . . . It was because, I don't know whether this is justified or not, but I felt that I had come so far, that I'd gone from not learning in high school to coming to Israel, and pushing my parents to let me come to Israel. And I had struggled to get into the learning in Israel and [was] winning that battle and becoming a serious learner. And I felt "haven't I earned these two weeks," and I felt that he wasn't seeing that. And I walked away from that conversation very frustrated. The other conversation I had was with Rav _____ about my learning, and he said "I know you're limping, just take it day by day." It was very practical, it wasn't profound, but the way he told me it struck as very straightforward, as something that I appreciated a lot. And I remember thinking of that in comparison to Rav _____, and one being very negative and one very positive. Both were trying to give me guidance and help me, and one was very effective and sincere, and the other struck me as very manipulative and unhelpful.

For many students with low-level psychological difficulties during study in Israel, Rebbes are able to help them with an encouraging approach: "my *rebbe* told me 'what you're going through, it's tough, but you're good the way you are or if you change.'" Another student explained the mechanism by which positive rabbinical feedback helped him to change.

> Rav _____ started to like me in January. Once he likes you, when he's nagging you . . . well first of all he always likes you, but until you know it. Then it started to feel like he liked me, then you like him back. My hatred of him only came because I thought he hated me . . . . In the beginning he would say a lot of nasty things, and then you realize he's just trying to get you riled up, so you think. Also some of his comments started to be good, you know, "you're doing good" . . . . you know he gets into this [*yeshiva*] family thing. And once you're part of the family you're in . . . . You have to work for him to show you love. You have to work for his love, but it's worth it.

The centrality of rabbis in the process of change is related to the developmental stage of students in Israel. In literature related to adult Christian converts, there is minimal discussion of the role of clergy. There are, however, several isolated discussions of the role of clergy in encouraging religious identity change and formation. Paavo Moilanen focused on the religious development of Finnish ministers, and corroborated the importance of relationships with clergy in the process of religious change. He also noted that discussion with a Christian authority figure was more integral in the change process of those who changed at a young age.[105] These phenomena make sense from the perspective of theories of separation and individuation. At a time when young men and women are going through the push and pull of becoming independent of their parents, an outside authority provides a sense of confidence and stability.

The phenomenon of students reaching out to *rebbeim* for psychological assistance is consistent with the practice of religious individuals across the spectrum of age and religion. Ann Hohmann and David Larson point out that clergy are often the frontline practitioners of mental health work for many reasons. First, religious people are used to sharing life-cycle events, along with their accompanying stressors, with their religious

---

105 Moilanen, P. (1974). "Family background and religious conversion in the Finnish ministry." *Psychiatria Fennia*, 83–90.

leaders. Second, clergy are immediately accessible in the individuals' communities. Third, people feel less stigmatized in bringing their problems to a religious guide than to a mental health professional.[106]

Among students with more serious psychological problems, however, there is variability in the capacity of *rebbeim* to properly diagnose and handle the clinical symptoms.

> And then when it really really got bad, I went to talk with my *rebbeim* but they didn't understand. I went and told them again that it's still bothering me. Sometimes I just broke down because I couldn't help it. But I didn't let it stop me . . . . I thought I needed help and went to a psychologist.

Clergy generally have little training in mental health issues. For instance, George Domino found that a wide variety of clergy had less diagnostic knowledge of psychopathology than undergraduates in abnormal and introductory psychology courses.[107] Thus, it would not be surprising if *rebbeim* in Israeli *yeshivot*, and clergy generally, had difficulty addressing cases of clinical psychopathology. That said, there are some *yeshivot* and seminaries that conduct in-service training for their teachers. Recently, Yeshiva University's Jerusalem office has also begun to offer psychological seminars for the staff of YU-affiliated programs.

Many *yeshiva* students develop close interpersonal relationships with their *rebbeim*. For some, the relationship serves as a surrogate parental relationship, which provides structure in the formation of religious identity. One student came to understand this more fully in retrospect.

> When I got to college, that support disappeared. It was the first time in my life when there were no *rebbeim* around. I guess the *rebbeim* play a really big deal in how I view Judaism/Torah. Because a lot of my belief and commitment derives from my relationship with *rebbeim* and teachers like ____. I respect them and

---

106 Hohmann, A. A., & Larson, D. B. (1993). "Psychiatric factors predicting use of clergy." In E. L. Worthington Jr. (Ed.), *Psychotherapy and Religious Values*. Grand Rapids, MI: Baker Books.

107 Domino, G. (1990). "Clergy's knowledge of psychopathology." *Journal of Psychology and Theology*, 18, 32–39.

I admire them. Without them it was a lot harder. Not because they were brainwashing or anything, but they created a family structure for me which, you know, I don't think I have at home . . . . so they fill in those roles.

Another student with a parental relationship with a *rebbe* found the relationship to provide emotional support.

I'm very friendly with everyone, but the next level of closeness [I only have with] Rav _____. I speak with him about everything. I had a "wacked-out" childhood a little bit, so he was like a parent . . . . Rav _____ always asks "how are you, how are you feeling, is everything O.K. That's always the first question." And then [asks] Torah questions.

Some students, however, have a meaningful experience without developing a close bond with a *rebbe*. Even those who are strongly influenced by a *rebbe* do not necessarily have a particularly close attachment to him: "I was never into the find a rabbi and stick with him and do everything he says and become like an apostle." While students are most likely to be religiously impacted by a *rebbe*, they are somewhat less likely to have had their closest relationship with him. Nonetheless, these findings do underscore the impact of Rebbes and mentors as not merely through preaching or teaching, but rather through a personal relationship.

Some students take on a non-rabbinic mentor as a significant religious influence. In the *yeshiva* setting, first-year students often have contact with second-year American students as well as Israeli and American rabbinical students. For many students, the influence of a mentor is similar to that of a *rebbe*, serving as a teacher and role model.

The *kollel guy*, he was a very pure person, personality-wise everything he does is straight. I just admired him a lot and tried to talk to him a lot. I tried to see his worldview and try to understand things better. You know a role model, so if you look at someone you admire you can see better where you're going.

Students also express similar concerns about the mentor maintaining a positive focus.

During my "down cycle" my *kollel* guy was disappointed . . . . He never raised his voice, but he was definitely disappointed. I had a *rebbe* who said "you're gonna end up marrying a *shiktza* and you're gonna have six *goyim* and sit in front of a Christmas tree celebrating Christmas." I told that to [the *kollel* guy] and I said "I know I accomplished so much. I keep kosher, Shabbat, I know I'll never intermarry. And here he is telling me I gained nothing." [The *kollel* guy] always expressed this concept to me that you can't measure yourself against someone else . . . . You came in from a different background, and sometimes from your background just gaining what you've gained is enough . . . . I would never tell you that you didn't gain anything. He never went for the method of that other rabbi that turned me off like crazy. He said you definitely gained a lot, I will never tell you that you haven't gained a lot. But will I tell you that you're done? I'll never tell you that because you have so much more potential. If he would have said the whole disappointment speech also, there's no way I would have gotten back up ever . . . I would have just folded into complete depression.

While many have a *rebbe*-style relationship with a mentor, other students are able to connect with a mentor in a manner that they could not with a *rebbe*.

In the beginning there was a *kollel* guy . . . . it was good to have a connection with him. He wore polo shirts and he seemed to have the same ideals as me. He was cool and funny. He kept me learning that whole time.

In understanding the difference between relationships with Rebbes in high school and during Israel study, context plays a critical role. Kenneth Pargament notes this phenomenon and explains that "availability, convenience, and accessibility are important factors . . . why people cope in religious ways."[108]

For other students, a friend serves as a major influence. The power of the peer group or congregation in the conversion process has similarly

---

108 Pargament, K.I. (1997). *The psychology of religion and coping.* New York: The Guilford Press.

been documented across many religions. Students give different explana-
tions of why they could not have been influenced by a *rebbe* or mentor
alone.

> I was scared into thinking that they brainwash you. I didn't
> know what that meant—I mean, you're sleeping and they send
> radio magnetic waves into your brain? I was definitely a little
> afraid of *rebbeim*. I didn't want them pushing something onto me
> that I didn't want. I was a little cautious.

Others emphasize the social and emotional reasons that friends serve
as an important religious influence.

> Growing together is easier than growing alone; it's like any-
> thing whether good or bad, it's easier to do things in a group.

Another student explained the mechanism for peer influence.

> My friends, I'm very close with [them] from high school. And
> they were all getting more religious, and I thought "my friends are
> getting more religious and look like they're having a great time—
> I want to do it." We were all moving together at the same time . . . .
> As the year went on, I saw the people who started quicker on a
> different level. And other friends of mine were at the same place
> I was, so we would work off each other. If he added something I'd
> add something, if I added something he'd add something.

While a number of students have a *rebbe* or mentor alone as their
influence, it is unusual for a friend to serve as the sole influence. Rather,
the influential friends support the process of change along with a mentor
or *rebbe*. The role of the *rebbe*, meanwhile, appears to be more central
than the role of the clergy described in adult conversion processes. It is
striking to observe the relatively small number who identify a friend as
their closest relationship during study in *yeshiva*. During adolescence,
peer relationships are particularly focal, allowing for exploration and providing support during stressful times.

Chapter 17

Parents and Visiting Home

"I remember when I was in Israel for the year. We actually spent the whole year in Israel. Nowadays, besides the constant distractions of cellphones and Treos, the students in our *yeshiva* all go back home for Pesach. Is there any silver lining in this bleak cloud of obstructions to their growth?"

Once upon a time, the year in Israel meant nine straight months away from home. Nowadays the large majority of students take a return trip to the U.S. during the course of the year. In some cases, this occurs early in the year for a family celebration. Most students, however, return during the Pesach break from *yeshiva*. The trip home is a mixed blessing for *yeshiva* students. For many of them the visit home is a distraction from the growth process, during which they regress spiritually. Although the trip is generally during Pesach break, when all of the students are on vacation, many students explain that leaving the country entirely makes it harder to pick up and continue upon return.

> The trip . . . may have been detrimental in progress. I don't feel this now, but I remember saying this then that . . . when I came back I couldn't pick it up again the way I had at first. I remember thinking that if I had not gone home, I don't know what could have happened.

For certain students, the trip stunts the process of change in a different way. Rather than simply slowing the flow of change, it changes the course. In these cases, returning home casts doubt on the veracity and desirability of change. One young man came to Israel with a weak religious foundation and was shaken by his Pesach visit:

> I came home for Pesach. It was hard; it gave me a taste of what it would be like after. It scared me a little bit . . . . Rav _____

prepared us by saying "relax, you're not going home to learn. If you learn an hour or two [a day], that's fine." So I expected myself not to learn. But then looking back at it, I think I was like a light switch: turn it on turn it off, do whatever I want . . . . I guess because I can see myself with religion without religion, with Torah without Torah. Maybe that's why when I came home, it wasn't plaguing me.

We can better understand the difficulty of integration in Israel and reintegration in the U.S. through the prism of the experiences of American university students during study abroad. David Nash has discussed the difficulty of integration into a foreign society, terming this the "U-curve." American students enter the foreign country with a high sense of well-being, which dips and then rises as the individual undergoes the process of integration.[109]

In tandem with this idea, others have written of a "W-curve," noting that the same phenomenon of adjustment occurs upon reentry to one's home society. Often upon returning home, travelers find that their families and old friends are not very receptive to their experiences and perspectives. Richard Raschio explained that they often have the need to find new friends with similar experiences to find support and validation.[110]

Although many educators bemoan the disruptive effect of leaving Israel for a month, for some students the trip home assists in the growth process. One strengthening element of the return home is in boosting the individuals' confidence in their ability to maintain their changes outside of the *yeshiva* environment. One student was surprised by his Pesach experience:

The most spiritual growth I had as an individual during the year was over Pesach. Even though I didn't learn so much, what I did learn was such a hard learning. The year before, during Pesach, I was the most friendly, outgoing guy in Florida, so at the _____ Hotel, I was the king. I was friends with everyone, boys, girls, everyone. I was very social. But the year in Israel, I was so

109 Nash, D. "The Personal Consequences of a Year of Study Abroad." *The Journal of Higher Education*, Vol. 47, No. 2, 191–203. Mar.–Apr., 1976.

110 Raschio, R. (1987). "College students' perceptions of reverse culture shock and reentry adjustments." *Journal of College Student Personnel*, March, 156–161.

worried about going and losing everything I gained. I was worried about sitting around and going to the beach . . . . you know there are stories about guys who just lose everything. So I spoke with a *kollel* guy for advice, and he said just pack your day with things. So I did, playing tennis, golf, but even so I managed to make 20 minutes to learn, and prepare a *dvar Torah* for every meal. The time learning was so much more powerful.

Similarly, another student experienced the return home as solidifying his new identity.

Pesach break was fine. It's good to show off and meet your friends who aren't religious. Especially the girls who expect hugs and kisses. But it's good when you go out with your friends, and you're wearing *tzitzit* and stuff. I don't know if it's a good thing, being proud . . . . For me it felt like doing the right thing and you're showing it off, I guess.

Another component of home visits that many students find helpful is in alerting them to the challenges at the end of study in Israel. This helps them focus on the needed strengthening of the change during the remaining time in *yeshiva*.

Besides the positive or negative effects, many experience culture shock.

It was a culture shock, I guess. Being in the atmosphere that I had been in before Israel, where I was an almost totally, well a very different person, and now I'm in the same atmosphere again as a new person. Even just sitting in my room, and walking up and down the streets in my neighborhood, there was an inner feeling like "where am I." It was a very changing experience.

Why do students have different experiences during their Pesach return? One explanation, alluded to above, is that the degree of preparation for the culture shock of return determines the student's ability to handle the experience. Among college students studying abroad and returning home, Jolene Koester noted that students who are unprepared for an adjustment period on their return experience added difficulty. Additionally, she pointed out that "the sojourners who experience the greatest difficulty in the home adjustment may be those who were most successful in adapting to the foreign culture."[111]

"My wife and I have been debating *shanah bet* with our son Max by phone. I'm getting nervous that we're doing permanent damage to our relationship with our son."

Students coming from all qualities of relationships with parents undergo meaningful change processes. Although there is a communal tendency to see religious change as a sign of disrespect or distancing from parents, most students have a good relationship during their study in Israel.

I spoke with my mom every day from Israel. I think you develop more of an appreciation of them. You can analyze your relationship with them and everything they've done for you when you're not really in it. Rav _____ also focused a lot on that.

Others reported more temporary causes.

Definitely while I was in Israel we were closer. We spoke on the phone a lot, and I was able to show maturity in helping with some problems with my younger brother. Absence makes the heart grow fonder.

Nonetheless, students suggested that remaining connected despite the distance allowed the relationship to grow along with the change.

My father came [to visit during] *shanah alef* twice . . . that was important. I wanted him to see who I was now and see what he thought. I was looking for acceptance, and he was very happy.

No clear pattern is discernible in the effect of the change process on the parental relationship. During study in Israel, some students' relationships with parents become closer or less conflictual, while others are the reverse. An essential element of identity development in this stage is the task of differentiating from parents. Historically, psychologists have

---

111 Koester, J. (1984). "Communication and the intercultural reentry: a course proposal." *Communication Education*, 33, 251.

viewed lower levels of conflict as demonstrating more successful separation. It is, in any case, a developmental phase during which it is very common for temporary changes in the nature of the parental relationship.

After their return from Israel, some students experience improved relationships for several reasons. For some, the face-to-face connection eased certain tensions that had built during the year.

> My mother thinks I'm a little crazy, but it's a lot better now than it was when I was in Israel. Now my mother sees me in person and sees that personality-wise I'm still the same. But while I was in Israel, my mom just heard my schedule for the day and it was very hard for her to adjust . . . . once I came home and she saw me, it eased a lot of the worries. I think also she has a friend whose son came back and was really *haredi* and stayed in Israel, and she was scared about me.

Others felt that their new maturity helped the relationship upon their return.

> I think that the way disagreements would play out are pretty much the same, but the content is different . . . . In high school, if I lost a disagreement with my parents, I'd be cursing them to myself. Now, I'd be more trying to understand their perspective. I'd understand that they are doing it because they care about me, not to be nasty.

There are certainly individual cases in which the post-Israel relationship is worsened. On the whole, however, most relationships continue based on their pre-Israel quality. Among the relationships that do experience ongoing change, there are instances of both improvement and worsening. This finding differs from the results of Rivka Eidex' dissertation on the relationships between *ba'alei teshuvah* and their non-Orthodox families. That study found tense relationships with family after the process of religious change. Feelings in the relationships included anger, resentment, confusion, and concern.[112] On the surface, this might be attributed to the

---

112 Eidex, R.M. (2000). "The effect of the Ba'al Teshuva phenomenon on non-Orthodox Jewish families of origin." *Dissertation Abstracts International*, 61(2-A), 640 (University Microfilms International).

degree of change. Unlike the *yeshiva* students, *ba'alei teshuvah* undergo more extreme change, which is thus more likely to create tensions with their families.

These findings regarding parental relationships also shed light on the literature on the U-curve and W-curve discussed above. While there are signs of the psychological impact of transitions going to and returning from Israel, these do not generally appear to have had a distinct impact on the parental relationship. Thus, the quality of parental relationships seems to remain stable despite the distance and change.

While change does not seem to affect the quality of parental relationships, the quality of parental relationships may affect the nature of change. Students' relationships with their parents are an intricate part of the change process. Although both the home and the external environment play a role in the creation of an individual's religious identity, Scott Myers found that parental religiousness is the most reliable predictor of a child's degree of religious commitment. The likelihood of a parent being able to pass on their perspective to a child, meanwhile, is dependent upon the quality of the parent-child relationship.[113] Lee Kirkpatrick and Philip Shaver found that subjects describing their mother as cold and unresponsive were more likely to undergo a process of religious change, rather than retain their parent's religious values.[114] Students with problematic relationships with their parents prior to *yeshiva* also appear more likely to change more intensely.

---

113 Myers, S. (1996). "An Interactive Model of Religiosity Inheritance: The Importance of Family Context." *American Sociological Review*, Vol. 61, No. 5, 858–866

114 Kirkpatrick, L.E. (1999). "Attachment and religious representations and behavior." In Cassidy, J. (ed.) & Shaver, P.R. (ed.). *Handbook of attachment: Theory, Research, and Clinical Applications*. 803–822. New York: The Guilford Press.

Chapter 18

Finding Your Place Back Home

"I grew and changed a lot during my year in Israel. After a summer and one month in college, I see that some of that Israel magic is gone. Is the remaining impact from the year a lost cause?"

About a decade ago, the Yeshiva University student newspaper, *Hamevaser*, critiqued the "Israel experience" in a cartoon satire.* In the image, a typical Modern Orthodox high school student enters the "year in Israel" revolving door and becomes *haredi* half way through the revolution. By the time, however, he has finished the revolution he has returned to his original self. Extreme cases of change and reversion to original self capture people's attention. Less noticed is the manner in which the person whose change sticks incorporates his period of change into his life trajectory and self-image.

Some students appreciate their Israel experience upon return more than they had while in the midst of their sojourn.

I didn't really appreciate the time so much while I was there. The time to just sit and learn and reflect, to really choose a path to live my life, that's cliché-ish, but I didn't appreciate the year as much as I do now.

For those expressing increased appreciation, there is often a growing feeling of the challenge to maintain and extend the progress made in Israel.

I definitely feel that while I was there I was growing, and upon return I'm trying to maintain it . . . . As time goes by, I think I look back at the time in Israel more fondly, and maybe remember things a little differently than they were. I long for those days. Now is the time to shape the inspiration from the time in Israel.

---

* See earlier, p. 58.

Some students explain that the increased appreciation stems from an internalizing of the degree and meaning of their change upon returning to the United States.

> As time goes by I realize how important my time in Israel was for me, and what I'd be like without it. When you first come back you think "O.K. this is how I am now" . . . . In general there's times I feel like, "if I didn't go to Israel I'd be like this guy I went to high school with or like that guy." And you just realize how lucky I was to go and how much I got out of it. At the same time, I realize, "oh I could have done so much more."

Many others, however, retreat from the changes they have undergone in Israel upon their return to the United States, but they have varied perspectives on this phenomenon. For some, this creates remorse over backsliding.

> I've kind of deviated in general attitude from what a *ben Torah* should be. My personality maybe and my demeanor maybe.

For other students, there is a definite feeling that this retreat is a correction of changes in Israel that were too extreme. Yet others are confused about the changes they have made, no longer sure whether the changes were positive or not.

Returning to the YU *Hamevaser* image, we can state that there is variation in the permanence of change in Israel. It is important to understand, however, that even among those who continue to describe themselves as having undergone meaningful change in Israel, there is sometimes a lessening of the degree of change.

> "*Yeshiva* in Israel was great! It's been three years since, and I can't see myself fitting into any community here in the States?! What am I supposed to do with myself?"

While students from Modern Orthodox high schools vary widely in their religious observance, by and large they share a religious self-identification as "Modern Orthodox." Among students experiencing meaningful religious change in Israel, however, there is variation in subsequent self-identification. There are many who still identify themselves as Modern Orthodox. Such individuals describe themselves as more religiously committed than before, but unchanged in fundamental perspective.

I'm not sure where I place myself. I guess closer to the _____ Yeshiva from what I hear. Modern Orthodox, but really being Modern Orthodox not just the name. But Riverdale is a good example, with the younger community as opposed to [my parents' community] where there's fifteen people at weekday *minchah* in a *shul* of 500 people. Rav _____ calls it the *kaddish minyan.* Eleven people including the rabbi, with nine people saying *kaddish.*

Others, however, change more fundamentally, and identify themselves as Yeshivish, apparently demonstrating the most change and furthest distancing from their upbringing.

My affiliation is very black (Yeshivish). I don't know how else to say it. You can't mess around because you might fall back. So I have to be as Right [wing] as possible.

Nonetheless, even among those who have become Yeshivish, many have hesitations about affiliating with the Yeshivish community. One student expressed disdain for the notion of having to label oneself.

I mean I'm [in a modern orthodox *shul*] every Shabbat . . . . I don't know. I don't care. That's stupid stuff; I mean [I'm] more Yeshivish, that's how I act, but that's because _____ is the only *Bet Midrash* that I'm comfortable learning in here. I got a lot of my *hashkafot* from _____—he's Yeshivish and not Yeshivish. He doesn't dress Yeshivish, but he thinks Yeshivish . . . . I wear a white shirt, but people get too caught up in it. _____ reminds me of that. He sits and learns in jeans and a t-shirt. That's also good . . . . People grow up Modern Orthodox with their shtick and become Yeshivish with some other shtick.

There is a similar discomfort with fully self-identifying as Yeshivish, even among those who essentially identify as such.

I met a guy in _____ College, who asked me if I'm *haredi*.
I told him I'm just a *pashute yid* (simple Jew). I mean this is a
Yeshivish place. I wear a black hat now, but I view it more as
political. If you're going to be in this group you're like this. How
I think is from my *rebbeim*. The way I dress looks Yeshivish so
other people may associate me with it. I felt different than the
Yeshivish guys when I came in, but I feel now that I have similar
perspective to other guys here. I mean we haven't discussed our
philosophy. I don't feel like an outsider here.

One of the most critical areas of misunderstanding in the Modern
Orthodox community is the existence of an intermediate group of
"straddlers," who do not identify fully with either the Modern Orthodox
or Yeshivish communities. For some students, this is a function of incom-
plete identity development.

I affiliate with whatever community I'm with at the time. A
lot of people don't feel that way. Most of my friends, I'd say, even
the ones who are Yeshivish or want to be Yeshivish, they're not
Yeshivish. They're Yeshivish within the Modern Orthodox community. The way I personally feel is comfortable anywhere, and
that's partially because of the varied backgrounds in my family.
So whoever I'm with I'll feel part of that. So I'm in YU now and
I feel a part of it, but when I was in Mir this summer, I had no
problem putting on a black hat and white shirt and making
friends, and fitting in there.

For others, however, it manifests an integrated identity, incorporating
the Israel changes while maintaining a connection with their roots through
the creation of a new community identity.

I guess Modern Orthodox is the schools I went to, but I don't
think Modern Orthodox is my view now. I'd say, well I honestly
don't like labels, they're man-made, but if you're asking, I guess
I'm the new post-Israel religion in one of its degrees.

One student provided another label for this group.

I don't know how to put it. The way I once heard someone put
it is the YU *Bet Midrash* [community]. I consider myself between

the more modern and more right-wing. I don't know if the word is strictly orthodox. I don't know. I consider myself to be pretty modern, but in some ways I'm more traditional and more strict. I don't know exactly where that puts me. I guess in terms of views I'm pretty positive about college education, very positive about Israel. In terms of dress and attitude toward other Jews, I'm pretty open-minded. But some of my attitudes are more traditional, as is my love of learning and level of observance.

The W-curve discussed above is of particular relevance to our *yeshiva* students. While there is much focus on the process of change in Israel, there is insufficient awareness and attention to the process of ongoing change and reintegration in the year or even years following return from Israel. It is especially challenging for straddlers who simply do not find an established group in the United States with which to identify.

Although it is difficult to pinpoint a qualitative difference between those who changed their self-definition and those who did not, these varying levels of change are similar to those described by Kenneth Pargament. He suggests that the practice of referring to individuals who switch religious denominations (e.g., Catholic to Protestant) as converts is misleading. In the process of conversion, there is a change in the goals of living. In denominational switching the end remains more or less the same, while the path to the goal changes. Similarly, among the *yeshiva* students, those who became Yeshivish experienced the change as more of a conversion process, while the straddlers are better described as denominational switchers.

An additional framework is also helpful in formulating the different levels of change. Pargament also suggests that one of the areas in which psychology and religion diverge is in their goals of change. In psychology, the goal is growth and improvement, while in religion the goal is a more radical conversion. While this may be true in some religions or circumstances, that is not necessarily the case for *yeshiva* students. Phenomenologically, the Yeshivish students may have had an experience akin to conversion, the straddlers experience something akin to denominational switching, and those who remained Modern Orthodox find an experience like the humanistic psychological notion of personal growth.

There are several additional trends related to Yeshivish students. Students who became Yeshivish seem more likely to have been rebellious in high school. Similarly, those who are "dissatisfied changers" seem more likely to become Yeshivish. This concept of shifting from one end of the spectrum to the other is widespread in popular wisdom, and is eloquently captured in a short story about a convert: in *The Man Who Saw Through Heaven* by Wilbur Steele, the narrator describes the protagonist's drastic change by noting "the blacker the heathen, the whiter the light they want."[115]

The students identifying as Modern Orthodox also demonstrate several possible trends. First, they are less likely than other changers to have an encompassing focus on Torah study. For them, Torah study is important, but only one part of their daily schedules, while with the students identifying as Yeshivish, Torah study becomes a main focus. This may also be related to the students' experience prior to study in Israel.

In addition to the content of their change, there may be certain aspects of the process of change that are associated with the Modern Orthodox students. On one hand, the less intense change of Modern Orthodox students does not seem to be a function of a lesser connection with the *yeshiva* environment. The Modern Orthodox students are as likely as others to perceive a *rebbe* as an important influence. However, in comparison to the Yeshivish students, Modern Orthodox students may be less likely to have their closest relationship with an authority figure. One Modern Orthodox student thus emphasized that his *yeshiva* and Rebbes had impacted him without his developing a close connection with a *rebbe*.

> I was never into the find a rabbi and stick with him and do everything he says and become like an apostle . . . . I think the entire experience as a whole has the imprint effect on me. I know some people put up pictures of Rav _____ on their door, but that's not for me.

This is different from Ken Pargament's depiction of the interplay of religious intensity and institutional connection among converts:

> Sacred power can be attached to the local mainstream congregation and clergy as well as the nontraditional group. The loyalty and devotion the individual feels for the neighborhood church and its leader can also become a new organizing force for the self.

---

115 Steele, W.D. in Haydn & Cournos eds. (1947). *A World of Great Stories*. New York: Crown Publishers.

This description of intense connection is more accurate for the Yeshivish students. In the case of the *yeshiva* students, it may also be that extreme change becomes less likely when students are less intimately connected with an authority figure.

Chapter 19

Developmental Stages
and Influences

"I was in Israel for the year about 10 years ago. It was great and so was college. My nephew seems to still be trying to find himself two years after returning from Israel. Should I be worried?"

Late adolescence is a time of change regardless of where our children may be. We must, therefore, see the change in students during their year of study in Israel through the prism of normal adolescent development. Erik Erikson expanded Sigmund Freud's model of developmental stages to later periods of life. Of most relevance to this discussion, he explained that the late adolescent years are marked by the task of solidifying an identity independent of one's parents. Older adolescents or young adults undergo this process, eventually reaching a point of identity confusion or identity integration.

Stable individuals will reach a stage of internal clarity regarding their identity, even though they will continue to grow spiritually within that identity. The process of identity development proceeds at widely varying rates; for most, however, it extends significantly past their return to the United States. For a minority this essentially occurs while still in Israel. One student explained how he had been able to solidify his change while still studying in Israel:

> I think I've basically settled in terms of who I am now. I can't define an exact moment when it happened. I think before Pesach [during] *shanah alef* [first year in Israel], I had already settled on these goals in life. I didn't feel strong enough that if I were thrown into the opposite I wouldn't go the other way, lose it. That definitely became stronger over the summer and *shanah bet.*

138

For most students, however, the encounter with the non-*yeshiva* aspects of their lives—family, friends, or environments—is a necessary step before identity formation occurs. One student, presently studying in an American *yeshiva*, explained the psychological and interpersonal manifestations of reaching identity integration.

> I went to Columbia University recently for Shabbat and I feel more comfortable there then I did previous times, because I'm now comfortable with who I am. The previous times I was sort of withdrawn. This time I was able to act like a normal human being. Not that I want to live there or be part of that community, but I could relate to them normally without withdrawing into a shell. Without feeling it would adversely affect me to be there.

Identity formation is a process that has an impact on areas such as choice of profession and spouse.

> I think I'm close, but I don't think I can say I've completed it. I think . . . more than fine-tuning, some things I still need to think about. There's a few multiple directions I could be headed. I'm in between, but my exact attitude toward the world outside Judaism, I'm not clear on yet. And I'm also not sure what I want to do with myself, whether I want to do something religious professionally. I hope to reach a resolution soon, but there's time over the next few years. Every once in a while I get nervous about it, but I'm not in any rush to get married, so I don't feel a rush regarding some of the hashkafic and professional things.

For a minority, the period of post-Israel identity formation is extended, and leaves the student in a limbo state.

> In a philosophical way, I think people change every day, and that's important to keep in mind. I mean I don't know how long this is going to last, I'm in college now and that's the mentality of many people in college, and that's a good thing. I don't know where my process of change is taking me; I don't know where I'm gonna go.

Erik Erikson called this phase prior to identity formation "moratorium." He suggested that going through such a phase is part of healthy development during this stage of life, as long as it is completed within a reasonable amount of time. Those in moratorium are primarily in one of two limbo states. Some of the students hover between being Yeshivish and being a "straddler." Other students hover between being Modern Orthodox and being a "straddler." Overall, the students in the former state of moratorium tend to be more comfortable with their exploration than the latter. This may be because the former are simply deciding how far to take the change they are approaching. The latter, however, are generally pulling back from their change and questioning the very change they have undergone, which consists of a stressful dilemma. In fact, these students also seem likely to have a longer road to identity integration.

Introjects

> "I enjoy my son Zach's email *dvar Torah* from his teacher each Friday, but I'm a little uncomfortable with the centrality of this *rebbe* in his life."

When asked to identify the person or people whom they experienced as an introject—"the people whose opinion of you mattered most"—before going to Israel, most students identify one or both parents. Surprisingly, after study in Israel, most students continue to identify their parent as an introject! One student illustrated why his parents remained his introjects even after he had differentiated himself from them through his process of change:

> All my *middot*, everything I have is from my parents . . . . [Even in the ritual realm], I don't look at it as I did terrible things and that person's not me. I feel like maybe if I hadn't been that, I wouldn't be who I am now.

A traditional developmental view might suggest that the students continuing to report deep attachment to their parents have not achieved as healthy or complete a process of individuating from their parents. More recently, however, Donna Schultheiss and David Blustein have framed healthy parental attachment as "an enduring emotional bond with parents." That is, psychologically healthy adjustment entails achieving autonomy within the context of "an interdependent, rather than an independent relationship with their parents."[116]

After study in Israel, however, most students also identify a *rebbe* as an introject. One of the critical questions in this arena is whether parents are replaced by Rebbes or others as the introject during study in Israel. Contrary to popular belief, for many, internalizing a *rebbe* figure is not an important aspect of change.

> I think the entire experience as a whole has the imprint effect on me. I know some people put up pictures of Rav _____ on their door, but that's not for me. Maybe I should, but I wanted to get something like a necklace or something as a symbol of the experience, but it was too weird. It's not the point to get something physical.

Much has been written in the literature of religion regarding the role of the search for a parental figure in religious conversion or switching. While searching for a parental figure may have played a role for some of these students, most of those who become closely connected with a *rebbe* have a good parental relationship prior to *yeshiva*. Moreover, most students maintain a parent as an introject alongside the *rebbe*.

Friends have an important role in this process as well, and not only in the form of peer pressure. In addition to parents, some students maintain a friend as a post-Israel introject who has deeply affected their spiritual psyche. One described the power of friendships during the process of change to leave an imprint.

> [My friend and I] were very close in high school, and when I left Israel in the middle of *shanah bet*, he cried and said "I see how much we've grown together, and I hope we can stay close." So even though our moral systems are pretty different, still I might carry his voice with me.

---

116 Schultheiss, D.E.P. & Blustein, D.L. (1995). "Role of adolescent-parent relationships in college student development and adjustment: Correction." *Journal of Counseling Psychology, 42*(3), 406.

This phenomenon is a part of the normal developmental pattern literature; Kenneth Rice notes that close relationships with friends have been found to be of particular import to college-aged men. While closeness to fathers is critical prior to identity-development transitions, afterward, peer support becomes more important.

Another student described the ongoing impact that a non-human introject had on his religious identity formation.

> When I first came back, I would just have the Kotel in my mind. If anything was leading me away, I would think "one or two months ago, I was sitting in the Old City [of Jerusalem] right across from the Kotel, and now you're gonna do something wrong, or not continue with what you did there" . . . . It was more of an image of the *Beit HaMikdash* over the Kotel, and a feeling of "how could I let go?"

Chapter 20

Conclusion

As mentioned in the opening of this section, this discussion is based on interviews of male *yeshiva* students. Certainly, many aspects of the process of change apply to girls as well. For instance, it seems clear that much of the content of change—such as observance and *weltanschauung* —is relevant in the development of girls' maturation as well. However, many questions remain in this area. Is the process of change also conversationally based in the class-focused seminary structure, or is that more specific to the boys' *yeshiva* atmosphere, with its extended hours of unstructured time spent in the *beit midrash*? Do maturational differences between genders render girls likely to change more quickly or more slowly? Unlike boys, girls are often preparing for marriage within several years of their year in Israel. How does the near overlap of the Eriksonian stages of identity-formation and intimacy-seeking have an impact on the change process? In particular, how does it affect the integration of change upon return to America? Psychologist Dodi Tobin notes more frequent communication with parents during the year in Israel among girls. How does this affect the change process? A number of psychological disorders have their onset among men in their mid 20's, but among women the same phenomena are seen when they reach their late teens. Is this evident in the year in Israel process for girls? A study led by Dr. David Pelcovitz that is currently underway should shed light on these and many other questions. It is my hope and *tefillah* that a deeper understanding of the psychological aspects of this formative year will assist students, teachers, and parents in making this the special experience that it is supposed to be for each student.

Section 3:
American Orthodoxy, Zionism and Israel

Chapter 21

American Religious Zionism

This essay is an analysis of American Orthodox community with special focus on the role of the Year-in-Israel program in and on American Orthodoxy. Although contemporary American Orthodoxy is overwhelmingly pro-Israel, as will be discussed, this was not always the case. To set the stage for the dramatic changes in American Orthodoxy during the second half of the twentieth century, we begin with a brief history of religious Zionism in America.

Historians are divided over the issue of the strength and influence of religious Zionism among American Orthodox Jewry at the beginning of the twentieth century. Marnin Feinstein and Naomi Cohen argue that both religious and political reasons explain the tepid support for Zionism within the Orthodox community of this time. Feinstein ascribes the slow development of Chovevei Zion, among others, to the general opposition of both Reform and Orthodox rabbis to Chovevei Zion, the Zionist movement that existed before the Zionist Organization was created.[117] "The ultra-Orthodox Jewish elements," he suggests, were bitterly opposed to the renewal of resettlement of *Eretz Yisrael* (pp. 42–43). Similarly, Naomi Cohen avers that "Orthodox Jews opposed a restoration contrived by man because it ignored the traditional belief in the role of a divinely commissioned messiah. They also objected to the secular and areligious cast of the Zionist movement."[118]

Evyatar Friesel and Melvin Urofsky present a somewhat different picture. They suggest that, although there were opponents to Zionism among the Orthodox, a significant portion of them demonstrated staunch empathy and support for both the notion of Zionism and for its organization. Friesel

---

117 Marnin Feinstein, *American Zionism: 1884–1904* (New York: Herzl Press, 1961), pp. 28–29.

118 Naomi W. Cohen, *American Jews and the Zionist Idea* (Hoboken, NJ: Ktav, 1975), pp. 6–7.

writes that there were two contrasting approaches to Zionism within the
Orthodox community at that time, one siding with Zionism and one oppos-
ing it; he then asserts that "The anti-Zionist segment, which had always
been a minority among the American Orthodox, became even smaller."[119]

Urofsky goes on to write of the Orthodox opposition to Zionism
both in Eastern Europe and in the United States, but he suggests that
"pietistic opposition to Zionism was limited to small, albeit vocal,
groups."[120] He also indicates the strong support for Zionism at the end of
the nineteenth century and the organization, in 1898, of the "Orthodox
Jewish Congregational Union of America," which explicitly supported
Zionism.

Jeffrey Gurock and Kimmy Caplan emphasize the spread of Zionism
within the American Orthodox community at the beginning of the twentieth century. Gurock describes the growing importance of the Mizrachi
Organization, in general, as well as its influence within the Union of
Orthodox Rabbis of the United States and Canada (*Agudat Harabanim*)
during the first decades of the century.[121] In his work, Caplan analyzes
the articles, letters, and sermons of American Orthodox rabbis during
that period, indicating their strong connections to Zion and the Zionist
idea.[122]

There were no doubt anti-Zionist elements in the Orthodox community of the time, some informed by their religious ideology and others bas-
ing their stance on socio-political factors. It must be recalled, after all, that
most of the Orthodox rabbis at the time were immigrants or children of
immigrants from Eastern Europe and, as Yosef Salmon indicates, the overwhelming majority of traditional rabbis in Eastern Europe did not support

---

119 "The Meaning of Zionism and Its Influence Among the American Jewish Religious
     Movements," in Shmuel Almog, Jehuda Reinharz and Anita Shapira, eds., *Zionism
     and Religion*. (Hanover, NH: University Press of New England/ Brandeis University
     Press, 1998), p. 177.

120 Melvin I. Urofsky, *American Zionism From Herzl to the Holocaust* (Doubleday:
     Garden City, NY, 1975, p. 101.

121 Jeffrey S. Gurock, "American Orthodox Organizations in Support of Zionism,
     1880–1930," in Almog et al., eds., *Zionism and Religion*, pp. 219–234.

122 Kimmy Caplan, *Orthodoxy in the New World: Immigrant Rabbis and Preaching,
     1881–1924* (Hebrew). (Jerusalem: Merkaz Zalman Shazar, 2002), pp. 285–303;
     Kimmy Caplan, "The Beginning of 'Hamizrahi' in America" (in Hebrew), *Yahadut
     Zemanenu* 13 (1999): 173–206.

Zionism after the Second Zionist Congress.[123] Likewise, the Jewish masses in the United States did not support Zionism at the time, and there were some who maintained their position even after the World War II. As Arye Goren indicates, "from 1898 until 1941, the Zionist movement was rather weak, entirely uninspired and irresolute."[124]

Accordingly, it is not surprising that religious Zionism was slow to become organized and established.[125] Remarkably, Mizrachi saw significant growth during and after World War I. An example of this can be seen in the first decade of the organization's existence: 30 representatives attended its first meeting in Cincinnati, Ohio, on May 1, 1914 (which, coincidentally, was 5 Iyar 5674); by its eighth meeting in 1923, there were 350 representatives. The number of branches in the country had grown to 230 in that time.[126] Mizrachi was supported by a majority in the Union of Orthodox Rabbis as well as by the Union of Orthodox Jewish Congregations,[127] and the movement even established a Teachers Institute which, subsequently, became an integral part of Yeshiva University.[128]

123 Yosef Salmon, "Zionism and Anti-Zionism in Traditional Judaism in Eastern-Europe," in Almog, et. al., eds., *Zionism and Religion*, pp. 25–43.

124 Arye Goren, "Zionism and its Opponents in American Jewry," in Haim Avni and Gideon Shimoni, eds., *Zionism and its Jewish Opponents* [Hebrew], (Jerusalem: Hassifriya Hazionit Publishing House, 1990), p. 357.

125 Friesel attributes the fact that the American Mizrachi was not organized until 1914 to "the internal weakness of Orthodox Jewry (as was the case in the Old World) in the American circumstance. The religious stance was at this time on defense and decline, fighting to preserve its realms . . . and it had no strength left to encourage and support new endeavors." (Evyatar Friesel, *The Zionist Movement in the United States: 1897–1914* [Hebrew] Tel Aviv: Tel-Aviv University and Hakibbutz Hameuchad, 1970, p. 137). Salmon disagrees and argues that the late founding of Mizrachi "can better be explained by the independent stance of the religious Zionists" who initially "remained aloof from the American Zionist leadership, which was western or central European and non-observant." Yosef Salmon, "The Mizrachi Movement in America: A Belated but Sturdy Offshoot," *American Jewish Archives* 18:2, 1996, pp. 161–175.

126 Aaron Halevi Pechenick, "Religious Zionism in America," (in Hebrew) Izhak Raphael and Sh. Z. Shragai, eds, *Sefer hazionut hadatit: Iyunim, ma-amarim, reshimot, te'udot*, Vol. 2, pp. 230–33.

127 Jeffrey S. Gurock, "American Orthodox Organizations in Support of Zionism, 1880–1930," in Almog, et. al., *Zionism and Religion*, p. 220.

128 Hyman B. Grinstein, "Orthodox Judaism and Zionism, in Isidore S. Meyer, ed., *Early History of Zionism in America* (New York: American Jewish Historical Society and Theodor Herzl Foundation, 1958), p. 221.

Another indication of religious Zionism's significance within the American Orthodox community in the 1910s and 1920s was the election of Rabbi Meir Bar-Ilan (Berlin) to head the board of Yeshiva College (later Yeshiva University).

At the same time, it should be recalled that American Zionism developed very differently from the way it did in Europe, including not only immigrants from Eastern Europe but leaders of American Jewry who claimed their origins in Central Europe. Within a few years, the movement included leaders of all three branches of American Judaism, including Reform Judaism. It should also be noted that, at the end of the nineteenth and the very beginning of the twentieth centuries, the designation "Orthodox" frequently meant anyone who did not identify explicitly as Reform.[129]

---

129 Yosef Salmon, "The Mizrachi Movement in America"; Jeffrey S. Gurock, "Twentieth-Century American Orthodoxy's Era of Non-Observance, 1900–1960," *Torah u-Madda Journal* 9, 2000, pp. 87–107.

Chapter 22

Between the Two World Wars

The American Mizrachi movement grew and, as Menahem Kaufman indicates, "The majority of Orthodox Jewry in the United States supported Zionism."[130] In commemoration of its 25th anniversary, the American Mizrachi organization received a warm congratulatory letter from the Union of Orthodox Rabbis.

Interestingly, the leader of Mizrachi, Rabbi Yehuda Leib Fishman (Maimon), expressed a nascent conflict within its membership. He noted that the body included a significant number of older American rabbis, born and raised in Eastern Europe; notwithstanding their personal support of Zionism, these rabbis did not publicly express that support, because they wanted to appear as "*haredim*" and "God-fearing" (*yirei Shamayim*). He wrote,

> Not too many of the Orthodox rabbis in America at that time enthusiastically joined Mizrachi. Many related to both Zionism and Mizrachi with apathy and indifference, and some opposed us. That was the situation within American Orthodox Judaism with respect to our organization. And the American *haredi* rabbis will excuse me if I say that the situation is evident even now to anyone who has the eyes to see and the heart to understand. The rabbis in America—I'm speaking of the older among them—have not forgotten that which they learned from their rabbis in Russia and Poland, and there are among them some Torah scholars, and for some reason even now I relate to them with all due respect, regard-

---

130 Menahem Kaufman, *Non-Zionists in America and the Struggle for Jewish Statehood: 1939–1948* [Hebrew] (Jerusalem: Hasifriya Hazionit, 1984), p. 7. Curiously, that statement is absent in the English translation of the book: Menahem Kaufman, *An Ambiguous Partnership: Non Zionists and Zionists in America, 1939–1948* (Jerusalem and Detroit: Magnes Press and Wayne State University Press, 1991). See p. 17.

less of whether their stance on Mizrachi is positive or negative, but I do allow myself to say that the competition among them over "the fear of God" (*yirat shamayim*) is what belittles their status and diminishes their appearance. There are rabbis whose Torah is in their stomachs and their Mizrachism is in their hearts, but when someone from Lithuania arrives—someone who considers himself or is considered to be a great Torah scholar ("*gadol hador*") who opposes Mizrachi from a "Fear of God" stance, and many rabbis dance around him—then even those who do support Mizrachi allow themselves to hide their Mizrachism and perhaps even to oppose our organization. That was the situation that I found among American rabbis more than thirty years ago and I found them just as pitiful when I most recently visited America, last year (1945). There is no consistency except among a few rabbis; the rest put on an understanding or welcoming face sometimes to Agudah and sometimes to Mizrachi. There was a time when the Union of Orthodox Rabbis was considered almost totally Mizrachi. It also sent special delegations to one of the Word Assemblies of Mizrachi in Europe and also to the conference of the Agudah in Vienna and it made all-out efforts to unite them. But since they were unsuccessful, because the Agudah wants the divisiveness, the Union of Orthodox Rabbis reverted to its previous position—half-awake, half-asleep—with respect to Mizrachi, and only a few of their rabbis remained loyal to us with all of the fibers of their souls.[131]

With all due respect to Rabbi Fishman-Maimon's impressions, most researchers hold that Mizrachi was the dominant organization in American Orthodoxy at that time. However, the organization declined subsequently, for a number of reasons that will be discussed below. At the outset, however, it must be emphasized that the decline of the Mizrachi Organization, which is now known as the Religious Zionists of America (RZA), does not necessarily indicate a decline of Zionism among American Orthodox Jews. On the contrary, it will be argued that Zionism—especially in the American

---

131 Rabbi Yehuda L. Hacohen Fishman, "*Toldot haMizrachi vehitpatchuto*," in Rabbi Yehuda L. Hacohen Fishman, ed., Sefer haMizrachi: Kovetz lezecher Hagaon Rabbi Yitzchak Ya'acov Reines ztz"l *limleot sheloshim shana lepetirato* (Jerusalem: Mossad Harav Kook, 1946), p. 188.

sense of the term—in the Orthodox community grew significantly in the second half of the twentieth century, even as the RZA declined.

The second half of the century also witnessed significant shifts within Orthodoxy itself. Specifically, the relative strength of Orthodoxy's two major philosophical stances—"Ultra-Orthodoxy" (i.e., the *haredim*) and "Modern Orthodoxy"—underwent major changes during this period.

In their European antecedents, as well as in their development in the United States for much of the past century, the distinct versions of Orthodoxy were rather clearly distinguishable on the basis of three major characteristics. The first involved stances toward the larger society in general and the larger, non-Orthodox Jewish community, with the *haredim* holding an attitude of isolation, as opposed to the inclusive attitude of the Modern Orthodox. The second was in reference to modernity, general scholarship, and science, with the Ultra-Orthodox serving as antagonists and Modern Orthodoxy accommodating, if not welcoming, a modern outlook. The third entailed a basic difference in perspective toward Israel and Zionism. Here we find Modern Orthodoxy supporting the State of Israel as having inherent Jewish religious significance and the Zionist goal of Israel as the spiritual center of the Jewish People, while the Ultra-Orthodox are represented, in the minority, by an overtly anti-Zionist position, whereas the majority hold a less adversarial, non-Zionist viewpoint, in the sense of attributing no religious significance to the State of Israel and rejecting cooperation with movements and organizations headed by secular Zionists.

As we have already seen, American Orthodoxy during the first half of the century took on a more modern stance, with pro-Zionists standing as the clear majority. Indeed, of those who sent their children to day schools rather than public schools, many did so in the hope that the schools would produce and reinforce in the students love for the Jewish People and their cultural heritage, as well as a strong connection with and commitment to Zionism.[132]

---

132 Joseph Nardi, "A Survey of Jewish Day Schools in America," *Jewish Education*, Vol. 15, No. 2, September 1944, p. 25.

Chapter 23

World War II and the Immigration of Rabbis and Roshei Yeshiva

This situation changed dramatically with immigration of Eastern European Jews precipitated by the Holocaust. Included among the new arrivals were a number of Orthodox leaders who had been heads of advanced rabbinical seminaries—*yeshivot gedolot*—in Eastern Europe. Almost immediately upon their arrival in the United States, they set about reconstructing those *yeshivot* on American soil. Such leaders as Rabbi Aaron Kotler, Rabbi Abraham Kalmanowitz, and Rabbis Eliyahu Meir Bloch and Mordechai Katz reestablished their advanced *yeshivot*—as well as their conceptions of Orthodoxy—in Lakewood, Brooklyn, Cleveland, and elsewhere, in the Eastern European mold. These institutions then spawned a generation of knowledgeable and ideologically committed Orthodox Jews, many of whom went on to establish other *yeshivot* in dozens of American cities.

The first wave of "new" Orthodox tradition in America came with the foundation of the National Society for Hebrew Day Schools, Torah Umesorah, in 1944 by Rabbi Shraga Feivel Mendelowitz. The objective of this society was to encourage and assist in founding Jewish day schools, elementary, and high schools in cities and neighborhoods across the country, schools which would provide an intensive Jewish education along with a quality secular curriculum.

Between the years 1940 and 1965, the number of day schools grew tenfold, and enrollments grew almost as impressively, with the rate of growth continuing to accelerate between the middle 1960s and 1975. These day schools and *yeshiva* high schools represented in Table 1 were located not only in the New York metropolitan area, but in 33 states across the country. By 1975, every city in the United States with a Jewish population of 7,500 or more had at least one day school, as did four out of five of the cities with a Jewish population of between 5,000 and 7,500. Among cities with smaller Jewish populations, one out of four with a population of 1,000 Jews had a Jewish day school.[133]

Table 1. Number of Hebrew Day Schools, Types, and Enrollment

	Day Schools	High Schools	Total Enrollments	Number of Communities
1940	335		37,700	337
1945	369	339	10,200	331
1955	180		35,500	68
1965	323	383	63,500	117
1970			72,000	
1975	425	138	82,200	160

It should be emphasized that instituting this type of day school was in itself an adaptation to modernity. Many of the very same rabbinic leaders who drove the day school movement had previously been adamantly opposed to this type of school, which combined both sacred and secular education.[134] Although, as indicated, a number of day schools had been founded early in the twentieth century, their numbers—and, hence, their impact—were relatively small.

With the efforts of the leadership spurred by new immigration, the picture of American Jewish education changed dramatically. There was a virtual boom in the growth of the day school movement from World War II to the mid-1970s and, since then, day schools have become recognized as valued institutions within Conservative and Reform Judaism as well. Indeed, by the 1990s, non-Orthodox day schools were the fastest growing phenomenon in the American Jewish community.[135] As indicated in a

---

133 Chaim I. Waxman, *America's Jews in Transition* Philadelphia, PA: Temple University Press, 1983, pp. 125–126.

134 Cf. Jacob J. Schacter, "Haskalah, Secular Studies and the Close of the Yeshiva in Volozhin in 1892," *Torah u-Madda Journal* 2, 1990, pp. 76–133.

135 Hanan Alexander, "Literacy, Education and the Good Life," paper delivered at the Workshop on Language, Culture, and Jewish Identity, Tel-Aviv University, School of Education, Dec. 28, 1998.

1994 study by the Avi Chai Foundation—which analyzed the self-identified denominational affiliation of day schools in the United States—of a total of 221 schools surveyed in New York State, 204 were Orthodox, eleven Solomon Schechter, five Community schools, and one Reform. In the rest of the country, a total of 280 schools were surveyed: 170 were Orthodox, 55 Community, 43 Solomon Schechter and twelve Reform.[136] Thus, in New York State, the Orthodox schools represented 92 percent of the total number of day schools—but the picture was very different outside of New York State. There, although Orthodox Schools were still a majority, they represented only 60 percent of the total.

As for the impact of day schools on Jewish identity, analysis of the 1990 National Jewish Population Survey (NJPS) data on baby boomers indicates that day school education correlates with almost all measures of Jewish identity and identification. For many of those measures, the correlation is much higher than it is with other types of Jewish education.[137]

Additionally, many members and some leaders of Hasidic sects among the World War II refugees settled in the United States. Among these, the prominent groups include the sects of Belz, Bobov, Chernobyl, Habad-Lubavitch, Lisk, Munkatch, Novominsk, Satmar, Skver, Stolin, Talin, Trisk, and Zanz. The Hasidim, perhaps even more than others, were determined to retain their traditional way of life even within the modern metropolis, and they were largely successful in achieving that goal.[138]

This new infusion of ideologically committed Orthodox Jews provided the numbers and the manpower for the renaissance that was to manifest itself almost a quarter of a century after World War II. It also played a role in the intensification of religious belief and practice among the Orthodox, as well as in the increasing rift between their communities and

---

136 Avi Chai, *Jewish Day Schools in the United States*. New York: Avi Chai Foundation, 1994, p. 4.

137 Chaim I. Waxman, *Jewish Baby Boomers: A Communal Perspective*. Albany, NY: State University of New York Press, 2001, pp. 112–114. See also Sylvia Barack Fishman, and Alice Goldstein, *When They Are Grown They Will Not Depart: Jewish Education and the Jewish Behavior of American Adults*, Research Report 8, Waltham: Brandeis University, Cohen Center for Modern Jewish Studies and the Jewish Education Service of North America, (March) 1993.

138 This theme is captured in the 1997 award-winning documentary film by Menachem Daum and Oren Rudavsky, "A Life Apart: Hasidim in America." See also Jerome Mintz, *Hasidic People: A Place in the New World*. Cambridge, MA: Harvard University Press, 1998.

those of the non-Orthodox.[139] The issue of "haredization" will be further analyzed at a later point in this chapter.

During the second half of the twentieth century, the more sectarian, "Ultra-Orthodox," or *haredi* variation became the dominant mode of American Orthodoxy, and Modern Orthodoxy, which had earlier been the dominant American variation, appeared to be a passing phenomenon. However, to paraphrase Mark Twain, reports of Modern Orthodoxy's passing seem to have been greatly exaggerated. As I have argued elsewhere, Modern Orthodoxy is still a significant element in American Orthodoxy and, since the closing decade of the twentieth century, has shown signs of strength and growth.[140]

American Orthodox Judaism does not exist in a vacuum, and its development during the second half of the twentieth century was not unrelated to its connections with Israel. Both the Modern and Ultra-Orthodox strengthened their ties with Israel during this period. Surveys from several decades during this period consistently showed that the extent of Orthodox Jews' attachments to Israel—however they were measured—greatly exceeded those among other denominations. The observed differences between Orthodox and non-Orthodox were sharpest with respect to the most demanding measures of involvement with Israel, whether this took the form of receptivity to *aliyah* in place of pro-Israel feelings, having closer ties with individual Israelis, or fluency in modern Hebrew rather than just a rudimentary knowledge of Israel's official language.[141]

139 Chaim I. Waxman, "The Haredization of American Orthodox Jewry" *Jerusalem Letter/Viewpoints*, No. 376, Jerusalem Center for Public Affairs, 15 February 1998; Samuel G. Freedman, *Jew vs. Jew: The Struggle for the Soul of American Jewry*. New York, Simon & Schuster, 2000. The "move to the right" in American Orthodoxy was already apparent in the 1960s. See Charles S. Liebman, *Aspects of the Religious Behavior of American Jews*, New York: Ktav, 1974, p. 150. That essay, "Orthodoxy in American Jewish Life," is reprinted from the *American Jewish Year Book*, Vol. 66, pp. 21–98. See also Haym Soloveitchik, "Rupture and Reconstruction: The Transformation of Contemporary Orthodoxy," *Tradition*, Vol. 28, No. 4, Summer 1994, pp. 64–130; reprinted in Roberta Rosenberg Farber and Chaim I. Waxman, eds., *Jews in America: A Contemporary Reader*. Hanover: Brandeis University Press/University Press of New England, 1999, pp. 320–376.

140 Chaim I. Waxman, "American Modern Orthodoxy: Confronting Cultural Challenges," *Edah Journal* 4:1, Iyar 5764/May 2004, http://www.edah.org/backend/JournalArticle/4_1_waxman.pdf

141 Chaim I. Waxman, "All In the Family: American Jewish Attachments to Israel," in Peter Y. Medding, Ed., *A New Jewry?: America Since the Second World War* (*Studies in Contemporary Jewry*, Vol. 8), New York, Oxford University Press, 1992, p. 136.

As indicated in the table below, Orthodox Jews visit Israel at a much higher rate than do Conservative or Reform American Jews.

Table 2: Respondents Who Have Ever Been to Israel, by Denomination, 2001 NJPS

	Orthodox	Conservative	Reconstructionist	Reform
Yes	81.4	61.2	34.6	37.8
No	18.6	38.8	65.4	62.2
Total	100.0	100.0	100.0	100.0

In addition, there is a similar pattern of denominational variation with respect to the number of times the respondent visited among those who have visited Israel. Twenty-five percent of the Orthodox respondents who had visited Israel did so more than 5 times, a statistic that far exceeds the percentages of other denominations who visited Israel more than 5 times. The only deviation from the denominational pattern previously noted is in the Reform respondents, whose answers indicated a higher percentage than the Reconstructionists who visited more than 5 times.

Table 3: Number of Times Visited Israel, by Denomination

	Orthodox	Conservative	Reconstructionist	Reform
1 time	27.5	52.3	51.8	71.2
2–4 times	38.7	29.7	38.2	19.4
5–9 times	14.1	8.0	–.–	4.8
10 or more times	15.1	5.2	–.–	4.0
Resided in Israel	4.7	4.8	10.0	.5
Total	100.0	100.0	100.0	100.0

Moreover, as the following table indicates, emotional attachment to Israel also varies considerably with denominational affiliation, with the Orthodox indicating much stronger emotional ties to Israel than did the Conservative and Reform.

Table 4: Level of Emotional Attachment to Israel, by Denomination, 2001 NJPS

	Orthodox	Conservative	Reconstructionist	Reform
Very	72.1	45.1	27.4	22.5
Somewhat	22.7	37.3	50.8	45.1
Not very	2.1	15.1	11.1	22.8
Not at all	3.1	2.4	10.7	9.7
Total	100.0	100.0	100.0	100.0

The argument is frequently heard that the reason the Orthodox have stronger connections with Israel is because of the Orthodox domination of establishment Judaism in Israel. The non-Orthodox, it is alleged, are less connected because they feel less comfortable in Israel, and they feel less comfortable there because of the Orthodox discrimination against them. However, the NJPS data do not appear to support this contention. As I have indicated elsewhere, the denomination variation manifests itself in a wide range of issues relating to both religious and communal identification, such as feelings of a common destiny with Jews elsewhere, and whether they attend an adult Jewish education class or any other kind of adult Jewish learning.[142]

---

142 Chaim I. Waxman, "Congregation, Community, and Continuity: Denominational Affiliation as an Indicator of Jewish Identity," in Sergio DellaPergola and Judith Even, eds., *Studies in Jewish Demography, 1997* (Jerusalem: Hebrew University, Institute of Contemporary Jewry, 2001), pp. 281–293; "The Enduring Significance of Denomination" [Hebrew], *Gesher: Journal of Jewish Affairs* 50, No. 150, Winter 2004, pp. 24–31.

Chapter 24

A Brief History of Year in Israel Programs

Today, it is almost the norm for both male and female Orthodox high school graduates to spend a year or more of study in Israel, primarily in a *yeshiva* or seminary. In his pioneering study of the phenomenon, Shalom Berger found that, by the middle of the 1990s, up to ninety percent of the graduates of Modern Orthodox high schools participated in such a program.[143] Although those figures may not be representative of all American Orthodox high school graduates, Jay Goldmintz indicates that

> there are graduates who report that their parents are forcing them to go to Israel for the year against their will and there are high schools who use the number of their graduates who go to Israel as part of their publicity campaigns for prospective students. There can be no doubt that the post-high school yeshiva experience has become a mass movement within the Orthodox community.[144]

Berger's analysis suggests the Israeli experience probably intensified their ties with the country and its Jews. In addition, their intensive experiences in the Israeli *yeshivot* probably contributed to greater ritualistic punctiliousness for many and they, in turn, promoted such rigorous practice when they returned to their American Orthodox communities.

There has long been a tradition for adult Jewish males to move to Torah centers, in keeping with the dictum of Rabbi Nehorai, "Exile yourself to a place of Torah."[145] As early as 1881–1883, at the very onset of the great

---

143 Shalom Z. Berger, *A Year of Study in an Israeli Yeshiva Program: Before and After* (Ph.D. Diss, Yeshiva University, Azrieli Graduate School of Jewish Education, 1996); see also his section in this volume.

144 Jay Goldmintz, "The Post-High School Yeshiva Experience in Israel," (*Ten Da`at*, V:2, Iyar 5751/Spring 1991, p. 32).

145 Avot 4:18.

wave of immigration from Eastern Europe to the United States, there is a record of an American student who studied at the *yeshiva* in Volozhin.[146] In his recollections of *yeshiva* days in Mir, Shlomo Zaltzman, later the director of Jewish newspapers in Russia, wrote of "several American students in Mir in 1887."[147] During the 1920s and 1930s, Americans were found in the major *yeshivot* in Eastern Europe, especially in Mir, Slabodka, and Telz, as well as in many others.

A well known biblical verse states, "For out of Zion shall go forth the Torah, and the word of God from Jerusalem."[148] As a result, there is in Jewish tradition a special value in Israel. Ancient Jerusalem was the first community to implement the notion of public Jewish education, based on that very verse,[149] and, thus, the notion of *Torah MiTzion*—Torah in and from *Eretz Yisrael*—has also enjoyed special status in the tradition.

During much of the two thousand years since the destruction of Jerusalem and the Second Temple, the small Jewish communities in *Eretz Yisrael* sent out emissaries to Diaspora Jewish communities, and one of the major requirements of those emissaries was that they bring Torah to the Diaspora communities.[150] It is therefore not surprising that, even when the Eastern European *yeshivot* were the most prominent, there were American Jewish young men who went to learn in *yeshivot* in the Holy Land, *Eretz Yisrael*. Jonathan Sarna relates that Behr Manischewitz—the founder of the well known B. Manischewitz matzah company—had very close ties with Jerusalem and, at the beginning of the twentieth century, sent two of his sons to study there. The first, Hirsch, started learning in *Eretz Yisrael* in 1901, at the age of ten, and remained there for thirteen years, during which time he studied at the *yeshivot* Etz Chaim (1901–1907), Torat Chaim (1908–1910), and Meah Shearim (1910–1914). The elder son, Max, went when he was older and also studied for the rabbinate at Yeshiva Etz Chaim.[151]

---

146 Nathan Kamenetsky, *Making of a Godol: A Study of Episodes in the Lives of Great Torah Personalities.* Jerusalem: 2002, p. 888.

147 Shlomo Zaltzman, "*Bayeshiva beMir*" [pp. 312–319] in Immanuel Etkes and Shlomo Tikochinsky, eds., *Memoirs of the Lithuanian Yeshiva* [Hebrew] Jerusalem: Zalman Shazar Center for Jewish History, 2004, p. 314.

148 Isaiah 2:3.

149 *Bava Batra* 21a.

150 Abraham Ya'ari, *Sheluhe Eretz Yisrael.* Jerusalem: Mossad Harav Kook, 1951.

151 Jonathan D. Sarna, "The Americanization of Matzah: Manischewitz and the Rabbis of the Holy Land," Graduate School of Jewish Studies, Touro College, 2005, p. 12.

R. Avraham Hezroni, of Rechovot, who lived in Jerusalem until 2006 and was at the *yeshiva* in Hebron in 1929, stated that there were approximately two dozen American students in attendance that year.[152] Several of them were killed in the infamous massacre; among them were William Berman and Benjamin Horowitz, who had previously studied for about a half-dozen years at the Yeshiva Rabbenu Yitzchak Elchanan (later, Yeshiva University), and Aaron David Epstein, the son of Rabbi Ephraim Epstein of Chicago and the nephew of Rabbi Moshe Mordecai Epstein, *Rosh Yeshiva* of the *yeshiva* in Hebron.[153]

Instances such as these continued and, after the destruction of European Jewry and its *yeshivot* and the establishment of the State of Israel, the numbers of American Jewish young men who studied at Israeli *yeshivot* increased. Until the later 1950s, however, all such activity was unorganized, on an individual basis, and on a very small scale.

The organized one-year post-high school *yeshiva* in Israel program was the brainchild of Rabbi Zevi Tabory, who was the director of the Torah Education Department of the Jewish Agency in New York. It was initiated in 1957 with a handful of students who went to the only Hesder *yeshiva* at the time, Yeshivat Kerem BeYavne (KBY). In 1958, another small group participated in this program, which continued with very modest numbers until the end of the 1960s. In 1968, the program consisted of 15 young men who went to KBY, and 30 young men and women who went to Machon Gold. In 1969, it was determined to separate the males from the females, and the Jewish Agency helped establish Beit Midrash LeTorah (BMT) for males. The head of the Torah Education Department in New York at the time was an Israeli *shaliach*, Tzvi Asa-El, Assistant Director of the Torah Education Department of the World Zionist Organization in Israel. Also in 1969, Rabbi Dr. Emanuel Rackman turned

---

152 Interview, Jan. 13, 2005.

153 See Leo Gottesman, *The Martyrs of Hebron*, originally published in New York, 1930 and now on-line at http://www.hebron.org.il/pics/tarpat/martyrs.htm#Aharon%20David%20Epstein. See also Reuben Rudman, "The Story Behind the Benjamin Hurwitz Award," in Menachem Butler and Zev Nagel, eds., *My Yeshiva College: 75 Years of Memories* (New York: Yashar Books, 2006), pp. 118–21, in which he relates how his uncle, Benjamin Hurwitz, a graduate of the high school and teachers institute of what is now Yeshiva University, who went to study in the yeshiva in Hebron, was killed in the massacre, and was subsequently memorialized with the innovation of a yearly award at Yeshiva University in his name.

to Torah Umesorah for a candidate to become Associate Director of the Torah Education Department in New York, requesting a person who would be acceptable to the *yeshiva* world and one affirmed as a Zionist. Rabbi Mallen Galinsky was recommended for the position and, when it was offered to him, he accepted it.

One of Rabbi Galinsky's first undertakings was to broaden the range of *yeshivot* where students would be sent. In consultation with Rabbi Meir Schlesinger, who headed Yeshivat Shaalvim, a program for Americans was undertaken there. Likewise, Yeshivat Har Etzion and Yeshivat HaKotel (although it initially resisted) also agreed to participate. In time, others followed suit.

Further, Rabbi Galinsky, in consultation with and with the assistance of *yeshiva* high school principals—the late Rabbi Simcha Teitelbaum of Yeshiva High School of Queens, Rabbi David Eliach of the Yeshivah of Flatbush's Joel Braverman High School, and Rabbi Yehoshua Bakst of the Ramaz School—initiated a "Tochnit Yud-Bet" program, in which seniors whose parents were not willing to send their children for an entire year were encouraged to spend the second half of their senior year in a program in Israel. The women's programs were mainly in Machon Gold, Michlala, and Machon Devora, at about the same time.[154] As a result of these initiatives, there are now several thousand young men and women annually participating in the Year in Israel program.

In addition to the organized program, there are many more young men who study in the more European-style, *haredi yeshivot*, such as Mir, Brisk, Ponevezh, Slabodka, Torah Ohr, and Ateres Yisrael, among other, and numerous Bais Yaakov and similar institutions exist for young women. The institutions in which these students study are somewhat more restricted and isolated from the larger Israeli society, but the students are equally influenced by their experiences. Although the primary focus of this volume is on those who participate in the Year in Israel program, these students should not be overlooked. They also have some impact on Israeli society during their time there, as well as on the Orthodox community in the United States when they return.

---

154 Interview with Rabbi Mallen Galinsky, Jan. 13, 2005.

Chapter 25

On College and University Campuses

One factor facilitating the re-emergence of Modern Orthodoxy in North America is the development of Jewish Studies programs in secular universities. There has been a dramatic increase of Jewish Studies on campuses across the United States since the discipline was first established in the early 1970s. In just the decade between 1993–2003, the Association for Jewish Studies doubled its membership of professors who teach Judaic Studies from approximately 800 to 1500. There has also been a proliferation of accredited classes in Jewish Studies at colleges and universities across the United States.[155] In conjunction with this, Jewish centers and organizations such as Hillel have become more intensively and extensively active, and they have provided a more inviting institutional setting for religiously observant students. Harvard, Yale, Columbia, Princeton, Rutgers, and the University of Pennsylvania—to name just a few in the Northeast—now have energetic, observant sub-communities of students and faculty, and the restrictions and limitations on those young college-age adults who wish to be both modern and religiously observant are much fewer than they were in past decades. Indeed, the Orthodox Union is exploring the idea of funding a *kollel* couple on the Rutgers campus, to further invigorate the campus and to provide a source of inspiration and assistance to observant students and faculty already there. On many campuses, developments such as these have been spearheaded by students who spent a year or more in the Year in Israel program.

Additionally, the 1960s and 1970s were decades of significant increases in programs and levels of Jewish education for Orthodox women. This was the time when the women's movement gained prominence in American society. The workforce participation rate of women rose dramatically, as did their levels of education. Increasing numbers of

---

155 Nacha Cattan, "Jewish Studies Classes See Enrollment Boom," *Forward*, January 23, 2004.

Orthodox Jewish women sought to advance their Jewish education, which was until then (even if available) largely limited to specific areas.[156]

The Year in Israel program played a role in the expansion of higher Jewish education for Orthodox women in a number of ways. Most basically, the dedication by young women of a year of post-high school intensive Jewish learning was, in itself, a new phenomenon. Even if they had chosen to pursue such Jewish learning in America, it would have contributed to greater Jewish educational status. In Israel, however, they were also frequently exposed to new fields, new approaches to texts, and new female role models such as the late Nechama Lebowitz, Bryna Levy, and Aviva Zornberg, among others. In addition, these and other Israeli scholars facilitated the development of new institutions of higher learning for Jewish women and groups of young female Jewish scholars—many of them former Americans—who serve as the core faculty in these institutions.

Rabbi Joseph B. Soloveitchik ("The Rav") provided renewed ideological validation of higher Jewish learning for women when, in 1977, he gave the inaugural lecture at the opening of the Beit Midrash program at Yeshiva University's Stern College for Women. Almost 40 years earlier, Rabbi Soloveitchik had espoused the goal of equal Jewish education for females in the Maimonides School, which he headed in Boston.[157] His lecture at the Stern College program was an indication of his support of

---

156 Deborah Weissman, "Bais Yaakov: A Historical Model for Jewish Feminists," in Elizabeth Koltun ed., *Jewish Woman: New Perspectives* (New York: Schocken.Books, 1976), pp. 139–48; Judith Tydor Baumel and Jacob J. Schachter. "The Ninety-Three Beit Yaakov Girls of Cracow: History or Typology?" in Jacob J. Schachter, Ed. *Reverence, Righteousness, and Rahamanut: Essays in Memory of Rabbi Dr. Leo Jung* (Northvale, NJ: Jason Aronson 1992), pp. 93–130; Jeffrey S. Gurock, *The Men and Women of Yeshiva: Higher Education, Orthodoxy, and American Judaism* (New York: Columbia University Press, 1988); Bonnie Morris, "Female Education in the Lubavitcher Community: The Beth Rivkah and Machon Chana Schools," in Wendy E. Chmielewski, Louis J. Kern and Marlyn Klee-Hartzell, eds. *Women in Spiritual and Communitarian Societies in the United States* (Syracuse, NY: Syracuse University Press, 1993) pp. 221–35; Sylvia Barack Fishman, *A Breath of Life: Feminism in the American Jewish Community* (Hanover, NH: Brandeis University Press/University Press of New England, 1993), pp. 181–99.

157 Seth Farber, *An American Orthodox Dreamer: Rabbi Joseph B. Soloveitchik and Boston's Maimonides School* (Hanover, NH: Brandeis University Press/University Press of New England, 2004), pp. 68–87.

educational equality at the highest levels. Drisha was founded within a few years after his 1977 talk; this institution achieved not only legitimacy, but a reputation for providing a first-class center for higher Jewish education for women. A significant percentage of its graduates have made *aliyah*, and some serve in Jewish educational settings in Israel. All of this has reinforced the connections between the Modern Orthodox communities in the United States and in Israel.[158]

For some students, the Year in Israel program may provide an incentive to be even more selective in the type of college or university they attend. For example, in a study of undergraduates of Yeshiva College that I conducted in the 1980s, one student said, "I wanted to combine the college education and to be able to continue learning in a *yeshiva* setting. I had experienced a special kind of learning in an Israeli *yeshiva*, and I wanted to continue that kind of learning while getting a broad-based liberal arts education."[159] Aspirations such as these provide an incentive for some returning young men and women to enroll in Yeshiva College, Stern College for Women, and Touro College. Others, desiring a broad college experience as well as an intensive Jewish environment, may choose from an increasing number of non-affiliated secular universities with strong traditional Jewish cores, such as Columbia University, Rutgers University, and the University of Pennsylvania.

---

158 Charles S. Liebman, "Modern Orthodoxy in Israel," *Judaism* Vol. 47, No. 4 (Fall 1998) p. 406; Yair Sheleg, *The New Religious Jews: Recent Developments Among Observant Jews in Israel* (Jerusalem: Keter, 2000) [Hebrew].

159 Chaim I. Waxman, "Orthodox Judaism and Modern Society: A Study of Undergraduates at Yeshiva University," paper presented at the Annual Meetings of the Israel Sociological Society, Bar-Ilan University, Feb. 7–8, 1990.

Chapter 26

Year in Israel and the Orthodox Community

Because of the deep and extensive ties of Orthodox Jews in the United States, as discussed above, it is not easy to indicate specifically the impact of the Year in Israel program on the American Orthodox community. American Orthodox Jews are intertwined with Israel in a myriad of ways and, as a result, Israel has had a far-reaching impact upon that community. Israel has affected the religious habits of American Orthodox Jews—for instance, many kosher food products available in the U.S. are produced in Israel; most American Jews who purchase ritual objects buy those produced in Israel, such as *etrogim* for Sukkot; many Orthodox Jews buy religious books from Israel, adopt Israeli religious music as their own and, as was indicated, travel to Israel frequently. For many, Israel is probably the only country outside the United States they have ever visited.

A number of customs connected with American Orthodox synagogue practice indicate one particularly influential area of association with the Year in Israel program. For example, until the 1960s, it was rare to find an American Orthodox synagogue where the Friday evening service, *Kabalat Shabbat*, was begun with the singing of *Yedid Nefesh*. That was an Israeli custom, which has now been incorporated into American Orthodox culture. Likewise, the *minhag* (local practice) in most Ashkenazi synagogues before the middle twentieth century was that the two chapters of Psalms said after *Kabalat Shabbat*—Tehillim 92, *Mizmor shir l'yom ha-shabbat*, and Tehillim 93, *Hashem malakh*—were said together, and the Reader, *ba'al tefillah*, repeated only the last verse of *Hashem malakh*. Since the 1960s, however, it has become customary for the congregation to stop after *Mizmor shir* and for the Reader to repeat the last two verses before everyone continues with *Hashem malakh*.[160] This,

---

160 This observation was confirmed to me by Cantor Sherwood Goffin, who teaches Cantorial Training, including Nusach of Tefillah, at Yeshiva University's Belz School,

too, is an adoption into American Orthodox culture of an Israeli custom. One other change in practice to be noted here is the reciting of *Birkat Kohanim* on the Shabbat of the Intermediate Days of a holiday, *Shabbat chol hamoed*. For whatever reason, the custom in Ashkenazi synagogues until, approximately, the 1960s, was not to recite this particular blessing on *Shabbat chol hamoed*. Since then, the custom of reciting *Birkat Kohanim* on a *Shabbat chol hamoed* has become prevalent, mirroring the practice in Israel.

In all of these cases, the changes were typically introduced by young men who returned from learning in an Israeli *yeshiva*, where they had seen the Israeli custom both in the *yeshiva* and in synagogues there. And just as these influences were subtle and, individually, almost unnoticeable, so has American Orthodox culture been influenced by Israeli culture in many other ways. Indeed, American Orthodoxy and Israel are so intertwined in their cultural and religious profiles that one can visualize an "Orthodox global village," with Israel as its center.[161]

Many of the young men who participate in the Year in Israel program arrive home from a very intensive year in which they were detached from synagogues and were strongly influenced by *roshei yeshiva*. Whereas prior to their Israel experience, their local rabbi, synagogue, and family were the authorities with respect to standards of proper behavior within the religious realm, in the *yeshiva* as encountered in Israel, it is the *roshei yeshiva* who stand as the authorities.

In addition, the setting of the *yeshiva* is very different from that of the synagogue. In contrast to many synagogues—where the emphasis is on form and inter-community gossip is frequently indulged in[162]—*yeshivot* typically emphasize "*ruchniut*," a intense spirituality that emphasizes

---

and has been the cantor of the Lincoln Square Synagogue in Manhattan for more than 4 decades. I also conducted an informal poll among a dozen Orthodox scholars above age 60, all of whom recalled these same patterns.

161 Some years ago, Prof. Menachem Friedman, of Bar-Ilan University's Sociology Department, suggested to me that the connections between the Orthodox in the United States and Israel could be appropriately analyzed within the context of such concepts as the "*haredi* global village" and "Modern Orthodox global village." The notion I suggest here is built on Friedman's suggestion but extends it beyond the confines of a particular Orthodox subcommunity.

162 Samuel C. Heilman, *Synagogue Life: A Study in Symbolic Interaction* (Chicago: University of Chicago Press, 1976.

kedushah, holiness and separateness.[163] Gossip per se is discouraged, while serious and enthusiastic prayer—"davening with *kavanah*,"—is striven for within *yeshivot*. The *yeshiva* experience works toward, and often represents a buttress for, resocialization, with the result that students return to their families and communities with not only more knowledge but with different interests and values than they had previously. Those returning from the program in Israel often find themselves at odds with their families and communities over this different practical outlook; it is not unusual to find stress in the families of returnees from the Year in Israel experience.[164]

On the communal level, the returnees frequently find themselves alienated from the synagogue and its rabbi. They may no longer look to the rabbi as either their Halachic or spiritual advisor. They may also be "turned off" by what they view as the pretentiousness, superficiality, and insincerity of much of what goes on in the synagogue. These returnees therefore frequently look for alternative places to daven (pray), and they contribute to a growing pattern of "shtibelization" within the Orthodox community; that is, a movement can be observed where small informal congregations have appeared, where members show an increasing reluctance to participate in, let alone join, the activity of formal synagogues. Much as these may be viewed, on a religious plane, as more personally beneficial, the pattern has serious communal consequences. In contrast to informal quorums—*minyanim* and *shtiblach*—formal synagogues typically provide for a range of communal needs well beyond prayer services and congregational membership. The process of shtibelization did not begin with the Year in Israel program, nor is this movement its main source of strength, but the returnees from the program frequently contribute to the split from formal synagogue communities as a result of their experiences in the intensive *yeshiva* environment.

Perhaps the most significant development in contemporary American Orthodoxy is the recognition that the notions of "*haredi*" and "Modern Orthodox" may no longer be appropriate for American Orthodoxy. As discussed above, Modern Orthodoxy has become more stringent in its

---

163 Charles S. Liebman, "Post-War American Jewry: From Ethnic to Privatized Judaism," in Elliot Abrams and David G. Dalin, eds., *Secularism, Spirituality, and the Future of American Jewry* (Washington, DC: Ethics and Public Policy Center, 1999), p. 23.

164 For a fictional but poignant portrayal of this phenomenon, see Tova Mirvis, *The Outside World* (New York: Knopf, 2004), pp. 26–50.

ritual observance. However, much of this "chumrazation" appears to have little to do with any power struggles or even conflicting ideologies between *haredim* and Modern Orthodox. It lies instead in the impact of both socio-economic advances and the emergence of a significant Jewish educational structure encompassing a vast network of day schools, *yeshiva* high schools, post-high school *yeshivot*, and *kollelim* in cities throughout the United States since World War II.[165] Already by 1976, David Singer has suggested, "the number of students . . . studying Talmud on an advanced level . . . (compared) quite favorably with the number who were enrolled in the great *yeshivot* of Eastern Europe during their hey-day—and this despite the fact that the *yeshivot* have made no concessions to modernity, and few to the American environment."[166] His assertions about a lack of concessions to modernity are debatable; I would argue that they have made numerous concessions to modernity, most basically—at least through the high school level— all of these institutions provide secular education; there are other concessions as well. Be that as it may, Singer is essentially correct. There has been a radical increase both in the extent of and the levels of traditional Jewish learning among Orthodox Jews in the United States, to the point that at least 12 years of *yeshiva*-day school education is the norm, and a significant number of the graduates of those institutions continue their studies for a year or more in *yeshivot* and seminaries in Israel or in the US.

In addition, there has been a dramatic increase in adult Jewish learning in the Orthodox community. This is evident is the popularity of the ArtScroll Schottenstein Edition Talmud, as well as English translations of many other texts of Judaica. It is also suggested by the remarkable increase of attendees at the celebrations of the *Siyum Hashas*, the conclusion of the seven-year cycle of daily Talmud study. The first public *Siyum Hashas* was in 1968 and had about 700 attendees. The figures rose to 3,200 in 1975; more than 5,000 in 1982; about 26,000 in 1991; 70,000, which includes those who participated via satellite, in 1997; and more than 100,000, including participants via satellite, in March 2005.[167]

---

165 Chaim I. Waxman, "From Institutional Decay to Primary Day: American Orthodox Jewry Since World War II," *American Jewish History* Vol. 91, Nos. 3–4, Sept-Dec 2003, pp. 412–14.

166 David Singer, "The Yeshivah World," *Commentary* 62: 4 (October), 1976, p. 70. Also see Herbert W. Bomzer, *The Kollel in America* (New York: Shengold, 1985).

167 Andy Newman, "Orthodox Jews Celebrate End of a True Sabbatical," *New York Times*, March 2, 2005, p. B3.

It seems reasonable to assume that increased Jewish knowledge will lead to a greater awareness of *halakha*, and that awareness may lead to changes in behaviors which may have been widespread in the community but which are not halachically sanctioned. For example, during the first half of the twentieth century, many Orthodox synagogues held dinners and balls that included mixed-gender dancing, frequently with partners other than one's spouse. Likewise, it was quite typical for Orthodox Jews to eat dairy meals, as well as fish, in restaurants which had no *kashrut* supervision. With increased Jewish knowledge, such behavior is now much less common and widely frowned upon in the American Orthodox community. To those who recall the earlier days, the shift may appear as "chumrazation" when, in actuality, these are not matters of "excessive stringency" but rather represent a straightforward interpretation of *halakha*.

In addition, technological developments in the food industry have made food production much more complex. Products whose ingredients were well known in the past, and which may not have required special supervision, today frequently require supervision because the ingredients are much less well known. As Haym Soloveitchik put it,

> Frequently, a new practice was being labeled a *"humra"* not because it was the more stringent of two valid views, but simply because it made stricter demands than what had been habitually required. More often than not, *"Humra"* meant simply "more than what one had been accustomed to." . . . Modern technology had created a cornucopia of new products which required religious definition, and the growing complexity of food technology had transformed many hitherto harmless products into questionable ones, from the point of view of kashrut. [168]

Indeed, there is historical precedent for developing a greater awareness and, thus, stricter behavior with increased levels of education, especially with the opening of *yeshivot*. As Judah Galinsky has shown, late thirteenth- and fourteenth-century Spain saw a growth in *yeshivot*, a number of which became quite prominent. These educational centers, in turn, attracted an increasing number of students who went on to become learned scholars. As a result, a scholarly class grew and more authors emerged from that scholarly class.

---

168 Haym Soloveitchik, "Clarifications and Reply," *Torah U-Madda Journal* 7, 1997, p. 137.

The growth of academies, in places where they did exist previously or had been unsuccessful, had the potential of changing not only individuals but entire families. In forming learned young men, one in essence created many new "textual communities." The young scholar served as the conduit of the written word to a religiously unschooled community, largely unable to understand the Hebrew language. Many more individuals, in various communities, could perform the task of being communal "readers," explaining in a variety of forums the contents of the books. Even the student that did not become a rabbi or a judge was nevertheless somewhat of a local authority on all aspects of the written lore. In short, as the academies expanded so did the pool of potential readers, at the primary and secondary level.[169]

These developments, in turn, led to increased religious observance.[170] In brief, the opening of *yeshivot* and the expansion of Jewish knowledge does, at times, lead to increased piety and a more rigorous observance of *mitzvot* and *halakha*, because the population is now more aware of areas of *halakha* than they were previously.

This is especially the case where the observant community has the economic resources to adopt more rigorous observances and, indeed, the American Orthodox community made significant socio-economic advances during the second half of the twentieth century. By 1999, the reported mean annual household income for American Orthodox Jews was approximately $42,500.[171] That is higher than the median household income for all Americans in the same year, which was $40,816, as well as the median household income in 1999 for the Northeast, which is where the majority of American Orthodox Jews live. The household income of American Orthodox Jews was almost identical with that of white Americans in 1999, which was $42,504.[172] In his analysis of the data from

---

169 Judah D. Galinsky, "On "Popular" Halakhic Handbooks and the Emergence of a Reading Audience in 14th century Spain," *Jewish Quarterly Review*, forthcoming; See also Judah Galinsky, "*Arba turim vehasifrut hahilkhatit be-Sefarad ba-meah ha–14: Apectim historiim, sifrutiim, vehilkhatiim,*" Ph.D. dissertation, Ramat Gan, Bar-Ilan University, 1999.

170 Judah D. Galinsky, "On "Popular" Halakhic Handbooks."

171 NJPS 2001.

172 United States Census Bureau, *Statistical Abstract of the United States: 2001* (Washington, DC: US Government Printing Office, 2002), pp. 433 and 434, Tables Nos. 661 and 663.

New York, Jacob Ukeles found that 52 percent of the Orthodox households had incomes of less than \$50,000 in 2002.[173] There is, however, another important side to the economic picture, which will be discussed later.

Despite chumrazation, the overwhelming majority of Orthodox Jews in the United States hardly qualify as *haredim* according to the usual definition of the term. Israel has great religious significance for them, in its position as *Eretz Yisrael*, the Holy Land, as well as being the home of (perhaps) the world's largest Jewish community and certainly the home of the largest number of Orthodox Jews. Contrary to popular mythology, the Orthodox are not overwhelmingly anti-Zionist and certainly not anti-Israel. On the contrary, as the 2001 National Jewish Population Survey (NJPS) reconfirms, Orthodox Jews in the United States—including the "Ultra-Orthodox," "Hasidic," or "*haredi*"—have much stronger ties with Israel than do other American Jews, as was indicated previously. Indeed, for the *haredim*, perhaps the only newspapers that they read (at least in public), are *Hamodia* and *Yated Ne-eman*. In Monsey, New York, there are today private homes with newspaper boxes out front specifically for the delivered *Hamodia*, an English-language edition of the Israeli newspaper of *Agudat Israel*. *Yated Ne-eman* serves as the English-language edition of the newspaper of the more Lithuanian-oriented *haredim* of the *Degel Hatorah* party in Israel. Both of these newspapers—as well as most of the domestic weeklies catering to the Orthodox community, such as the *Jewish Press*—focus heavily on Israeli news and events, and they cater to and foster deep and perhaps penultimate ties between American Orthodoxy and Israel.

These patterns, although quite a contrast from the stereotypical image of *haredim* as anti-Zionist and isolationist, are not all that surprising, especially for those in Western societies. Even in Israel, research indicates a growing "Israelization" of *haredim*, politically, linguistically, and in many other cultural patterns.[174]

As for general education, large numbers—and they are increasing yearly—of so-called *haredi*, or "Ultra-Orthodox," American youth go to

---

173 Jacob B. Ukeles, "Modern Orthodox Jews in the New York Area: How Many are We, What are We Like and How are We Different?" *Edah Journal*, Vol. 5, No. 1, Tammuz 5765/June 2005, p. 10, Exhibit 11.

174 See, for example, Kimmy Caplan, *Internal Popular Discourse in Israeli Haredi Society*, (Jerusalem: Zalman Shazar Center, 2007 [Hebrew]); Kimmy Caplan and Emmanuel Sivan, eds., *Israeli Haredim: Integration without Assimilation?* (Tel Aviv: Van Leer Jerusalem Institute/Hakibbutz Hame-uhad Publishing House, 2003 [Hebrew]).

colleges and universities today. In fact, there is at least one institution, Touro College, which is specifically designed to attract this segment of the population. Some might argue that "college" and "university" mean something other for the Ultra-Orthodox than they do for the Modern Orthodox, in that, for the Modern Orthodox, education is an inherent value, whereas for American *haredim* it is simply a means to the end of getting a good job and making a living. That argument, however, does not appear to hold any weight in the face of evidence suggesting that the majority of those Modern Orthodox who attend college and university also do so for no reasons other than getting a better job and making a better living. The data in the survey of Yeshiva University undergraduates cited above support this conclusion. In fact, the vast majority of Americans, in general, who go to colleges and universities, do so for pragmatic purposes. As indicated by the president of the American Association of Higher Education, in the quarterly publication of the National Center for Public Policy and Higher Education, "When asked why they go to college, most students put 'getting a good job' high on their list."[175] It would thus seem that the commitment of the Modern Orthodox to the value of education and knowledge, per se, is rather overrated and overstated.

Finally, with respect to involvement with the larger Jewish community and the larger society, by the end of the century the *haredim* were heavily engaged in religious outreach in, among other organizations, the National Jewish Outreach Program (NJOP), the Association for Jewish Outreach Programs (AJOP)—with which hundreds of Orthodox outreach organizations are affiliated, and in the Orthodox Union's National Conference of Synagogue Youth (NCSY).[176] Ironically, the Modern Orthodox who pio-

---

175 Margaret A. Miller, "The Meaning of the Baccalaureate," *National Crosstalk* Vol. 6, No. 4 (Fall) 1998, p. 13.

176 Rabbi Avi Shafran, "I Have a Dream," http://www.jlaw.com/Commentary/ihavead-ream.html. Habad-Lubavitch, the most prominent Hasidic movement in the United States, was a notable exception to this pattern. Its major focus has been consistently on religious outreach to all Jews, and it utilizes cutting-edge technology in its outreach and public relations activities. Since the death of their *Rebbe*, Rabbi Menachem Mendel Schneersohn, in 1994, the movement has experienced struggles internally as well as with some other Orthodox groups, because of its increasing proclamations of him as the Messiah, a notion that others view as antithetical to Judaism. See Janet S. Belcove-Shalin, ed., *New World Hasidim: Ethnographic Studies of Hasidic Jews in America* (Albany, 1995); Lis Harris, *Holy Days: The World of a Hasidic Family* (New York, 1985); Sue Fishkoff, *The Rebbe's Army: Inside the World of Chabad-Lubavitch*

neered religious outreach have turned inward and, institutionally, are hardly engaged in such activity in the early twenty-first century. Instead, for the most part the Modern Orthodox have become defensive and are much more likely to engage in intellectual discussions among themselves rather than actively reaching out beyond their borders. Likewise, as Adam Ferziger has demonstrated, Modern Orthodox rabbinical seminaries have turned more inward and emphasize Halachic expertise, while the more "right-wing" institutions have programs which train rabbis in religious outreach.[177]

To some extent, this also reflects the "modernity" of the Modern Orthodox. Their very modernity means that they are less likely to be affiliated and actively involved with communal organizations. This is a phenomenon characteristic of the larger American society and culture, and not unique to the Modern Orthodox. Robert D. Putnam amassed considerable data indicating that Americans were, at least until the 9/11 attacks in 2001, increasingly detached from social groups such as community, and were increasingly less likely to join parent-teachers associations, unions, political parties, as well as a host of other social groups.[178] Although there is recent evidence of Modern Orthodox strength and institution-building,[179] the contemporary focus appears to be on intellectual discussion among

---

(New York, 2003); Shaul Shimon Deutsch, *Larger Than Life: The Life and Times of the Lubavitcher Rebbe, Rabbi Menachem Mendel Schneerson*, 2 vols. (New York, 1995); David Berger, *The Rebbe, The Messiah, and the Scandal of Orthodox Indifference* (London and Portland, OR, 2001). One other exception to the pattern was the Rabbinical Seminary of America, Yeshiva Chofetz Chaim of Queens, N.Y., which had a specific outreach component, and in the past several decades has opened branches in cities across the United States as well as in Israel.

177 Adam Ferziger, "Training American Orthodox Rabbis to Play a Role in Confronting Assimilation: Programs, Methodologies and Directions," Bar-Ilan University, Faculty of Jewish Studies, Rappaport Center for Assimilation Research and Strengthening Jewish Vitality, Research & Position Papers, 2003; Adam S. Ferziger, "Between Outreach and "Inreach: Redrawing the Lines of the American Orthodox Rabbinate," *Modern Judaism* 25:3 (October) 2005, pp. 237–263; Adam Ferziger, "Charles S. Liebman's American Orthodoxy: A Reexamination After Forty Years," paper presented at the 14th World Congress of Jewish Studies, Hebrew University, Jerusalem, August 3, 2005.

178 Robert D. Putnam, *Bowling Alone: The Collapse and Revival of American Community* (New York: Simon & Schuster, 2000).

179 Chaim I. Waxman, "American Modern Orthodoxy: Confronting Cultural Challenges," *Edah Journal* 4, no. 1, (2004; Iyar 5764).

peers rather than on active engagement and involvement with the broader population of America's Jews as well as the larger American public.

The *haredim*, on the other hand, have moved precisely in the opposite direction, into outward involvement. Thus, Agudath Israel, for example, became very active in the public sphere during the second half of the twentieth century. The organization has a full-time office in Washington, D.C., as well as others across the United States, and actively lobbies all branches of federal, state, and local government on issues it perceives as having Jewish interest. Its public relations specialist frequently writes columns in Jewish newspapers across the country and internationally, expressing the Agudah perspective on broad issues of Jewish interest. Indications are that American *haredim* are increasingly attached to the larger society and view living their Orthodox lifestyle as a right within the larger society rather than as set apart from it. One possible indication of their emotional attachment to the larger society may be reflected in the widespread display of American flags on homes and businesses in heavily Orthodox neighborhoods following the 9/11 attacks. Though inconclusive in and of itself, the additional fact that the national office of Agudath Israel sent out strongly worded letters imploring its members to contribute to the fund for families of firefighters and police victims of the disaster appears to indicate a deep sense of identification with the tragedy as Americans, and to reflect a sense of being an integral part of the society rather than remaining isolated from it.

It should be noted that this may also be a consequence of a basic difference between Christian and Jewish conservatives and how they carry out their lives as cognitive minorities. For Christians, the symbol is the "mighty fortress," which, according to Martin Luther, stands for God who acts as a trusty shield and weapon; Christian fundamentalists interpret this as reason for removing oneself from involvement in the larger society. For conservative (that is, Torah observant) Jews, the objective is to build a fence (*seyag*) around the Torah, to shield it from distortion but not to refrain from societal involvements. Socio-historical circumstances in Eastern Europe did encourage isolation from society, which carried over to the initial interaction of Jewish immigrants with American society. However, once they felt physically secure and legitimately autonomous in a religious sense, the Orthodox began to feel themselves as part of the society and to praise the political system supporting their lifestyle and traditions. They also began to feel comfortable enough to partake in some arenas within the popular culture previously alien to traditional Judaism, such as sports and music. As Jeffrey Gurock indicated, the notions of "recreation" and "leisure time" were unfamiliar to Jewish immigrants[180] and, I would add, to traditional Judaism. With respect to sports, it is com- monplace to find American *haredi yeshiva* students intimately involved as ardent fans of professional sports, even participating in betting pools as well as engaging in athletics, albeit non-professionally.[181] Exercise is now a "kosher" activity,[182] as are sports; there is even a "Kosher Gym." That the very notion of "leisure time" was alien in *haredi* circles in Eastern Europe may be further support for Alan Wolfe's thesis of the transformation of American Religion through the influence of American culture upon it.[183]

With respect to music, there is today what might be called parallel structure to the American pop culture music industry, with a broad new genre of American *haredi* music being created, much of which signifi- cantly resembles mainstream popular music but with a Jewish twist.[184] *Haredim* have also developed a genre of literature—namely, fiction— which had been alien to conservative, traditional Orthodoxy.[185] All of this is possible in an American society tolerant of, if not openly encouraging, both religion and religious diversity.

Haredim have now adopted modern methods of inspirational self- help. Agudah conventions and *Haredi* publications are replete with "cut- ting edge" psychological, educational, and medical discussions. Both the producers and the consumers of these materials are not isolated and do not retreat from the larger society and culture. They are very much engaged in it, having learned to dwell within it and to use it for their ends.[186]

---

180 Jeffrey S. Gurock, *Judaism's Encounter with American Sports.* (Bloomington: Indiana University Press, 2005).

181 Ibid.

182 Zlati Meyer, "*Shvitzing* to the Oldies: Why is This Gym Different From All Other Gyms?," *New York Magazine*, Feb. 6, 2000; Shira Klapper, "Muscles Meet Maimonides At Brooklyn's Kosher Gym," *Forward*, July 13, 2001.

183 Alan Wolfe, *The Transformation of American Religion* (New York: Free Press, 2003).

184 www.shlockrock.com, www.veroba.net—Mattisyahu, Blue Fringe, Soul Farm, The Chevrah, and even Mordechai Ben-David and Avraham Fried, to name a few.

185 Yoel Finkelman, "Medium and Message in Contemporary Haredi Adventure Fiction," *Torah Umadda Journal*, Vol. 13, 2005, pp. 50–87.

186 See, for example, the highly popular books by the psychiatrist Abraham J. Twerski, especially *Getting Up When You're Down: A Discussion of Adult Malady*

When a *Haredi* legal scholar recently became the dean of a law school in New York, it warranted an article in the "Long Island" section of the *New York Times*, but only because of Aaron Twerski's atypical appearance, including his garb. However, he made a point of emphasizing that, "We are insular in terms of our private lives and our institutions and all the rest, but we are not insular in terms of being a vital part of society."[187]

Depression and Related Conditions. Brooklyn, NY: Shaar Press/Mesorah, 1995; *The Shame of Silence: Spouse Abuse in the Jewish Community*. Pittsburgh, PA: Morkov, 1996; *Successful Relationships: At Home, At Work, and With Friends: Bringing Control Issues Under Control*. Brooklyn, NY: Shaar Press/Mesorah, 2003. Also see the works of Akiva Tatz, *Anatomy of a Search: Personal Drama in the Teshuva Revolution*. Brooklyn, NY: Mesorah, 1987.

187 Marcelle S. Fischler, "Hofstra's Law Dean Stands Out, but Still Fits In," *New York Times*, September 18, 2005, Sect. 14LI, P. 4.

Chapter 27

Year in Israel and Aliyah

American *olim* arrive in Israel with more extensive Jewish education than is typical of the Jewish population in the United States, according to all studies addressing this subject. About 22 percent of the American Jews (by religion), ages 25–45, who responded to the 1990 National Jewish Population Survey said they never received any Jewish education. Of those who did, about 10 percent said that day school was their major type of Jewish education.[188] By contrast, more than a third of the American *olim* had at least a day school education.[189]

In analyzing the denominational affiliations of America's Jews as indicated in the 1971 National Jewish Population Survey, Lazerwitz and Harrison[190] found that 11 percent identified with the Orthodox, 42 percent with the Conservative movement, 33 percent with Reform, and that 14 percent had no denominational affiliation. By contrast, both Goldscheider and Jubas found that 37–42 percent of the American *olim* in their surveys identified as Orthodox. The percentage of Orthodox among those American *olim* was also higher than among those in Engel's 1950–66 sample, and much higher than among pre-State American *olim*.[191]

In their study of older immigrants in Israeli society, Lache and colleagues found that almost three-fourths of the middle-aged and retired

---

188 Waxman, *Jewish Baby Boomers*, pp. 109–10.

189 Calvin Goldscheider, "American Aliyah: Sociological and Demographic Perspective," in Marshall Sklare, ed., *The Jews in American Society*, (New York: Behrman House, 1974), pp. 335–384; Harry Lieb Jubas, "The Adjustment Process of Americans and Canadians in Israel and Their Integration into Israeli Society" Ph.D. dissertation, Department of Secondary Education and Curriculum, Michigan State University, East Lansing, MI, 1974, p. 108.

190 Bernard Lazerwitz and Michael Harrison, "American Jewish Denominations: A Social and Religious Profile." *American Sociological Review* 44, 1979, pp. 656–66.

191 Gerald Engel, "North American Jewish Settlers in Israel," *American Jewish Year Book* 71, 1970, pp. 161–187.

North American *olim* they interviewed classified themselves as "religious." However, these researchers used the prevalent Israeli categories
"religious," "traditional," and "nonreligious." This categorization is inap-
propriate for American Jewry, among whom Orthodox, Conservative, and
Reform might identify themselves as "religious." On the other hand, since
it is doubtful that an Israeli researcher would classify most Conservative
and Reform Jews as "religious," the data of Lache and colleagues would
seem to confirm that a disproportionately high percentage of American
olim are Orthodox.[192] Goldscheider found that patterns among the
American *olim* "of over-concentration and selectivity among religious and
Orthodox Jews relative to the American Jewish population" also mani-
fested themselves in their patterns of synagogue attendance and ritual
observance.[193] Specifically, among the *olim* the rate of synagogue attendance and observance of such rituals as fasting on Yom Kippur and dietary
regulations was disproportionately high when compared to the rates for
the Jewish population of the United States.

Data from Israel's Central Bureau of Statistics likewise indicated the
disproportionate religiosity of American *olim* and the increasing proportion of the religiously observant among them. Of the 1978–80 North
American *olim*, a majority—54 percent—identified themselves as "religious," 21 percent as "traditional," 11 percent as "not very religious," and
only 14 percent as "not religious at all."[194]

Since those studies were performed, strong indicators of a significant
increase in the percentage of Orthodox among American *olim* have
appeared, despite the fact that their percentage in the American Jewish
population has increased moderately at best. For example, it has been
reported that "of the [approximately] 1,900 [*olim*] who arrived from the
United States [in 1986] more than 1,200 are Orthodox Jews and the

---

192 S. Y. Lache, Dorota Teczniczek, Beatriz Mann, and Ron Lahav, *The Absorption
      Problems of Older Immigrants in Israeli Society* (Jerusalem: Henrietta Szold
      Institute, 1976).

193 Goldscheider, "American Aliyah," pp. 381–82.

194 Central Bureau of Statistics, State of Israel, *Survey of Absorption of Immigrants:
      Immigrants of the Seventies—The First Three Years in Israel*, Special Series No. 771.
      (Jerusalem: Central Bureau of Statistics, 1986), pp. 14–15; see also Sergio
      DellaPergola, "Demographic Trends of Latin American Jewry," in Judith Laiken
      Elkin and Gilbert W. Merkx, eds., *The Jewish Presence in Latin America* (Boston:
      Allen & Unwin, 1987), pp. 85–133.

remainder defined themselves as somewhat religiously observant, etc."[195] This report is consistent with 1976 estimates of the assistant director of the Aliyah Department of the World Zionist Organization-American Section, and discussions with others connected with that department at the time, both of which state that about 60 percent of current American *olim* are Orthodox.[196] More recent estimates by the major American *aliyah* organization, Nefesh B'Nefesh, suggest that 79 percent of contemporary American *olim* are Orthodox.[197]

The high proportion of Orthodox among American *olim* raises two questions. The first is, why are they over-represented? The second, why is their overrepresentation growing so rapidly? The source of the disproportionate number of Orthodox among the *olim* is most likely rooted in the ideological-cultural and social-psychological characteristics of American Orthodoxy. In the ideological-cultural sphere, the American Orthodox rabbinic leadership—more so than in other denominations—defines living in Israel as a religious norm. Thus, shortly after the Six Day War, Liebman queried Orthodox, Conservative, and Reform rabbis and synagogue presidents, as well as the presidents of their respective national Jewish organizations, about their agreement or disagreement with a number of statements relating to Israel. Significant as regards the specific subject of this article, one finds a majority—69 percent—only among the Orthodox rabbis agreeing with the statement: "A Jew who really wants to do what Judaism requires of him should move to Israel." The percentages indicated for the other groups was: Conservative rabbis—25% ; Reform rabbis—10% ; Orthodox synagogue presidents—37% , Conservative—12% , and Reform—5% .[198]

In his study of American *olim*, Avruch suggests a social-psychological basis for the *aliyah* witnessed among the American Orthodox. He found that they tend to be people who, "in America, by investing heavily or increasingly in their Jewishness, effected a primordialization of their

---

195 *Barkai* 4, 1987, p. 408.

196 I conducted the interviews and discussions.

197 Gaby Wenig, "Making Dreams of Israel Come True," *Jewish Journal of Greater Los Angeles*, August 15, 2003).

198 Yesha'yahu (Charles) Liebman, "The Role of Israel in the Ideology of American Jews." *Dispersion and Unity* 10, 1970, pp.19–26.

social identities."[199] In other words, these are individuals who define themselves primarily in terms of their Jewishness. Their Jewishness took precedence over other aspects of their identities, and their *aliyah* was an attempt to live their lives as Jews within the family of Jews. Orthodox Jews are overrepresented among the American *olim*, Avruch suggests, because they are more likely to have been those for whom, in America, Jewishness took precedence over other aspects of their identities.

My analysis of American Orthodox Judaism provided an explanation both ideological-cultural and social-psychological in nature. It suggested that the two major approaches adopted by Orthodoxy in its confrontation with modernity have been those of compartmentalization and expansionism.[200] In compartmentalization, a sharp boundary is drawn between the world of the sacred and the world of the secular, and those adopting this approach seek to live their lives as much as possible within the world of the sacred. When necessity requires that they leave the world of the sacred and enter that of the secular, they are shielded from the impact of this movement by their consciousness of its secular, transitory quality and, hence, worthy of no real value. In expansionism, on the other hand, there is no clear boundary between the worlds of the sacred and the secular, and the two are not kept totally apart. On the contrary, the expansionist attempts to bring sanctity to the secular: to make the secular sacred. This approach, which has among its ideological fathers Rabbi A. I. Kook, is one exhibited by the Modern Orthodox in principle; that is, we find this attitude in those who view integrating sacred learning with secular knowledge, *Torah U'Madda*, as an inherent value—a *"l'chat'chilah"*—rather than as a necessary evil—a *"b'dieved."*[201] Those who adhere to expansionism seek wholeness in their lives and thus, perhaps, are more likely to go on *aliyah* as part of their quest for leading more whole, complete Jewish lives. It was also suggested that this might also explain the disproportionate number of Americans among the settlers in Judea and Samaria.[202]

---

199 Kevin Avruch, *American Immigrants in Israel: Social Identities and Change* (Chicago: University of Chicago Press, 1981), p. 117.

200 Waxman, *American Aliya*, pp.119–38.

201 Norman Lamm, *Torah Umadda: The Encounter of Religious Learning and Worldly Knowledge in the Jewish Tradition* (Northvale, NJ: Jason Aronson, 1990).

202 Waxman, *American Aliya*, pp. 167–68.

Chapter 28

Orthodox Institutional Structures Promoting Aliyah

Structural factors can, of course, slow down or speed up the rate of *aliyah* among the Orthodox. Interestingly, economic factors have been suggested as both impediments and as promoters of *aliyah* within the American Orthodox community. Thus, Isaac Berman[203] argues that, even though ideology is an important variable influencing *aliyah*, so is reality—which is to say, economic conditions. All other things being equal, he maintains, the *aliyah* rate goes up when the economic conditions in Israel are good, and the rate declines when the conditions decline. When one examines the figures on American *aliyah* (shown in the table below), it appears that factors other than economic conditions in Israel determine the rate of emigration to Israel. The patterns of ups and downs do not seem explicable in terms of trends in the Israeli economy. For example, the figures on American *aliyah* for the years 2001–2004 indicate a consistent rise, despite the fact that during those years the Israeli economy was in a rather poor state.

---

203 Isaac Berman, "Immigration to Israel: Ideology vs. Reality," *Forum* 50, 1983–84, pp. 25–30.

Table 5: American *Aliyah*, 1948–2006[204]

1948 (from May 15)	301	1985	1915
1949	584	1978	2921
1950	761	1979	2950
1951	568	1980	2312
1952	292	1981	2384
1953	202	1982	2693
1954	294	1983	3469
1955	321	1984	2581
1956	187	1985	1915
1957	277	1986	1968
1958	378	1987	1818
1959	330	1988	1551
1960	413	1989	1383
1961	313	1990	1370
1962	619	1991	1538
1963	868	1992	1804
1964	1006	1993	2057
1965	924	1994	2118
1966	749	1995	2253
1967	665	1996	1990
1968	932	1997	1858
1969	5739	1998	1605
1970	6424	1999	1515
1971	7364	2000	1237
1972	5515	2001	1250
1973	4393	2002	1536
1974	3089	2003	1687
1975	2803	2004	1891
1976	2700	2005	2045
1977	2571	2006	2157

204 The data in this table are from monthly and annual reports published by Israel's Central Bureau of Statistics.

On the other hand, economic factors might, in part, explain the *aliyah* figures during those years, if we can assume that the vast majority of those *olim* were Orthodox. Carmel Chiswick offers a somewhat unique economic basis for the *aliyah* of the Orthodox. She attributes at least part of their higher rate of *aliyah* to the fact that

> the greater the emphasis placed on traditional observance, the greater the conflict between rhythms of Jewish and secular life and hence greater the lifestyle cost of being Jewish. Within the American Jewish community, the more observant the family the greater the lifestyle costs of being Jewish and hence the greater the "savings" achieved by moving to Israel. Thus the rate of return to *aliyah* would be higher among more religiously observant Americans, and immigration to Israel would have been stimulated by a revival of Jewish observance among Jews with high-level secular occupations in the United States.[205]

Indeed, as I indicated in my study of Jewish baby boomers, the 1990 National Jewish Population Survey data indicated that Orthodox Jewish baby boomers had lower family annual incomes than did Conservative and Reform families, and that the "cost of Jewish living" was higher for Orthodox than for others:

> . . . there is a gap of more than $10,000 between the mean family incomes of Orthodox and Conservative, and a similar gap between the mean family incomes of Conservative and Reform baby boomers. Almost two-thirds of the Orthodox baby boomers reported combined annual family incomes of less $45,000, whereas only half of the Conservatives and 42.5 percent of the Reform did . . . Since Orthodox have more children than Conservative and Reform do, this means that the economic constraints are even greater than these data indicate. The lower income of the Orthodox, combined with their larger families, means they have considerably less disposable income than others. In addition, their ideological commitments compel them to join synagogues at

---

205 Carmel Ullman Chiswick, "Impact of the Six-Day War on American Jewry: An Economic Perspective." Paper presented at the conference on The Impact of the Six-Day War, The Hebrew University, Institute of Contemporary Jewry, Jerusalem, Israel, December 19–21, 1994.

a higher rate than others, . . . and to send their children to private
day schools, as well as to contribute to a variety of other Jewish
communal institutions. There is, thus, ample evidence that the
Orthodox are disproportionally affected by what has been called,
"the high cost of Jewish living."[206]

The lower income of the Orthodox continued to be evident in the 2001
NJPS. For example, of those identifying as Orthodox, 80 percent had
incomes of less than $100,000, as compared to 77 percent of those who
identified as Conservative and 73 percent of those who identified as
Reform. Five percent of those who identified as Conservative had incomes
of $300,000 or more, as compared to 3 percent for the Reform and only
one percent for the Orthodox. These figures assume that the family sizes
are the same, but, in fact, we know that they are not and that the Orthodox
have larger families. In other words, the significantly higher cost of Jewish
living for the Orthodox persists.

Lest there be any question about the high cost of Jewish living for
Orthodox families, it should be noted that at least 12 years of *yeshiva* education is today the norm in the Orthodox community. In the summer of
2005, I inquired about tuitions at Modern Orthodox high schools in the
New York–New Jersey area, and found that tuition and other required fees
at the high schools of HAFTR, HALB and Yeshiva of South Shore, in the
Five Towns, Nassau County, New York, were approximately $18,000 in
that year. Kushner Yeshiva High School, in Livingston, New Jersey,
charges similar fees, as do the high schools of Yeshiva University, Yeshiva
of Flatbush, Ramaz, and a number of others

If it is assumed, therefore, that the declining economic conditions in
the United States during 2001–2004 had even greater consequences for
the Orthodox—because their "lifestyle cost of being Jewish" in America
resulted in their having even less "disposable cash" than other American
Jews—they would have had a greater incentive to go on *aliyah*, even if the
Israeli economy was faring poorly because their religious-lifestyle cost
would be much lower in Israel.

Indeed, the major organizations promoting American *aliyah*, Nefesh
B'Nefesh and the American branch of the Israel Aliyah Center, are direct-
ing their messages to Orthodox families with small children, the most

---

206 Waxman, Jewish Baby Boomers, p. 35.

likely candidates for *aliyah*, and emphasizing the economic incentive of *aliyah*.[207] There has been some debate about the wisdom of this approach, but it does reflect the reality of the immediate economic concerns of young American Orthodox families.

On the other hand, relative to American society as a whole, the economic status of the Orthodox is higher than it had been in the past. With mean family incomes of approximately $48,000 in 1989, Orthodox Jewish baby boomers were clearly no longer the working class. They had improved their economic status, and higher educational status, both of which would appear to foster opportunities for *aliyah*.

In fact, there is evidence of a growing phenomenon of transnational commuting among American *olim*, much of which is predicated on relatively high occupational status.[208] Recent adult *olim* have typically completed their education and bring with them several years of work experience. They are exceptional in terms of the occupations they choose, and it is this uniqueness that accounts for the relatively large numbers of commuters to the United States. Overwhelmingly, the commuters are professionals—accountants, physicians, surgeons, lawyers, computer specialists and other high-tech professionals—and there is a greater demand for their services in the U.S. than in Israel. Data from Israel's Central Bureau of Statistics (CBS), the 2000–2001 National Jewish Population Survey (NJPS), and the U.S. Bureau of the Census starkly demonstrate that there is a higher rate of professionals and managers among American *olim* than among Jews who remain in the U.S. There is also a higher rate of professionals and managers among American Jews in general than among the overall white American population. Thus, among employed adult white Americans, 38 percent of the adult males and 41 percent of the females were found to be in managerial or professional positions in 2000. Among employed adult American Jews, however, 80 percent of the males and 74 percent of the females were in professions or managerial positions. And among American *olim*, 82 percent of those with known occupations were in professions or managerial positions.[209] As suggested, it is pre-

---

207 Uriel Heilman, "Shh! Don't Tell Them its Aliya," *Jerusalem Post*, July 21, 2005, p. 5.

208 Dodi Tobin and Chaim I. Waxman, "The Transatlantic Commuter—Living in Israel, Working in the States," *Jewish Action*, Vol. 66, No. 2 Winter 2005/5766, pp. 44–48.

209 I thank Prof. Barry R. Chiswick, University of Illinois at Chicago, and Dr. Uzi Rebhun, The Hebrew University of Jerusalem, for providing me with these data.

cisely individuals in those types of positions—professions and managerial positions—who are more likely to commute between Israel and the U.S., because these positions are much less likely to require 9–5, Monday–Friday schedules and they are much more amenable to telecommuting innovations.

Economics aside, the disproportionate number of Orthodox Jews among American *olim* may also be a byproduct of the growing popularity of the Year in Israel program. In many of the *yeshivot* and seminaries involved, *aliyah* as a religious obligation—a mitzvah—is strongly emphasized. In addition to talks by the heads of the *yeshivot* on the subject of *aliyah*, in almost every *yeshiva* where we find Israelis in addition to Americans—and especially the *yeshivot hesder*, those with a strong Religious-Zionist ideology and who combine study with military service —there is very strong peer-group pressure from the Israelis for the Americans to commit themselves to *aliyah*. As Shalom Berger's data suggest, the year spent in Israel has a significant impact on *aliyah* plans, and a two-year stay has even greater significance. For example, in the pretest administered prior to their year's study in Israel, 17 percent said it was "Very Likely" that they "will make *aliyah*," and 37 percent said it was "Somewhat Likely." After a year in Israel, 37 percent said that it was "Very Likely" and 44 percent said that it was "Somewhat Likely." After two years, 50 percent said that it was "Very Likely" and 35 said that it was "Somewhat Likely." In other words, after two years, about 85 percent said that it was very or somewhat likely that they would go on *aliyah*. These patterns indicate a rise in interest with regard to making *aliyah* coinciding with the amount of time spent in Israel. Although no systematic study of the impact of the year or two spent studying in Israeli *yeshivot* has yet been completed, it is evident that this pattern has increased dramatically over the past 25 years. For example, of the 1994 graduating class at the Yeshiva University High School for Boys, 121 out of 137 (88 percent) spent the year after graduation studying in a *yeshiva* in Israel. Similar percentages were reported for the girls' high schools, as well as for other *yeshiva* high schools, such as Hebrew Academy of the Five Towns and Rockaways (HAFTR) High School, a large Modern Orthodox *yeshiva* high school in Cedarhurst, Long Island, New York. Yeshiva of Flatbush, in Brooklyn, had a lower rate, probably due, in part, to the high percentage of students of Syrian background in the school. Syrian parents are much more likely to insist that their children remain nearby after graduating high school. Among the Ashkenazi students there, the percentages were similar to those in the other schools mentioned.

Reports from a number of the *yeshivot hesder* suggest that a high percentage of Americans who studied there for at least one year subsequently go on *aliyah*. For example, data obtained from Yeshivat Sha'alvim indicate that 123 of the 614 Americans who studied at the *yeshiva* during the years 1985-95 (20 percent) have already gone on *aliyah* and are currently living in Israel. Consequently, support groups and other *aliyah*-oriented groups—*garinim*—are much more highly visible in those institutional locations in which young Orthodox men and women are likely to be present, and organizations such as Tehillah and Nefesh B'Nefesh promote pilot trips and in other ways create direct contact between potential *olim* in the United States and their American counterparts in Israel. This enhances the perception, discussed by Avruch, of Israel as a "*mishpachah*," as one large family of Jews. Be that as it may, it does appear that *aliyah* derives from what have become the normal institutional patterns of socialization within a significant segment of American Orthodoxy.

For the years 2001–2006, in particular, it should be noted that the increase in American *aliyah* may be due to the active efforts of Nefesh B'Nefesh, which is now a full partner with the *aliyah* department of the American branch of the World Zionist Organization.[210]

---

210 For more information, see http://www.nbn.org.il.

Chapter 29

Recent Questions About Aliyah

Recently, a number of questions have been raised in the American Orthodox community concerning American *aliyah*. Much of the questioning may be attributed to ingenuous expectations about *aliyah*. All too often, either as the result of misinformation or disinformation by formal *aliyah* emissaries,[211] *olim* arrive in Israel ill-prepared for the challenges they and their families will face.

Many of the challenges are common to all *olim* and are the natural result of immigration and learning a new culture. Some, however, are specific to religious families, especially those with young children. One of the first to address these issues was Yair Spolter, an American *oleh*, in an article published in the *Jewish Observer*.[212] In an attempt to encourage rather than discourage *aliyah*—while still contributing to its success—Spolter surveys a series of educational and child-rearing challenges young American families will likely face upon their *aliyah*. Whether or not one agrees with all of his specific suggestions and recommendations, there is little question that "the many issues and challenges involved in *aliyah* and integration into Israeli society . . . can make moving to Israel a difficult task. Being aware of the risks and difficulties that *aliyah* entails can help parents make an educated decision and plan a successful *aliyah* for their family."[213]

Some of the issues raised by Spolter with respect to *olim* apply similarly for American students in the Year in Israel program. Often, the students themselves are swayed by where their friends are going, without having any idea about what those *yeshivot* are actually like and what they expect from their students. The Orthodox Caucus, in particular, has recog-

---

211 Jay Shapiro, *From Both Sides Now: An American-Israeli Odyssey* (Tel Aviv: Dvir Katzman, 1983), esp. Part II, Pp, 153ff., "Lies My Shaliach Told Me."

212 Yair Spolter, "Grasping the Kedusha, Avoiding the Pitfalls: When American Families Move to Eretz Yisrael," *Jewish Observer*, December 2004, pp. 6–12.

213 Spolter, "Grasping the Kedusha," p. 7.

nized that parents frequently have very little information and guidance when it comes to their children's study in Israel. To assist both parents and prospective students, the Caucus has posted a detailed "Israel School Guide" for "Post High School Study in Israel" on its website.[214]

Some American Jews have suggested that *aliyah* drains the Jewish community in America of its leadership, in that the *olim* are often among "the best and the brightest." As was indicated above, there are those who attribute the decline of the Mizrachi Organization in the United States to the *aliyah* of the most committed and dynamic of the religious Zionists. The persuasiveness of that argument is limited by the low rate of American *aliyah* as well as by the strong ties that American *olim* retain with the United States and with the American Jewish community. In fact, data on *olim* suggest that perhaps as many as 30 percent of the American families who made *aliyah* in the past decade have a family member who commutes to work in the U.S.[215] Nor does *aliyah* from the United States entail cutting connections with the American Jewish community. Quite the contrary: it often generates energies and activities that contribute to a strengthening of leadership, particularly for the Orthodox community in America, because of its strong Israeli ties.

In January 2005, one severe manifestation of a problem associated with the Year in Israel program came to public attention with the death by drug overdose of an American student studying in an Israeli *yeshiva*, and the arrest there of four others on suspicion of peddling drugs to many of their fellow *yeshiva* students.[216] This problem is related to a broader one within the American Orthodox community, namely, the growing evidence of substance abuse, especially among youth, in the American Orthodox community. In the face of a deeply ingrained tendency to deny and cover up problems within the Orthodox community—much the way there is a tendency within families to deny and cover up internal problems—a number of Orthodox psychologists, social workers, and other substance-abuse professionals have striven to publicize the problem, in order to compel the Orthodox community to confront this issue and undertake efforts to change the structural conditions which contributing to the growth of such

---

214 www.ocweb.org.

215 Tobin and Waxman, "The Transatlantic Commuter."

216 Mati Wagner, "Student Came for Torah, But Found Heroin," *Jerusalem Post*, January 20, 2005.

problems. The Orthodox Union has taken a leadership role in publicizing the problem,[217] and has urged synagogues to adopt a ban on "kiddush clubs," in general, and the serving of alcohol, in particular, within the synagogue. Although there is no evidence of any widespread adoption of those bans, there does appear to be a greater public awareness of not only substance abuse but other problems among Orthodox teens. In the Fall of 1999, the *Jewish Observer* published a "Special Issue" dedicated to the topic—"Children on the Fringe—and Beyond"[218]—and it is reported to have been very widely distributed. It appears that the American Orthodox community is finally beginning to confront, if not actively address, a range of problems within its midst, including spouse and child abuse.[219] It should be emphasized that there is no evidence that these problems are more prevalent within the Orthodox community than elsewhere; on the contrary, there may well be a significantly lower rate within the Orthodox community. But they clearly do exist, and may play a role in the defection of Orthodox Jewish youth from the community.[220] These are serious problems and, as has been indicated, it appears that the community is beginning to face up to them. Perhaps more serious are issues that the community apparently continues to avoid—indeed, the community appears to be in almost total denial about them.

American Orthodox Jews, Modern as well as the *haredi*, project a sense of self-assuredness and a conviction that their lifestyle immunizes them against the challenges confronting other American Jews, especially from the problem of intermarriage. They and some others are convinced that day school education is the key and guarantee against intermarriage. Until recently, the empirical data appeared to firmly support such convictions. In my analysis of the 1990 NJPS, I found that, among those who were raised

---

217 Benzion Twerski, "Orthodox Youth and Substance Abuse: Shattering the Myths," *Jewish Action*, Vol. 58, No. 2, Winter 5758/1998.

218 Vol. 32, No. 9, Kislev 5760/Nov. 1999.

219 Rabbi Abraham J. Twerski, M.D., "Tackling a 'Shondeh'," *Jewish Action*, Vol. 58, No. 3, Spring 5758/1998; Abraham J. Twerski, *The Shame Borne in Silence: Spouse Abuse in the Jewish Community* (Pittsburgh, PA: Mirkov Publications, 1996); and the range of articles on the web site of Ohel Children's Home & Family Services http://www.ohelfamily.org/articles.cfm.

220 Faranak Margolese, *Off the Derech: Why Observant Jews Leave Judaism* (Jerusalem and New York: Devora Publishing, 2005). For examples of such in the Hasidic community, see Hella Winston, *Unchosen: The Hidden Lives of Hasidic Rebels* (Boston: Beacon Press, 2005).

Orthodox and had twelve or more years of day school education, the rate of intermarriage was statistically insignificant.[221] However, the data from the 2001 NJPS indicate that the intermarriage rate among that population has risen. Although still much lower than in the overall American Jewish population, there was an increase from zero in 1990 to 5 percent in 2001. Nor can this be attributed solely to problems with the survey.[222] Interviews and discussions with rabbis and lay-persons in the Orthodox community revealed a number who could personally point to more than a few intermarried individuals, people raised Orthodox and who had 12 or more years of day school education. Disturbing as this may be, it should not be surprising. Jews have never been immune to the social patterns in the surrounding environment. Rather, what is surprising is that so many in the Orthodox community believed—and many still believe—that the behaviors and trends within contemporary American Orthodox are inherently different.

Perhaps the obliviousness of the Orthodox to the phenomenon of Orthodox intermarriage is related to that of defection from Orthodoxy. Hundreds of books, articles, and lectures have been written on the "*ba'al teshuvah*" phenomenon—that is, the turn to Orthodoxy by either those who had previously left it or, more typically, those who were never raised Orthodox. Despite a dearth of hard data, many, especially among the Orthodox, are convinced that the phenomenon entails large numbers and that those numbers are ever-increasing. At the same time, few appear ready to accept, let alone publicly address, the reality of the phenomenon of defection from Orthodoxy, despite the fact that its existence is obvious in virtually every Orthodox community.

Perhaps, too, it is human nature to place emphasis on the positive and, indeed, the Orthodox community does have reason to bask in some positives. Demographically, the data indicate growth. For example, decades of available data indicate that the American Orthodox birth rate is higher than that of Conservative, Reform, and unaffiliated Jews. However, although the average number of children of Orthodox females (2.2) was found to be somewhat higher than that of the others (1.9), they continued to decline in size.[223] More recently, data from the 2001 NJPS indicate that the Orthodox birth rate has risen significantly. Whereas the overall average of children for

---

221 Waxman, *Jewish Baby Boomers*, p. 113.

222 The 2001 NJPS was and remains the subject of some controversy; cf. Nacha Kattan, "National Population Survey Postponed—Again," *Forward*, April 11, 2003.

223 Waxman, *Jewish Baby Boomers*, p. 57.

Jewish women has declined to 1.86, the average for all sectors of Orthodoxy has climbed: 3.3 for the Modern Orthodox, and 7 or 8 for *haredim*. As a result, the Orthodox now enjoy a significantly higher proportion of minor children, ages 18 and below (19 percent), than do other American Jews (less than 12 percent). This should certainly have an impact upon the relative size of the Orthodox component of the American Jewish community.

However, what these figures do not indicate is the rate of defection from the Orthodox community of even those with extensive and intensive *yeshiva* education, as well as the non-affiliation of religiously observant Jews. Some *ba'alei teshuvah* defect for the same reasons they were initially attracted to Orthodoxy, namely, they were "seekers,"[224] and they still are. Others, *ba'alei teshuvah* or "ffb's" ("*frum* from birth") leave regardless of whether they stopped seeking or never began; either way, they have come to terms with their newfound non-Orthodoxy. Again, this is not limited to those with little *yeshiva* education: it is the case with some who have had extensive *yeshiva* experiences as well. According to estimates of some who have participated in the Year in Israel program (as well as some administrators of *yeshivot* in the program), more than 10 percent of the participants leave Orthodoxy within 5 years of returning home.

There are, most assuredly, many reasons why individuals opt out of Orthodoxy, and there may well be nothing the organized community can do to forestall defection entirely. However, there is one source of disaffection which the community may be able to control. Mention was made earlier of the economic status of the Orthodox and the cost of maintaining a household among the observant. In a recent essay on the consequences of the high cost of Jewish living, Gerald Bubis highlighted the cost across the board but appeared to downplay its significance for the Orthodox. He argues that the Jewish identity and identification of the Orthodox is almost total, and that

> [t]he potency of the community and its institutions serves to support these values and practices. Thus the economic hardships of the most impoverished are often mitigated, to a degree, by the readiness of community members and institutions to help.[225]

---

224 Wade Clark Roof, *A Generation of Seekers: The Spiritual Journeys of the Baby Boomer Generation*, (San Francisco: Harper Collins, 1993).

225 Gerald B. Bubis, "The Costs of Jewish Living: Revisiting Jewish Involvements and Barriers," American Jewish Committee, Contemporary Jewish Life Department, 2005, p. 8.

Bubis assumes that cost is not a barrier for the Jewish community because their Jewishness is the most important aspect of their identity. However, what he does not consider is that cost is also a factor for many Orthodox Jews as well, and may play a role in the fact that Orthodoxy has not grown as rapidly as one might have expected. Although, as indicated above, the Orthodox birth rate is higher than that of the non-Orthodox, the 3.3 average number of children for the Modern Orthodox might well be higher were it not for the high cost of Jewish living in the Orthodox community. Also, it seems reasonable to assume that there are religiously observant families and people who have been forced to curtail their communal involvements and, perhaps, cease entirely to affiliate communally because they could not afford the *shul* membership, which includes a large building fund, day school tuition, and the cost of summer camps.

In addition to the issue of cost, there is another aspect of the school-educational issue that encourages leaving the Modern Orthodox community in particular. If it is assumed, as many in the Modern Orthodox community do, that there is some correlation between academic ability and financial success, the structure of the community favors the elite and alienates the non-elite. Orthodox day schools are designed for the academic elite—"average" students are viewed by others, and often by themselves, as "flunkies." Unless they happen to have financially affluent parents, they are often made to feel unwelcome. The schools do not cater to them and, as a result, they frequently do not develop proficiency in Hebrew and other skills necessary to fully participate in Orthodox Jewish communal life, such as adult Talmud classes, *shiurim*. As a result, they drop out of communal life.[226]

The problem associated with the cost of *yeshiva* education has become even more critical recently, and a number of public efforts aimed at addressing it are ongoing. The Orthodox Caucus has an initiative to deal with "The Rising Costs of Day School Tuition" but, at the time of this writing, the program is much too new to evaluate its effectiveness. There have been few, if any, practical suggestions for dealing with the problem of costly *yeshiva* education, other than broadly calling for public support in the form of school vouchers, an issue on which the American Jewish community is bitterly divided. The Orthodox generally support vouchers, while

---

226 I thank Myron Wurzburger for this observation.

most of the non-Orthodox staunchly oppose their use.[227] The United States Supreme Court has ruled school vouchers Constitutional, but it is an issue that will no doubt come before the Supreme Court once again in the near future. Another, in some ways more radical, approach calls for a communal tax to support day-school education. The brainchild of George Hanus—an attorney, real estate developer, and Vice Chairman of the United Jewish Federation in Chicago—"Operation Jewish Education: The 5 Percent Mandate" calls upon every Jew to set aside a minimum of five percent of their estate for an endowment fund for a local day school. The program's objective is to establish local endowments that would be large enough to cover the tuition for all of the children in the community. Hanus maintains that his idea is not new, that the notion of the organized community, *kehillah*, imposing taxes for communal needs has been around at least since the time of the Talmud.[228] Be that as it may, there has not been any significant response to this initiative.

The costs of tuition for a *yeshiva* education have become intolerable to a growing number of Orthodox families, and some of have taken a radical step and approached the local public school system to discuss the feasibility of having their children educated in the public schools for part of the day. The children would be part of the regular public school system and would receive their religious education in the same building after school hours, taught by a teacher whom the parent body would hire.[229] After a spate of publicity, widespread discussion and debate, this proposal came to nothing more than any of the other initiatives, and the issue of the cost of Jewish living continues to loom larger than ever.

---

227 Barry Rosen, "Are School Vouchers Un-American," *Commentary*, Vol. 109, No. 2, February 2000, pp. 26–31; Barry Rosen and Critics, "Are School Vouchers the Answer?" *Commentary*, Vol. 109, No. 6, June 2000, pp. 16–29; the entire "Education" section of *Jewish Action*, Vol. 66, No. 1, Fall 2005/5766.

228 http://www.jewishsf.com/content/2-0-/module/displaystory/story_id/11802/edition_id/227/f ormat/html/displaystory.html.

229 Jonathan Isler and Kenny Gluck, "A Radical Proposal Whose Time Has Come," *Jewish Action*, Vol. 66. No. 1, Fall 2005/5766, p. 36.

Chapter 30

The Politics of the American Orthodox

The strong ties between American Orthodox Jews and their counterparts in Israel have reinforced their political attitudes and behavior. There has long been evidence that American Orthodox Jews are more politically conservative than non-Orthodox Jews. The latter are typically liberal, have long been so and, despite repeated predictions that they are becoming more conservative, show no signs of shedding their liberalism.

The more conservative political beliefs and behavior of the Orthodox are not unusual. Quite the contrary, religious conservatism generally tends to coincide with political conservatism. In recent decades, however, a much more overt and active political conservatism has appeared than was previously evident. Much of this is probably due to the broader national move toward conservatism and the presidential election victories of George W. Bush. In addition to his social conservatism, with which many Orthodox Jews tend to feel comfortable, he has been viewed as a staunch ally of Israel. So it should come as no surprise that he had enthusiastic support in Orthodox neighborhoods during his two presidential campaigns.

However, it is somewhat surprising that there was not much discussion in Orthodox circles of some of the basic differences in approach between national socio-political conservatism and Orthodox Judaism. For example, although both oppose abortion on demand, many socio-political conservatives would oppose it even if the safety of the mother is at stake. Also, although many Orthodox Jews are not, in principle, opposed to prayer in public schools, they presumably support it only when the prayer is completely non-denominational,[230] whereas many socio-political conservatives want to see specifically Christian prayer in the public schools. Above and beyond differences in specifics on the socio-political issues are more general differences in personality and perspective. For at least the

---

230 R. Moshe Feinstein, *Igrot Moshe*, *Orach Chaim*, Part II, No. 24.

past century, a strong representation of nativism and fascism has been espoused by the political right, and this is something of which all Jews, including Orthodox Jews, are probably wary. In addition, Jews have long feared "gun-toting," and are much less opposed to gun-control legislation than is the National Rifle Association.

Growing Orthodox support for the American political right has been reinforced by the ties between American Orthodoxy and its counterpart in Israel, which has seen the growth of religio-political radicalism. Both in Israel and in the American Jewish community, a significant transformation in perceptions has taken place, focusing on the relationship between religiosity and political radicalism in Israel. As analyzed by Eliezer Don-Yehiya,[231] the religious tradition was, until recently, uniformly understood as a source of passivity or political moderation. In contemporary Israeli society, by contrast, it is widely perceived as a factor that encourages radical nationalism and extremist political activism.

Since 1967, the National Religious Party—the "official" party of religious Zionism—has become much more overtly nationalist and "hawkish." Interestingly, the relationship between the views of the party leadership, as compared with those of the membership, is almost the reverse of what it is within the *haredi* parties. Much of the leadership of the NRP has taken staunchly nationalist positions and has played up the appearance of its membership as being in full support of those positions. This was glaringly evident in the campaign against the "Disengagement" from Gush Katif, the "*hitnatkut*," in the summer of 2005. The extent to which the NRP leadership reflects the political positions of its electorate is somewhat questionable. Some studies suggest that, on average, NRP voters were no more hawkish than Likud voters, with both falling between the polar extremes on a hawk-dove scale; in addition, the studies find that a significant minority of NRP voters—about one third—hold rather moderate positions with respect to the Administered Territories and the establishment of a Palestinian state. Even in Gush Katif itself, one study of the evacuated Israeli citizens indicated some diversity; the overwhelming majority—three-quarters—defined themselves as "right-wing," with 15 percent as

---

231 Eliezer Don-Yehiya, "Does Place Make a Difference?: Jewish Orthodoxy in Israel and the Diaspora," in Chaim I. Waxman, ed., *Israel as a Religious Reality* (Northvale, NJ: Jason Aronson, 1994), esp. pp. 58–74.

center or left, and about 10 percent as "extreme right-wing."[232] And, in the final analysis, the Disengagement proceeded with almost no violence and without the active opposition of the overwhelming majority of NRP voters.

The leadership of American Orthodoxy was relatively passive with respect to the Disengagement from Gush Katif. For example, the major organizations of centrist and modern American Orthodoxy—the Orthodox Union and the Rabbinical Council of America—issued calls urging restraint, civility, and sensitivity, but were not in the least critical of the Israeli government.[233] However, after the violent dismantling of Amona in early 2006, they were pronouncedly more critical of the Israeli government. The Orthodox Union wrote a strong letter to the then Acting Prime Minister Ehud Olmert

> to express our deep dismay regarding the violent scene that was broadcast around the world from Amona last week. We cringed as we viewed the images of members of the elite Yassam unit, tasked with carrying out the rule of law, enter a house and proceed to mercilessly beat fellow citizens who were merely sitting on the floor exercising their right to civil disobedience. We never thought we would see such a dark day in the State of Israel where Israeli citizens are trampled by the horses of their own police force.

The letter continued with more harsh criticism of the police, with only part of one sentence directed at the actions of the protesters: "While we reject the actions of the those protesters who resorted to violent tactics such as throwing stones, bricks, glass and paint at soldiers, ..." The contrast between the positions of the Orthodox Union vis-à-vis the disengagement from Gush Katif and that of the dismantling of Amona appears to be

---

232 Steven Hobfoll, Daphna Canetti-Nisim, Eran Halperin and Oren Shapira, "On the Eve of the Evacuation of Jewish Settlers from the Gaza Strip: The Psychological and Political Effects of the Disengagement Plan on the Settlers," Background Paper: The National Security Studies Center—University of Haifa, 2005.

233 For a critique of, as well as a rationale for, the official position, see the debate between Emanuel Feldman and Yosef Blau, *Jewish Action* 66:2, Winter 5766/2005, pp. 38–42.

reflective of a broad shift in opinions of American Orthodoxy regarding both the Israeli government and perhaps even the broader, non-Orthodox, Zionist movement.

With respect to the *haredi* parties, the *haredi* masses are today among the most nationalistic in Israeli society. Surveys consistently reveal that the overwhelming majority of *haredi* respondents hold strong nationalistic views. Contrary to the widely circulated notion that the Sephardim of Shas and the Ashkenazi *haredim* represented by the Degel Hatorah party are, in principle, amenable to territorial compromise on the basis of *pikuach nefesh*, that is the primacy of life and saving life, the evidence indicates otherwise. Although it has been assumed that the respective leaders of Shas and Degel Hatorah, Rabbi Ovadia Yosef and the late Rabbi Eliezer Shach, were supportive of territorial compromise on that basis, their followers staunchly oppose such compromise. It is, therefore, no surprise that a very small percentage of *haredim* supported the Oslo peace accords. One survey found that "only 9 percent of the *Haredi* respondents were in favor of the peace process, as opposed to 24 percent among the national-religious and 56 percent among the secular."[234] Indeed, already in 1994, only 4 percent of the haredim supported the Oslo negotiations, whereas among religious Zionists four times as many, 16 percent, supported them.[235] And, in 1998, when Netanyahu signed the Wye Accords, Habad cut all ties with him and indicated that he was no better than Ehud Barak.

Be that as it may, both major factions of Israeli Orthodoxy are highly nationalist, and they look to their Orthodox fellows in the Diaspora, including the U.S., for economic, political, and moral support. The close ties between the American and Israeli Orthodox communities documented above has fostered a strong support for the right-wing politics of the Israeli Orthodox within the American Orthodox community. A look at any of the American Orthodox weekly "newspapers" quickly brings this home in their editorials, articles, and advertisements. The right-wing positions on Israeli politics, in turn, generate and reinforce right-wing positions on American political issues, especially when a conservative President who is viewed as being highly supportive of Israel is the incumbent.

---

234 Shahar Ilan, "They Believe in the Booth," *Ha'aretz*, March 31, 1998.

235 Ilan 1998.

There are reasons to suggest, however, that the Disengagement from the Gaza Strip/Gush Katif and the dismantling of settlements such as Amona now present a significant challenge to educating Religious Zionism and Modern Orthodoxy. This is an issue—perhaps even more so —for Israeli Religious Zionism, but it is also one that may well concern American Modern Orthodox educators for the foreseeable future.

Glossary

Acharonim—Early and late Talmudic commentaries.

Aliyah—Immigrating to Israel.

Am Yisrael—The Jewish people.

Asher Yatzar—The blessing recited after going to the bathroom.

Assur—Religiously prohibited.

Avodah—Service, worship.

B'dieved—Only allowed after the fact, secondary, not really permissible.

Ba'al Tefillah—Reader who leads the synagogue in services.

Ba'alei Teshuvah—Returnees to Orthodox Judaism.

Bein Adam L'chaveiro—Interpersonal commandments.

Bein Adam La-Makom—Commandments dealing with one's relationship with God.

Beit Hamikdash—The Temple in Jerusalem.

Beit Midrash—A yeshiva's study hall.

Berachah (pl. Berachot)—Blessing.

Bereshit—Genesis.

Birchot Ha-Torah—The blessings recited prior to studying Torah.

Birkat Hamazon—Grace after meals.

Birkat Kohanim—Priestly blessings during prayer services.

Chametz—Leavened bread that one is forbidden to eat on Passover.

Chavruta (pl. Chavrutot)—Study partner, generally for Gemara.

Chazar—Review of one's studies.

Chessed—Helping others.

Choref Zeman—Winter semester.

Chumash—The five books of Moses.

Chumra (pl. Chumrot)—Stringencies in religious practice.

Daf Yomi—A popular daily program of Talmud study.

Dati Le'umi—Religious Zionist.

Daven—To pray.

Davening—Prayer services.

Dvar Torah (pl. Divrei Torah)—Torah thoughts, often relayed in a speech.

Emet—Truth.

Emunah—Faith.

Eretz Yisrael—The land of Israel.

Eretz Yisrael Ha-Shelemah—The complete and expansive land of Israel.

Erev—The evening before a holiday.

Etrogim—Citrons used on the Sukkot holiday.

Frum—Religiously observant.

Ga'avah—Haughtiness.

Gadol Hador—The greatest Torah scholar of a generation.

Galut—Exile.

Garinim—Group of like-minded aliyah-oriented people.

Gemara—The later section of the Talmud, completed approximately 450 CE.

Gemilut Chassadim—The offering of help to others.

Hakadosh Baruch Hu—God.

Halachah (pl. Halachot)—Jewish law.

Hanhalah—Administration.

Haredi (pl. Haredim)—Ultra-Orthodox.

Hashkafot—Religious philosophies.

Hatmadah—Studiousness.

Havdalah—Ceremony that concludes the Sabbath.

Hitnatkut—The disengagement from territory in the land of Israel.

Humra—See chumra.

Kabalat Shabbat—The service at the onset of the Sabbath.

Kaddish—The mourner's prayer.

Kashrut—Jewish dietary laws.

Kashyas—Questions, often on complex Talmudic topics.

Kavanah—Concentration, focus.

Kayitz Zeman—Summer semester.

Kedushah—Holiness.

Kehillah—Organized Jewish community.

Keriat Ha-Torah—Torah reading.

Kiddush Club—Groups that drink liquor and eat cake in a side room of a synagogue during a part of services.

Kiddush Hashem—Sanctification of God's name.

Kippah—Skullcap, yarmulka.

Klal Yisrael—The Jewish people.

Kohen Gadol—High priest.

Kollel (pl. Kollelim)—Full-time Talmud program for married men.

Kotel—Western Wall.

Kumsitz—Inspirational gathering of singing and story-telling.

L'chat'chilah—The proper thing to do.

Lashon Hara—Gossip.

Lehavdil—Differentiating between sacred and profane subjects.

Limudei Kodesh—Religious subjects.

Lishmah—Doing something for the proper religious purpose.

Machshavah—The subject of Jewish Thought.

Machzor—Holiday prayerbook.

Madda—Secular subjects.

Madrich (pl. Madrichim, f.pl. Madrichot)—Counselor, supervisor.

Mashgiach—Religious supervisor, director of religious growth in a yeshiva.

Mazel—Luck.

Mechanech (pl. Mechanchim)—Teachers.

Megillah—The scroll of Esther, read in synagogue on Purim.

Mesorah—Tradition.

Midbar—Desert.

Middot—Ethical virtues.

Midrashah (pl. Midrashot)—Study programs for women.

Minchah—Afternoon prayer service.

Minhag—Local custom.

Minyan (pl. Minyanim)—Prayer quorum.

Mishnah (pl. Mishnayot)—The earlier section of the Talmud, completed approximately in the year 200 CE.

Mishpachah—Family.

Motzei—The evening after a holiday.

Mussar—Ethical texts.

Negiah—The religious obligation to refrain from touching a member of the opposite sex that is not a close relative.

Neshamah—Soul.

Netilat Yadayim—The ritual washing of one's hands.

Nevu'ot—Prophecies.

Nichshal—Stumbling religiously, failing to observe.

Oleh (pl. Olim)—One who immigrates to Israel.

Parashat Chayei Sarah—The weekly Torah portion of Chayei Sarah.

Pashute Yid—A simple Jew.

Pikuach Nefesh—The primacy of life and saving life.

Rabbanim—Rabbis.

Ramim—Rabbinic instructors in a yeshiva.

Rebbe (pl. Rebbeim)—One's personal rabbi or mentor.

Rishonim—Medieval rabbis.

Rosh Kollel—Dean of a kollel.

Rosh Yeshiva (pl. Roshei Yeshiva)—Dean of a yeshiva.

Ruach—Spirit, inspiration.

Ruchniut—Spirituality.

Seder—Special Passover ceremony in which the story of the Exodus is told.

Sefer (Sefarim)—Religious books.

Sefer Torah—Torah scroll.

Semachot—Family celebrations.

Semichah—Rabbinic ordination.

Seyag—A preventive ordinance.

Shabbat (pl. Shabbatot)—The Jewish Sabbath, from sundown Friday night through nightfall on Saturday.

Shabbat Chol Hamoed—The Sabbath during the intermediate days of a holiday.

Shabbaton—A Sabbath retreat.

Shaliach—An emissary who encourages people to immigrate to Israel.

Shalosh Seudot—Saturday evening meal, towards the end of Shabbat.

Shanah Alef—A first post-high school year of study in Israel.

Shanah Ba'aretz—A year of study in Israel.

Shanah Bet—A second post-high school year of study in Israel.

Shemirat Ha-Mitzvot—Observance of the Torah's commandments.

Shemot—Exodus.

Shep Nachas—Enjoy, have pleasure in.

Sherut Le'umi—National service.

Shiktza—Derogatory term for non-Jewish woman.

Shiur (pl. Shiurim)—Torah class, lecture.

Shofar—Ram's horn that is ritually blown on Rosh Hashanah.

Shtiblach—Small informal synagogues.

Shtuss—Nonsense.

Shul—Synagogue.

Sichot—Lectures.

Siyum Hashas—Celebration of the conclusion of a full cycle of studying the Talmud. See Daf Yomi.

Sugya—Talmudic passage.

Sukkah (pl. Sukkot)—Booth sat in during the holiday of Sukkot.

Talmid (pl. Talmidim)—Student.

Talmid Chacham (pl. Talmidei Chachamim)—Torah scholar.

Tefillah (pl. Tefillot)—Prayer.

Tefillin—Phylacteries worn during weekday morning prayers.

Tehillim—Psalms.

Teshuvah—Repentance.

Tish—Inspirational gathering of singing and story-telling.

Torat Yisrael—The Torah of the land of Israel.

Tzeniut—Modesty.

Tzitzit—Fringes ritually worn by males.

Yamim Noraim—High Holidays.

Yeshiva (pl. Yeshivot)—Schools of higher Torah learning for men.

Yeshivat Hesder (pl. Yeshivot Hesder)—Yeshivot that combine Torah learning with army service.

Yeshivot Gedolot—Same as Yeshiva.

Yeshivot Gevohot—Same as Yeshiva.

Yetzer Hara—Evil inclination.

Yichud—Forbidden isolation between an unmarried man and woman.

Yiddishkeit—Judaism.

Yirat Shamayim—Fear of God.

Yirei Shamayim—Those who fear God.

Yishuv—Settlement.

Yishuv Ha-Daat—Calmness of spirit.

Yom Tov—Holiday.

Tables for Section 1

Sample questions asked to students about their Israel experience. The full questionnaire can be found at http://www.YasharBooks.com/Israel.html.

	Always	Usually	Sometimes	Never
PRE				
h. Recite Bentching after eating bread	36	26	35	3
i. Recite Asher Yatzar after the bathroom	38	11	17	34
POST				
h. Recite Bentching after eating bread	64	24	10	1
i. Recite Asher Yatzar after the bathroom	66	15	11	8
ONE-YEAR LATER				
h. Recite Bentching after eating bread	70	22	8	1
i. Recite Asher Yatzar after the bathroom	75	11	8	6

* *

	Very likely	Somewhat likely	Somewhat unlikely	Very unlikely	Not sure
PRE					
l. make Aliya	13	30	22	15	20
m. serve in the Israeli army	6	15	23	46	10
POST					
l. make Aliya	31	37	11	6	15
m. serve in the Israeli army	8	15	21	45	12
ONE-YEAR LATER					
l. make Aliya	29	39	12	8	12
m. serve in the Israeli army	6	19	21	41	14

* *

	Very comfortable	Somewhat comfortable	Somewhat uncomfortable	Very uncomfortable	Not sure
PRE					
d. attending a movie rated "R" for its sexual content	28	30	24	17	2
f. going "mixed swimming"	35	25	22	16	2
POST					
d. attending a movie rated "R" for its sexual content	12	25	27	32	5
f. going "mixed swimming"	12	15	29	38	6
ONE-YEAR LATER					
d. attending a movie rated "R" for its sexual content	11	15	34	38	2
f. going "mixed swimming"	10	11	18	60	2

* *

Level of competence

	Excellent	Good	Fair	Poor
PRE				
d. reading an Israeli newspaper	3	12	39	47
POST				
d. reading an Israeli newspaper	3	19	43	35
ONE-YEAR LATER				
d. reading an Israeli newspaper	5	23	42	30

Index

K

Kalmanowitz, Rabbi Abraham, 154
Katz, Rabbi Mordechai, 154
Kaufman, Menahem, 151
Kehati, 37
Kellerman, Faye, 68
Kibbutz Shaalvim, 25
Kibbutz Yavneh, 25
Kirkpatrick, Lee, 130
Koester, Jolene, 111, 127
kollel, 26–27, 38, 72
Kollel Torah MiTzion, 71, 161
Kook, Rav Avraham Isaac, 51, 55, 182
Kook, Rav Zvi Yehuda, 55
Kotler, Rabbi Aaron, 154
Kushner Yeshiva High School, 186

L

Lache, S.Y., 179–180
languages, foreign, 21–22
Larson, David, 120
lashon hara, 49
Lazerwitz, Bernard, 179
Lebowitz, Nechama, 165
Leibman, Yesha'yahu, 181
Levy, Bryna, 165
Lichtenstein, Rav Aharon, 30, 92
Likud Party, 198
Lincoln Square Synagogue, 74
long-term vs short-term effects of
  studying abroad, 58–67
Luther, Martin, 176

M

Machon Devora, 163
Machon Gold, 31, 162–163
Maimonides School, 11, 165
maintaining Israel experience at
  home, 131–142
Manischewitz, Behr, 161
Manischewitz, Hirsch, 161

Manischewitz, Max, 161
Man's Search For Meaning, 92
MASA grants, 69
Mea Shearim, Israel, 98, 105
Mendelowitz, Rabbi Shraga Feivel,
  154
mental illness, 106, 110–112, 121
mentors for *yeshiva* students,
  118–124, 141–142
Michlala, 163
middot, growth in, 47–50, 93–95
military service. *see* army
Mir Yeshiva, 23, 86, 134, 163
Mirvis, Tova, 68
Mizrachi Organization, 148–149, 151,
  191. *see also* Religious Zionists of
  America
modern Orthodoxy
  changing of definition, 74–76,
    169–178
  origin of, 11
  vs National Religious, 55
  vs ultra-Orthodoxy, 133–137,
    169–170, 173–174, 176–178
modesty, 41–46, 50, 60–61, 66–67
Moilanen, Paavo, 120
morality, growth, 47–50, 93–95
Myers, Scott, 130

N

Nash, David, 126
National Center for Public Policy and
  Higher Education, 174
National Conference of Synagogue
  Youth (NCSY), 174
National Jewish Outreach Program,
  174
National Jewish Population Survey
  American Orthodoxy and zionism,
    173
  day school and Jewish identity,
    156–159
  denominational affiliation, 179